Scratching
the toe of
Italy

Scratching
the toe of
Italy

Expecting the unexpected
in Calabria

Niall Allsop

Text © Niall Allsop 2012
Photographs © Niall Allsop and Kay Bowen 2012

ISBN-10: 1468147668
ISBN-13: 978–1468147667

Published by **In Scritto** *Italy in writing*
www.inscritto.com

Cover and book design by Niall Allsop – niallsop@mac.com

Main text set in Sabon and Caecilia
Additional text, headings and captions set in Frutiger
Cover titles set in His Name is Honey, cover text in Frutiger

For all the people in Calabria who have helped us with our adventure and in particular the people of Santa Severina.

More importantly for three young children, unborn when we arrived, but who have since become part of our lives and we a part of theirs.

For **Eleanora, Giulia** and **Giovanna**

Also to the memory of a dear friend, and part of the extended Gerardi family, who brought much warmth to all who knew him.

To **Nino Biondo**

who passed away in January 2014

Acknowledgements

This page has been, by far, the hardest to write. This is the fourth version. The problem has been listing everyone in Santa Severina deserving of mention.

I started with the comprehensive list but then ran out of paper and time. So I decided to narrow it down to our first few months in Santa Severina but then found this list was pretty lengthy too and I kept thinking of other people to add ... and so it went on.

I went for the blanket 'Everyone in Santa Severina' but felt that this did not do justice to a few people in particular. So this is my best shot, a compromise that highlights the few, the very few, but acknowledges many, many more.

I am indebted to the following who helped us leave Bath: Vanessa Ashton, Joe Ashton, Jon Green, Michael Simpson, Mike & Carole Gay, Sharon Tuttle and Catriona Henderson

Also the following in Calabria who played a part in preparing the way ... Elvira Aggazio, Roberto Bisceglia, Dott. Rocco de Rito and Silvana Mancini

I am particularly indebted to all those in Santa Severina, too numerous to mention by name, who, through their tolerance, help, hospitality, friendship, courtesy and goodwill, have made us feel at home in their town. Also those others, mainly in and around Crotone, who have likewise helped us muddle our way through.

I would like to single out three particular groups of people:

Without Le Puzelle and the special people who live and work there, we could not have made such a move: Vincenzo Bisceglia & Elvira Aggazio, Beniamina Bisceglia & Vittorio Isabella, Roberto Bisceglia, Giuliano Stoica, Salvatore Vona, Angela Gigliotti, Martino Carvelli and Gabriella Capozza; also Gino Aggazio & Rosetta Catera, Luigina Tolomeo and Roxana Stoica.

Without the Gerardi family and their many kindnesses, individually and collectively, we would not have somewhere to call 'home': Mario Gerardi & Emelia Galasso, Silvana Gerardi & Raffaele Vizza, Aurelio Gerardi & Rosanna Stefanizzi, Antonietta Gerardi & (the late) Nino Biondo, Anna Maria Gerardi & Attilio Pugliese and Sergio Gerardi & Angela Alfonsi.

Without the Rosa dei Venti bar, both as a watering hole and a dropping-off point for a lethargic courier, our days would have been less rewarding: Carlo Tigano & Anna Maria Toscano, the extended Tigano and Toscano families, everyone we met there and all those with whom we shared an *aperitivo*.

Contents

Part one: Getting there

Getting there was the hardest part. Ten weeks of ups and downs and frenetic and intensive dedication to one goal, a single day in September when our lives would change for ever.

Part two: The first year

From our first faltering footsteps as Santa Severina residents to the time we began to walk upright with a modicum of confidence to become part of this Calabrian community.

Part three: The second year and beyond

The learning curve became less steep and, for others, our 'novelty' factor was increasingly wearing off. We moved on from being mere observers of life in and around Santa Severina to becoming contributors to it.

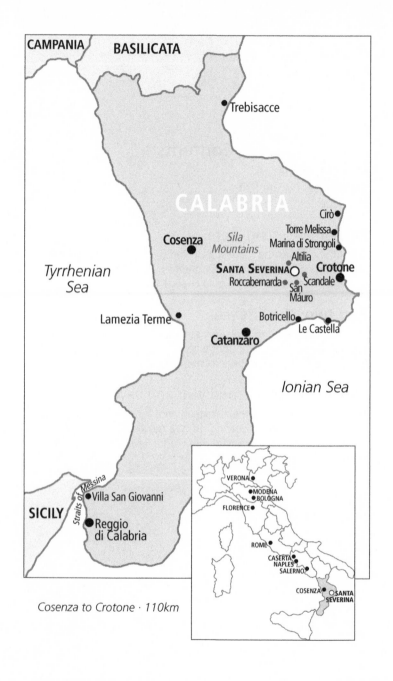

Cosenza to Crotone · 110km

Some notes on the text

If you read the original edition of *Stumbling through Italy* you may expect to read about Siberene and L'Oenotri and not Santa Severina and Le Puzelle. They are of course one and the same ... I decided to ignore the advice I was originally given to change both names.

Most of the place names mentioned in the text are on the map opposite. The inset map only includes the main location names between Verona and Santa Severina.

I have introduced Italian words and phrases which either have an obvious meaning or add flavour to a book about Italy and Italians.

I have used international English throughout rather than American English: autumn for fall; colour for color; centre for center; boot for trunk; realise for realize ... and so on. Most readers will be conversant with the language of both cultures. The most difficult cultural characteristic to overcome is the realisation that American football and football (soccer) in the rest of the world are two different games.

Finally, this is my version of the story. Kay and I generally did things together so will have had similar experiences; of course, our interpretation of these experiences may not always have coincided.

Prologue ... Hallowe'en

Kay and I wake up to a bright sunny morning two years to the day since we first woke up in this cosy Calabrian house. It is 31 October 2010.

It's Sunday morning and, as normal and in no particular rush, we drive the twenty-five kilometres to Crotone to go to the Farmers' Market where we can purchase all manner of fresh produce in season.

We are at our favourite cheese stall when we hear familiar voices and stop to chat to our friends Domenico Stumpo and Francesca Loria. Unusually they are without their charismatic daughter, Carmen; they look relaxed.

We have a coffee together in the centre of Crotone and, as we are returning to our respective cars, Stumpo (we have become used to calling him by his surname) suggests the four of us have lunch together.

We follow Stumpo and Francesca out of Crotone and along the *Strada Statali* that traverses the Sila mountains to a restaurant fifty kilometres away which is packed; there is no room at the inn.

We head back towards San Giovanni in Fiore, Francesca's home town, and stop at a redundant railway station, now a smart restaurant, Casello 65, where we eat well. Francesca has to leave early as she has an appointment at a television studio where she is adjudicating in the search for new, under-fourteen, singing talent in Calabria.

It is mid-afternoon and Stumpo drives *our* car into San Giovanni, parks up and takes us on a walking tour of the town's *centro storico*. We catch occasional glimpses of young kids, mostly girls, dressed up for Hallowe'en, playing their part in the Americanisation of the planet.

We stop off at Francesca's erstwhile home for a toilet break ... her parents (whom Kay has never met) are not in, nevertheless Stumpo shows us round their house and in particular the wonderful wooden furniture that his *suocero* (father-in-law) has crafted.

En route out of town we drop Stumpo off in the centre where he will reconnect with Francesca.

As we drive back to Santa Severina we muse about the day's trip to the Farmers' Market and how it turned out ... we have come to expect days like this, days when the unexpected is the way of things. But this day is not done.

We have arrived back in Santa Severina and are parking up by the Middle School and edging slowly into a space when, from nowhere and incredibly fast, backwards *and* uphill, comes another car that goes straight into the driver's (my) door. Kay and I are shaken but otherwise unhurt. The same cannot be said for the car and my door won't open and I have to get out the passenger side.

Luckily there are witnesses to the event and the young driver is very shaken, very apologetic. He uses his *cellulare* to call his father who appears a few moments later and agrees to pay for all the damage including a new door. There is no exchange of insurance details; instead we exchange phone numbers and shake hands.

I complete my parking manoeuvre and wearily we walk home where we are greeted by a small group of ten year-old witches, all daughters of friends. They *were* expected and we part with a few packets of pre-prepared goodies. ... our contribution to the aforementioned importation of Hallowe'en.

Home at last, and before rounding off the evening with a few glasses of red wine and a movie, I text Stumpo to explain why it is that I won't be able to take him to Crotone station on Wednesday as arranged.

*

This was neither an ordinary day nor an extraordinary day, it was simply one of many days that never turned out quite as we planned.

We did however make two new friends that day – Salvatore the teenage driver of the car that hit us and his courteous and helpful father, Giovanni. By the time this book is published Salvatore will be reading law at Rome University.

All we had expected of this day was to buy some fresh cheese, a few packets of home-made pasta and half a dozen free-range eggs at the Farmers' Market.

But no day in Calabria is *ever* what you expect.

*

If you have read *Stumbling through Italy* (and there is absolutely no excuse for not having done so) you will know that our route to Santa Severina began nearly a decade earlier when we visited Italy for the first time and ended in September 2008 when we returned to Calabria to live.

We had arrived home in England early in July 2008 fully expecting to fly back to Calabria as tourists the following year. Instead, just over ten weeks later, we arrived back in Santa Severina with all that was important to us crammed into our newly-acquired left-hand-drive Renault Clio.

What follows is the story of how this came about, of what happened in those ten weeks and how two people, in their sixties and with very basic Italian, have coped with being the only English-speakers in a small hilltop community in the toe of Italy.

It is the story of how we ended up scratching the toe of Italy to see what lay beneath; it is the story of how, day by day, we have come to expect the unexpected.

Part one
Getting there

Getting there was the hardest part. Ten weeks of ups and downs and frenetic and intensive dedication to one goal, a single day in September when our lives would change for ever.

Option three

We returned to England mid-week, the first week in July, and were soon absorbed into our work routines.

For me that meant catching up with clients for whom I worked as a graphic designer and for Kay it was the daily trudge into Bath to take up the reins again as the HR Manager of a large, ancient and wealthy charity that provided sheltered accommodation for the elderly.

Over the previous year there had been dramatic changes at Kay's workplace which culminated in the appointment of a new Chief Executive. On her return she was therefore not surprised when he announced that he wanted to speak with all members of staff individually the following Monday.

There were to be sweeping changes and some jobs would go, others would have their salaries frozen and some job descriptions would change; all staff could, as was the law of the land, opt to accept a redundancy package instead. Everyone had four weeks in which to decide what to do.

In Kay's case, apart from her job title, her work would change little in the shake-up while the package offered reflected her long service. However, her inclination was to carry on as before.

Her (our) options were limited in that we rented a three-hundred year-old stone-built cottage on the outskirts of Bath that we could never afford to buy but we were aware that, as and when we retired, we might have to move to a less expensive part of the country. We had to balance this against the knowledge that Kay's redundancy package was a one-off offer; it would not be on offer again.

It was while we were mulling over these choices that an idea came into my head and I spent an afternoon neglecting my clients and penning instead Option Three. That evening I showed Kay the result of my labours.

The premise of Option Three was simple – neither of the other options we seemed to be wrestling with was ideal, so why not indulge in a bit of lateral thinking and consider something completely different. That 'something' was to move to Calabria and to Santa Severina in particular.

In Option Three I set out the financial, social and family advantages and disadvantages of such a move and although, in retrospect, a few of my figures were wildly inaccurate (in both directions) overall they proved to be just about right. On the whole, the financial side was more endowed with pros, the social side had a mix of pros and cons while the family side generally had the monopoly on the cons.

Kay was not sold on the idea and so for about a week no further mention was made of it. As Kay was slowly changing her mind in favour of the notion, I was changing mine in the opposite direction and so, the next time the subject was broached, we found ourselves equally willing to look at it as a 'possible' option; but no more than that.

We discussed and examined the idea from almost every conceivable angle until, almost imperceptibly, we realised we were increasingly talking about it in real terms; we were not yet talking in terms of 'when …' but we had elevated the idea to 'if …'.

During the third week in July, less than a fortnight before Kay had to formally advise her employer of her decision, we arrived at the 'when' moment and from then on we were planning a strategy that, we hoped, would get us back to Calabria sooner rather than later.

For three summers we had stayed at the *Agriturismo Le Puzelle* near the hill-top town of Santa Severina in the province of Crotone where we had unwittingly created our own little support group for just such an eventuality. And so it was to English-speakers Roberto and Elvira, the son and partner of Vincenzo, Le Puzelle's proprietor, that I sent emails to test the water.

Within five hours Roberto emailed back … he had found us a house. His mother, Silvana, who lived in Crotone itself, also had a small house in Santa Severina which we could rent for as long as we wanted. A few days later he took some photos which he also emailed to us.

These two, Elvira and Roberto, made the Calabrian side of the move so easy; back in Bath we were wrestling with the feasibility of winding up our affairs, our home, our animals, our lives, in just eight weeks.

Where we were leaving; where we were heading

Eight weeks and three cubic metres

It wasn't that we were in a hurry to leave the UK but, we reasoned, the longer we stayed the more our limited funds would be depleted by the massive rent we were paying monthly.

Kay and her other colleagues would each meet with the Chief Executive early in August to pass on, in writing, their decision. Those that chose to leave would automatically work a month's notice which in Kay's case, and taking holiday entitlement into consideration, would mean she could actually finish work before the end of the month. The sooner we could leave after that, the more we would save.

The first major logistical problem we had to solve was actually how we would travel to Calabria and, related to that, what we would (or could) take with us. Everything would depend on that.

Less of a logistical problem, more of an emotional one was how and when we would explain our plans to offspring and family. In this respect telling Kay's daughters was easier in that they both lived in the London area and this we were able to do quite quickly.

When, in early September, Kay returned to London to say

her final farewells, I flew to Northern Ireland to do the same. In one sense this was much easier for me in that there has always been a flight involved for us to see each other ... the flight in future would just be longer or, more likely, two or even three flights. In another sense it was more difficult for, unlike Kay, I had a grandson across the Irish Sea.

There was, of course one other person that needed to know what was planned ... Kay's employer. August came and Kay and her colleagues each had their head-to-head with the Chief Executive to present and talk through their decision.

Ironically, because Kay had been employed longer than anyone else and also because her job description was not changing dramatically, everybody assumed that she would definitely remain in her post ... just shows how wrong some people can be.

So she went to great pains to pen a letter that pressed all the positive buttons about her work environment and to give the impression that she was staying ... until the very last sentence ... when off the page sprang something along the lines of: " ... nevertheless I have decided to take the money and run."

It was a shock, and the one outcome that nobody had reckoned on. Apart from family, we could finally go public and let our friends know.

There was of course an ulterior motive in spreading the word. We needed to find homes for all our furniture and worldly goods and, except for family, we were hoping for some sort of token financial contribution or just lots of cash.

Everything was for sale: beds, wardrobes, cupboards, shelves, bookcases, books, CDs, chairs, tables, fridge, freezer, washing machine, cooker, garden implements, tools, anything and everything that wasn't nailed down ... and some things that were.

As well as advertising on the internet and in the local newspapers, we became regulars at some of the local car boot sales, generally the best place to buy other people's rubbish. Every other Sunday we stuffed the car with all sorts of useless paraphernalia that we had accrued over decades, separately and together; hidden among our junk there might just be the very thing that some other hoarder desperately needed to make their life complete.

We became quite adept at shouting the odds and enticing people to our stall to have a browse ... we even offered CDs, priced at £3 each, at the bargain price of three for £10 and, yes, some people were taken in by this very special 'offer'.

I suppose we made about £250 in this way which probably didn't compensate for the energy we expended in doing it. Nevertheless it got us out of the house, a house slowly being denuded of everything that had made it a home.

The logistics of the move itself were beginning to become clearer. Initially we had thought of hiring a van and driving to Calabria, but that would have meant that we (for 'we' read 'I') would have had to drive the van back to the UK as one-way hire didn't seem to be available over such a distance. We considered paying for international movers to take everything over and we would fly but, as Calabria was almost as far as you could go in western Europe, the cost of this was astronomical. I checked out U-Haul's website in the off chance that they were going to launch a Europe-wide network before the middle of September. No such luck.

It was only when Kay found Euroman and Van on the internet that everything started to fall into place. This small three-man business was based in Devon and regularly made forays across the Channel to all parts of Europe, though most frequently to France and Spain. As luck would have it they had a delivery to Pescara on Italy's Adriatic coast scheduled for mid-September though at the time the exact date was still to be confirmed, as was the amount of room that might be available to us.

These two issues soon resolved themselves and Euroman and Van confirmed that they could pick up on 11 September and drop off in Santa Severina five days later; we were allocated up to three cubic metres of space.

Booking Euroman and Van to take our three cubic metres to Calabria was only one half of the equation ... *we* had to get there too and, of course, we had to leave Bath on or around 11 September and make sure we were in Santa Severina by the time the van arrived. Having looked at all the options, we came up with a novel plan. We decided to drive there.

First of all we had to get rid of our less-than-a-year-old right-hand drive car and find a second-hand, left-hand-drive substitute. It sounded simple on paper but this was late summer 2008 and there was talk of recession and cut-backs in the air. When I say "in the air", what I really mean is that the media were having a ball painting ever-darker pictures of gloom and doom; the phrase 'self-fulfilling prophecy' comes to mind.

Selling the car on eBay (which I had done once before) and through the local newspaper proved impossible so we were forced to sell it back to the dealership at a price which should make them blush with embarrassment ... it's all I can do not to include their name and address in the hope that they lose a few sales or, better still, pay back some of the money they stole.

Still, I thought, finding a left-hand-drive car should not be too difficult ... I had seen lots advertised on eBay. What I didn't realise initially was that most of the people using eBay to sell their apparently left-hand-drive cars were complete imbeciles. One of the 'fields' that sellers have to complete on the eBay questionnaire is to indicate whether the car for sale is left- or right-hand-drive; almost everyone, it seemed, was 'clicking' the left-hand drive box because they *drove* on the left-hand side ... in a right-hand-drive car! They might be able to use a computer but could they walk upright, I wondered?

Browsing through the left-hand-drive-cars-for-sale section I came across dozens of cars that were described inaccurately ... usually just one look at the photograph was enough to tell me that it was actually an erroneously described right-hand-drive car. In the end I just gave up emailing these people to 'thank' them for wasting my time and turned my attention instead to the websites of the various specialist left-hand-drive car dealers, based mainly in the south-east of England.

We were looking for a small, low-mileage, five-door diesel ... and at Basingstoke found a Renault Clio that indeed had a low mileage but which had three doors and was petrol-driven; apart from which it was perfect. Everything that didn't fit into three cubic metres would have to fit into a Renault Clio.

The Clio was in the process of being registered in the UK – had I seen it a week earlier it would have still have had its Italian numberplates indicating that it had been 'born' in Naples. When I went to collect it ten days later, I also had to buy all the extra bits and pieces (fluorescent tops, emergency triangle, replacement light bulbs, fire extinguisher *et al*) that were safety requirements in some of the countries we would pass through. How much simpler it would be if all members of the European Union had the same safety equipment requirements.

The car located, another related problem raised its ugly head, something that I had not thought of, another little headache to while away the time ... insurance.

For a decade or more I had been insured through

the Automobile Association but when I enquired about transferring my insurance to the Clio which I would be driving to Italy and which wasn't coming back, they didn't want to know. I was politely told to bugger off and insure elsewhere.

Eventually I managed to do this but in so-doing found myself in a 'Catch 22' loop. I had no option but to insure the car for a year but I knew that, within six months of it being in Italy, I would have to re-register it as Italian; then, once the car had Italian number plates, my English insurance would be invalid. I only really needed insurance for six months.

My new insurers were very helpful and said that, as and when I re-registered the car as Italian, they would refund me the balance of the premium less an administration charge. They kept to their promise.

While the car search was still ongoing, we were planning how we were going to get our new 'imaginary' car from Bath to Santa Severina and decided that we could use this journey as an opportunity to do some things we'd never done before ... like go through the Channel Tunnel and put the car on a train, sleep overnight on the same train, eat in the restaurant car and perhaps even solve the murder, maybe even commit one.

So, while Kay was working her notice or busy online closing down standings orders and direct debits for gas, electric, phone, internet and the like, I was online investigating, and eventually booking, our route across Europe. The plan was taking shape.

We would leave Bath on the evening of 11 September and drive to Folkstone in Kent where we would stay overnight at a hotel right beside the Channel Tunnel; the next morning we would go through the Tunnel and drive from France to and through Belgium and Holland and on to Düsseldorf in Germany, where we expected to arrive around four that afternoon.

At Düsseldorf we would put the car on the train where we would eat and sleep for sixteen hours as it hurtled across Europe to arrive at Verona in northern Italy, sixteen hours later, at ten on Saturday morning.

We would then drive south from Verona and break our journey to stay overnight in the small spa town of Triflisco in the Caserta area and then, on the Sunday, we'd drive down to Santa Severina where I expected to arrive at Le Puzelle (to stay for one night only) about four in the afternoon, a mere seventy-four hours after we left.

We had arranged to meet Euroman and Van and our three cubic metres on the Tuesday morning at Le Puzelle. Although we expected to move into 'our' house later the same day, we were not sure to what extent it was accessible by van.

As we were now able to be precise about the date, all the various service contracts could be terminated and, generally, there were few problems. The only one of note was with our new phone/internet suppliers with whom we had signed up some six months earlier. A microscopic review of the small print confirmed that the contract was indeed for a minimum of a year and so we could only terminate it by paying for the remaining six months.

Some paperwork was easier to wind up than others ... it just went straight into the wastepaper bin which gradually became two huge black plastic bags, one upstairs, one downstairs. These in turn became mere transit points en route to the shredder, itself another transit point en route to the bonfire at the bottom of the garden.

Every night we warmed our hands as a lifetime of bank statements, cheque stubs, payslips, love letters, gas, electric and phone bills and the like, went up in flames. Every night we added to the flames the other detritus of life and living that is so easily accumulated and which, in moments such as this, becomes as singularly unnecessary and unwanted as it was unremitting.

In fact we also managed to destroy our poor, overworked shredder in those eight weeks and had to invest in another more robust model, something that wasn't anticipated in the Option Three cash flow, though we did manage to sell it on to someone else.

For me there was the added headache of bringing all my business paperwork up to date and making sure it was in good order to pass on to my accountant. This I managed to do and still remember the look of surprise on his face when I turned up with everything much earlier that I ever had done before ... hitherto I had been very much a 'last-minute' person when it came to such things.

The accompanying letter explained everything. I watched as he read (yes, some accountants can also read) that I had decided to wind up the business as from the end of July and that I was now officially retired. The punch line about our imminent move to Italy was in the last sentence along with my new address. He was speechless.

Indeed he remained speechless for quite some time for, out of sight, out of mind, my paperwork went to the bottom of the pile. Despite being almost five months ahead of myself at the time, it was almost another two years before my accountant got off his ass and got round to finishing off what I began in that mid-August meeting.

I was not best pleased, particularly as I was fined by the Inland Revenue for late receipt of my accounts. (I must control this urge to name names!)

As the shutters were gradually closing down on one life,

those on another were slowly opening; every day they let in a little more light as the things we needed to do to end up as Italian residents became that much clearer.

We looked at ex-pat websites which, in theory at least, should have been the ideal place to tap into other people's experiences of doing the same. In theory, yes, but it gradually became all too apparent that more often these sites were no more than an outlet for people to complain about this or that aspect of Italian bureaucracy.

So it became clear that, as ever, those who had encountered problems complained and those who had few or none rarely felt the need to contribute to such forums. Also, we discovered, these rants were often completely out of date, as likely as not referring to circumstances and procedures that no longer existed.

Something else became clear from such sites ... many of the bad experiences that people complained about were self-inflicted, they arose because people had not done their homework, were not willing to accept that they were living in a different country with different ways of doing things. More than once I had to resist the temptation to email these folk to humbly suggest that possibly such situations arose *because* they had moved to Italy and were *not* in the UK.

There was a mindset too that said, 'if all Italians had been educated and trained in Britain and spoke the Queen's English fluently, then we ex-pat types wouldn't be having any of these problems.'

But, were that the case, Italy wouldn't be Italy would it? It's really simple ... don't move abroad it you don't want to cope with people speaking a foreign language and doing things a bit differently ... isn't that sort of what 'abroad' means?

This is not to say that we didn't glean *any* useful information from such forums but insightful gems were few and far between. So we complemented this online research by buying two books that purported to do more or less the same thing. I found these to be equally frustrating; yes, there were some useful tips but these were embedded in a framework of contradictions and inaccuracies not unconnected with their different dates of publication. It should have been obvious; anything in print about something so complex and fluid is likely to be out of date before the ink is dry.

The best source for up-to-date, uncomplicated information turned out to be a government website and the British Embassies in Rome and Naples. Here we found facts, figures and practical offers of assistance rather than some third-party whining because he or she had forgotten that they had moved to another country where they did have roast beef for dinner on Sundays and drove on the other side of the road.

From within this jigsaw we were trying to extract the corner and edge pieces, the key bits of information relating to what we could or should do about ensuring we had medical cover in Italy.

As we had already discovered, European Union rules were continually being reviewed or changed in an effort to make the sort of thing that we were planning easier, a little less complicated. For example, had we been making such plans a year earlier, we would have had to acquire our *permesso di soggiorno*, permission to stay, when we got to Italy. This changed in January 2008 and so our subsequent paper-chase was less complicated.

The regulations around medical care were no exception. For non-pensioners there was really only one option: private medical care. Of course, apart from financial considerations, there was no reason why pensioners couldn't also take out private medical insurance.

We therefore had a problem, we couldn't afford the private

insurance and neither of us was officially a pensioner. I would become of pensionable age the following year and Kay, who *was* of pensionable age (at the time this was sixty for a woman in the UK) had already opted to keep me company and to work on until she was sixty-five.

On paper, the way out of this conundrum was complicated but, in the end, proved reasonably straightforward.

The essence of the regulations was that, if one partner was a pensioner, then he (or she) could join another (EU) country's healthcare system and any partner would also be embraced as a dependent. In simple terms: if I had been a pensioner, then, as far as Italian healthcare was concerned, Kay would receive the same treatment (pun intended) as she would be seen as my dependent.

So *we* had to reverse the process. Kay decided that she would officially retire and take her state pension immediately so that, as a pensioner, she would be welcomed into the Italian healthcare system, with me running along behind as *her* dependent. To the credit of the UK's Pension Service (and Kay who did the donkey work), all the paperwork for this about-turn was completed before we left and we had received all the necessary documentation that we would need in Italy.

All we had to do was to see if it worked at the other end ... not just in Italy but in Calabria.

Over in Calabria Elvira was her usual helpful self with our questions about the Italian side of the medical equation.

She consulted with her doctor friend Rocco de Rito, whom we also had met a few times at Le Puzelle, and he told us we'd have to visit the ASL (Aziende Sanitarie Locali) in Mesoraca to do the paperwork when we got there. None of which, at the time, meant a great deal to us but it was good to know that somebody was on the case.

Rocco also insisted that we become his patients which is what we hoped he would say.

If either Kay or I had been confronted with a theoretical situation where we had to encapsulate our lives into three cubic metres and the back of a Renault Clio, we would have baulked at the very notion and, if pressed, probably taken weeks to come up with a list. When needs must, it's different.

We began by buying various sizes of heavy duty cardboard packing cases; as we knew their exact dimensions it was easy to work out how many would make three cubic metres. Nevertheless we made sure we were under the three metres to accommodate our work tables, a couple of sun loungers and a flat-folding, wrought-iron corner unit, none of which would fit in the boxes.

We continued to sort and clear, becoming increasingly ruthless as we did so. What didn't find its way into one of our boxes usually ended up in one of six categories: for shredding and/or burning; to take to the local tip for disposal or recycling; to sell at a car boot sale; to offer or give to friends and family; to sell. Sometimes things started off in one category and got demoted to another ... most often from car boot sale to tip or even the bonfire.

The sixth category? Well, there was of course the little pile of things that, space permitting, we would have liked to take but could live without if there wasn't the room. This was our 'pending' tray; it got smaller day by day.

We also had to decide what would go in the car with us and what would go with Euroman and Van, who I think now deserve names – Mark, Jeff and 'our' man, Ian.

Apart from overnight bags for the journey, we decided that our computers, a few paintings and, as padding and protection for these, bedding and duvets should go in the car. Also destined for the car were clothes we might need if Ian got delayed and bulky or heavy items that might prove too much for our packing cases, things such as our two metal document boxes, the breadmaker, the coffee maker, some of our larger pots and pans and my toolbox.

Basically anything we thought we might need in the first few days or en route, plus the things that were most precious to us, would go by car.

On-going was the problem of the animals: one cat, seven chickens and a couple of dozen fish. One solution would have been to feed the fish to the cat, then let the chickens and the cat fight to the death ... only problem was that the cat was shit-scared of the chickens and would have given up too easily and that would have still left us with seven chickens.

In the end the fish were relatively easy to re-house; we had a good friend with a pond and over a couple of days, as gradually I drained the pond, he gained twenty or so fine specimens ... the ones the heron didn't seem to like the look of back in April.

The chickens proved easier than we expected as a near neighbour, whom we had only recently got to know, also kept chickens and was more than happy to take ours, our chicken house, the fencing and all the other related paraphernalia that we had accumulated over the years so that we could eat the most expensive eggs in the known universe.

From the outset we were pretty sure we'd found a home for our jet-black, scaredy-cat, Sebbie. By late August however it was clear this was not going to happen. Nobody seemed to want poor Sebbie.

I spent a frustrating couple of weeks emailing, leaving messages for and speaking to almost every cat home and sanctuary in the area but to no avail. There was, it seemed, an unexpected glut of cats looking for new homes; quite simply, in the cat world, we were moving away at the worst possible time.

It was early September and there was only one cat sanctuary that had not got back to me; I had left a message on their answer machine about four days earlier and, ever the optimist, remained hopeful that they might be able to help.

And eventually they did call and their offer to help find a new home for Sebbie was very much appreciated but just less than an hour too late. No, he was still alive, but that same morning a friend of Kay's who had stayed with us overnight en route from Bristol Airport to her home in Wales offered to take him back home with her. Like our cottage, her rural house in Pembrokeshire backed onto a wood; he would feel at home, just a different mummy and no daddy.

After lunch we said our goodbyes to Sebbie, a faithful companion for fourteen years. He, of course, was none too pleased and protested vociferously from the confines of the cat basket that we knew he hated.

By the beginning of September the house was looking very sorry for itself. Upstairs there were two bedrooms, one of which we were still using as such but without the wardrobes that had already been sold. The other, also without its wardrobes, was full of packing cases, a few sealed, most pending; all labelled and their contents listed.

Downstairs, the main living room looked as if a bomb had just hit it. Most of the furniture was either gone or dismantled and awaiting collection by its new owner.

One half of the room was taken up with piles of books, already catagorised and awaiting pricing and, hopefully, purchase by a local bookseller. He did indeed buy the lot and, in so doing, paid for our overnight train trip from Düsseldorf to Verona.

Then, out of the blue, disaster struck. My bridge, the sophisticated repair my dentist had made to my enigmatic smile when we returned from Apulia three years earlier, snapped off. Up to this point that bite of Apulian bread, made specially for us by the wife of a single-toothed, octogenarian gardener, had cost me around seven hundred pounds and two trays of pastries. (The minutiae of this story are unravelled in the 'Back to Apulia' chapter of *Stumbling through Italy*.)

So now, within a few days of returning to Italy to live, I was once again sitting in the dentist's chair in the hope that he could glue the bridge back in place and that the repair would last. My enigmatic smile restored, I paid up albeit with the knowledge that such repairs did not last for ever – I was told I could expect another two or three years from it, particularly as he had used the latest sophisticated laser technology which would guarantee a stronger bond. (You've probably guessed where this sarcasm is heading.)

Even as I shook my dentist's hand and he wished us well in Calabria, little did I realise that this episode was destined to haunt me for well over a year and, more to the point, to cost me almost another two thousand euro.

As 11 September approached, we had to plan exactly how it was we would leave an empty shell of a house that evening, how and when we would finally wave goodbye to the cooker, the fridge and the bed and all the other things we couldn't reasonably do without until the last minute.

We decided that, if needs be, we could eat out for a few nights so could live without the cooker; for sustenance we would have our coffee machine which was going with us in the car. And there was always the local supermarket for a lunchtime sandwich.

A week earlier a man in his early forties, let's call him David, had answered an advert to buy the bed and arrived to take a look at it with his eleven-year old son Martin. He was happy to come back on our last day to collect it and we agreed a price. He asked about a couple of other things so I suggested he have a look round and, while he was doing so, I had a chat with young Martin.

When the boy told me the story of how his mother and father had split up and how his father was struggling to make a new start and how difficult it was for him, I decided to offer David everything that was still in the house on 11 September when he came to collect the bed. If he was lucky he would have the basics for furnishing a new home and our house-clearance problem would be solved.

September 11 dawned.

After we got up I dismantled the bed and we brought it and the mattress downstairs.

By mid-morning Kay's daughter and her partner had been and gone, their van full to bursting with all the things they had reserved.

I made one last trip to the local tip, bought lunch and filled the car with petrol.

Back 'home' I started to pack the car.

We finally taped up the last of our three cubic metres of packing cases and manhandled them down the stairs in readiness for Ian.

Our neighbour popped round to take the last of the garden tools.

A friend, Jon, arrived to make a few last trips to the tip for us.

David arrived with a van and a friend and loaded everything that wasn't going in our car or with Ian and *his* van.

I realised that my metal document box had vanished and called David.

David returned the document box he'd taken by mistake.

Kay read all the meters and filled in the last of the forms.

We continued to pack the car.

Mark (and not Ian as we had been expecting) arrived on behalf of Euroman and Van and I moved the car to make it easier for us to pack his van.

Never did three cubic metres seem so little, so much and so heavy.

We waved goodbye to Mark as our three cubic metres disappeared down the lane, turned left at the bottom, and headed for Calabria.

We finished packing the car and, with difficulty, I finally managed to shut the boot.

Mark phoned to say that he had heard on his radio that there had been a fire in the Channel Tunnel. He promised to keep us posted.

Kay and I walked round the house, in and out of each room, to check that we've left it more or less as we found it.

Half an hour later, at six-thirty, we locked the door on nine years in our little stone cottage, fourteen years in this village.

We got into our Clio, laden from floor to ceiling, and drove down the lane, turned left, stopped at the postbox to send the last of the bills on their way and joined the main road north to the motorway and the beginning of a new adventure.

The journey

The fifteen-minute drive to the motorway passed in silent contemplation.

In our own ways we were reflecting on the enormity of what we'd managed to achieve in just eight weeks. It was as if we'd completed the largest jigsaw in the world and, with our brief stop at the postbox, we had put the last piece in place.

Our heads were spinning with feelings of exhaustion, relief and exhilaration: exhausted after eight weeks of mental, emotional and physical mayhem; relieved that we'd accomplished what sometimes had seemed impossible in the time frame we'd set ourselves; exhilarated by the prospect of the journey and the new perspectives to come.

We were on the motorway heading east towards London when our contemplations were interrupted by the first call. It was Mark again, the news was not good on the Channel Tunnel. He thought we should know in case we needed to change our plans.

Our friend Mike, he of the garden pond full of fish that weren't eaten by the heron, called with the same gloomy news and thereafter became 'mission control' keeping us up to date with events underground and, when it became increasingly clear that our first underground crossing of the Channel was not going to happen, checking on the alternatives.

Of course, there was only one alternative, the ferry from Dover; it was when this sunk in that I realised I knew absolutely nothing about the geography of south-east Kent and had to ask Mike how far it was from Folkstone to Dover.

They were closer than I thought, just seven or eight miles he said, so there didn't seem any point in changing our overnight arrangements at Folkstone. Mike also confirmed that ferry operators would honour Tunnel bookings. We would just have to have an earlier start than planned.

We were on the last leg to Folkstone when we pulled off the motorway to have something to eat at a service area; I also bought a map of Kent just to be sure that I had the morning's route to Dover imprinted on my brain ... I knew I could follow signs to Dover the next morning but I needed to 'see' it beforehand, I needed to have that visual version in my head.

When we reached our hotel, it was clear that Closed-Tunnel-Mania had already taken up residence ... we were not the only ones asking for an early call the next morning for the dash to Dover and an early ferry.

It was late, we were tired ... a restless sleep beckoned.

Scarcely refreshed, we woke to a dank, drizzly morning; a typical English morning on the cusp of autumn. Just below our feet there was a tunnel; it all should have been so easy but here we were, driving in the opposite direction, following the road signs to Dover.

The route to the ferries was well sign-posted and, once inside the harbour complex, I stopped to confirm with one of the orange-coated stewards (the none-too-bright one) that our tickets for the Tunnel were valid. He told me they were and soon we were in the queue at one of the drive-by kiosks to board the ferry.

It was our turn and Kay passed our tickets through to the operator who then asked for our ferry tickets; she looked blank – we had, it seemed, missed out on a part of the process. When we entered the port complex we should have first called in at the terminal office where we would have had our Tunnel tickets validated before we were issued with replacement tickets for the ferry.

We had to go back and start again; I was crestfallen for I was pretty sure that if we missed this particular ferry we would be lucky to make our train connection at Düsseldorf by four-fifteen in the afternoon. I kept my thoughts to myself ... I was concentrating on sticking pins in an effigy of the none-too-bright, orange-coated steward.

The man at the kiosk gave us a pass whereby we could return via an, otherwise off-limits, serpentine route to the terminal over a mile back the way we'd come. Here we had to queue for about ten minutes to 'exchange' tickets before shooting back to the ferry which I knew was due to sail at any moment.

We joined the queue to the same kiosk as before and, papers all in order, drove onto the boat; there were only two other vehicles behind us.

A quarter of an hour later the whitish cliffs around Dover were no more than a greyish blur. France beckoned and with it my first chance to drive our little left-hand-drive Clio on *its* correct side of the road.

France was dank and depressing and soon became Belgium. We had been on the road over an hour in miserable weather conditions that required focussed concentrated driving when I realised I needed to stop and have a short sleep. I pulled off the road and parked outside a small cafè where I slept for

Sailing from Dover; all aboard at Düsseldorf

almost half an hour before we went inside for a strong coffee and a snack.

Belgium became Holland. We were making good time and, approaching Antwerp, were even pondering when and where we might stop for lunch. But Antwerp had other ideas. For no obvious reason, other than volume of traffic, we were reduced to a slow crawl for well over an hour and, suddenly, all thoughts of a lunch break were abandoned and in their place a mad dash to Düsseldorf was now the order of the day.

Holland became Germany. Outside the weather was brightening; inside the mood was gloomier as, approaching Duisburg around three, we hit more heavy traffic. Finally we were following signs down towards Düsseldorf. We left the *autobahn* and followed signs to and through the outskirts of the city. I stopped to ask for directions to the station; foolishly I thought it would be well signposted. It had just gone four.

We were now in downtown Düsseldorf and the signs to the *Hauptbahnhof* that I had been following had suddenly petered out (I had thought that was only an Italian phenomenon). I parked on a corner just beyond what I thought might be a railway bridge and ran across several lanes of traffic to a parked police car I'd spotted and asked a grumpy policeman where the station was. He looked at me as if I were a cretin and pointed. We were parked outside the back entrance.

I crossed the road to tell Kay. She already knew. A man had come out of the nearby tobacconists and asked her if she needed help. It was thirteen minutes past four. A minute later we were in the queue to load the car onto the train.

By four-thirty the car was loaded and we were heading on foot with our overnight bags into the station itself for something to eat and drink. We wouldn't be able to board the train itself for another hour by which time passenger coaches and car wagons would be as one.

Each carriage had a single door-side corridor, with a bathroom at each end; also at one end there was a small compartment for the carriage's guard; somewhere up ahead was the restaurant car. Each compartment could sleep up to six but could be reserved, as we had done, just for two. By five-forty-five we had settled into our mobile home for the next sixteen hours.

Right on schedule at six, we stood by the window and watched as we crept out of the station and left Düsseldorf behind to head south into the German countryside. As I watched the towns and stations flash by it occurred to me that if we had come through the Tunnel as planned, we would have arrived in France later than we actually did and so, given the traffic we encountered, there was a fair chance that we might have missed this train. It didn't bear thinking about.

I was watching out for one particular town south of Bonn, a little place close to the river Rhine called Bad Honnef. When I was seventeen I came to Germany by myself to improve my German and found ten week's work in a small jam-making factory in Bad Honnef called Dienel und Jakob. From the internet, and Google Earth in particular, I knew that the rail-side factory, just along from the station, didn't exist anymore but I was interested to see if there was anything of this little place that I might recognise after nearly fifty years.

There wasn't. We were travelling too fast and the light was fading. But it didn't stop me momentarily reflecting on a time that I recall as if it were yesterday. Every day during my lunch break at the factory I crossed these tracks via the footbridge and went into the large engineering works on the other side. Here I innocently joined the queue at the works canteen, collected my tray and proffered my bowl for the daily soup and bread which I consumed in silence before walking back across to Dienel und Jakob.

I was the only one to think of this, it just seemed like a good idea at the time; it was free and warming and nobody ever queried the fact that I didn't actually work there. I obviously looked the part.

After the muted excitement at seeing a part of my youth flash by, we had a couple of hours in which to stretch out in our little overnight kingdom before dinner.

This was the first opportunity we'd had to relax for weeks; we didn't have to do anything, see anyone, be anywhere, focus on a deadline, check emails or tend the bonfire. This time, this space was our own and we relished the freedom just to sit back and do absolutely nothing and marvel at the fact we'd got this far in one piece, to wonder what these next days and weeks would bring.

By eight-thirty we had returned to the real world, albeit a long and narrow world, and walked along the corridor to the restaurant car where we had to wait almost half an hour to be seated. But it was worth it.

We'd eaten on moving trains in the past but this was an altogether different experience. This was no two- or three-hour jaunt, this was coursing through Europe for sixteen hours in an olde worlde romantic setting that was the stuff of Agatha Christie whodunits. There was just the slightest hint of intrigue as we surveyed our fellow diners for that tell-tale mannerism that said there was more to him or her or them than met the eye.

Each table had its quota of suspects, their faces only partially given form by the brash yellow glow from the stylish semi-circular table lights. Which one, I wondered, would be the victim, who was the spy on the run, apart from me, who was the other internationally famous sleuth pretending to be interested in no-one, but missing nothing?

In reality we were the ones with the story to tell – we were the ones who had defied all the odds and got ourselves onto this train. We were not running away but, for me, this part of our journey created the inexplicable sensation of fleeing, we were on the run, and tomorrow we would wake up safe and sound in Italy.

We were joined at our table by a German couple who used this route to Italy regularly; it was so simple, they said in almost embarrassingly perfect English, it cut out most of the driving and, of course, the fuel, the tolls and the alpine tunnels.

Still in international murder mystery mode I made what I thought was a comical quip about already having solved the crime. Our German friends didn't understand my humour until I explained about *Murder on the Orient Express*. Even then I'm not sure they really got it.

As it happened they were from the Bonn area and knew Bad Honnef well. They confirmed that Dienel und Jakob had indeed gone and also, they thought, the engineering works where I lunched every day, had also closed down or was about to do so. They enjoyed my story about the free lunches there and promised not to report me to the authorities.

We shared our adventure with them, the only part of which they found difficult to grasp was why we were going to Calabria. They had been to many parts of Italy but had clearly avoided the deep south; they had, I guessed, succumbed to the oft-broadcast notion that the south was the pits, the arsehole of Italy, the unsophisticated and uninviting rump of a fragile nation.

We were not unaware of this reputation, this stereotypical view of a part of Italy that has had such a chequered and uncompromising history, home to ruffians, kidnappers, brigands, and their modern incarnation the 'ndrangheta, that even some Italians would think twice about setting foot in it.

(The *'ndrangheta* is Calabria's equivalent of the mafia. Despite its lesser international status it has a reputation for aggressive criminality and violence equal to the Sicilian mafia; its main organisational base is said to be in Reggio Calabria. Its main claim to international notoriety was when, in 1973, they kidnapped the 16-year old Paul Getty III and then sent one of his ears to his father in the post in an effort to focus his attention in meeting their ransom demands. It worked.)

I'm not sure we convinced our German friends that we wouldn't be on the same train as them in three week's time; they heading back home to Bonn, we scurrying post-haste back to England. Or perhaps they saw us as another couple of ruffians that would fit in just fine in Calabrian society.

We woke up to a bright alpine Italian morning, just as the train was pulling out of Bolzano where the German couple got off and where one of the car wagons was unhitched ... I just hoped it was the right one and strained to pick out our little Clio as we rounded some of the sharper bends when the cars at the back of the train momentarily came into view.

Our steward/guard knocked on the door, passed us our breakfast and confirmed that we were on schedule (as if we ever doubted it) and would arrive in Verona in a little over an hour.

Just before ten we were cruising gently through Verona's outskirts and, as the minute-hand on the station clock visibly clicked onto ten o'clock, came to a gentle halt alongside the platform. Here everyone disembarked before the train's remaining cargo of cars was shunted round to another part of the station complex to where we and our fellow passengers headed on foot.

By eleven we were once again driving in Italy, heading south on the *autostrada* towards Modena.

It was lunchtime and we had reached the Bologna area and were looking forward to a brief pit-stop and something to eat when we drove into and through a ferocious rainstorm. We had encountered such weather once before in southern Calabria and Sicily, the sort of weather that literally brings many Italian drivers, unaccustomed to such downpours, to a standstill. More at home in such conditions, we pressed on south towards Florence, postponing lunch until the rain abated.

Back on the *autostrada*, the sun finally making a unconvincing breakthrough, we headed towards and round Rome, south of which we, and the car, were back on familiar territory. An hour later we arrived at our overnight destination, Triflisco near Caserta just north of Naples, and settled in to the inaptly named Hotel Miami.

Our fatigue was countered by the knowledge that the next day, Sunday, we could have a late start and enjoy a more leisurely drive. We would be on our last leg south, skirting Naples and Salerno, heading out of Campania to briefly traverse the spur of Basilicata that dares to reach out to touch the Tyrrhenian Sea before crossing an unseen border into Calabria.

And, despite everything that these last few days had thrown at us, it looked as if we would arrive at Santa Severina bang on schedule.

It was three-thirty as we turned right off the SS107, the *Strada Statali* that spectacularly crosses the Sila mountains to link Cosenza and Crotone, the west coast with the east coast, the Tyrrhenian Sea with the Ionian. We crossed the river Neto and caught our first glimpse of that uncompromising slab of rock atop which Santa Severina clings with, it sometimes seemed, unjustified optimism.

Five minutes later we turned the last bend on the climbing,

winding approach and were confronted with the close-up of the town, with its lofty *centro storico* lit up by the late afternoon sun, that still left me as breathless as it did the first time we rounded that same bend.

Finally, some three days after we left an empty cottage near Bath, at twenty-to-four on Sunday 14 September, we turned into Le Puzelle's driveway to be welcomed, as usual and as expected, by Mara the dog.

No 26 Largo Borelli: outside and inside

Day one

Other welcomes followed. Vincenzo (Le Puzelle's owner), Elvira (his partner), Roberto (his son), Salvatore (the chef), Martino (the waiter) and Giuliano (who did almost everything else) were all there and all had to be greeted and told that 'yes' we had returned to live in Santa Severina *per sempre*, for always.

I could detect that, although we said *per sempre*, we were not being taken literally. Either we were not using *per sempre* correctly or I had not got the message across to Elvira and Roberto clearly enough in my emails. We took Elvira aside and explained that, in effect, we had nothing in England we were here for good, this was day one of the rest of our lives.

Like everyone else it seemed she had thought we'd come back to stay for a few months, maybe a year or two, maybe we'd buy a house and use it as a holiday home. She hadn't quite appreciated the finality of the situation and, when she did, she hugged us with such welcoming generosity and a tear in her eye that we were left in no doubt she both understood and approved.

I took Giuliano aside to ask for his version of what had happened on our last morning at Le Puzelle back in July when, uncharacteristically, he hadn't turned up to prepare the breakfasts and to say goodbye to us. "That was your fault", he said, "You gave me the wine." I had no idea what he was talking about until he reminded me that I had given him a bottle of wine for his birthday and that particular night, the night before we left, he decided to share it with a Romanian friend ... it was clearly *my* fault that he had overslept!

We were joined by Salvatore who, like Giuliano, was still trying to get his head round the idea that we were here in Santa Severina for good. I had an idea and put my hand in my pocket to take out a small bunch of keys.

I explained that these keys were the keys to our house in England ... this was the front door, this the garage, this the shed, holding each one up in turn. I then walked to the edge of the garden where the land dropped away over a broad and deep valley and hurled them as far as I could down into the sparsely wooded slopes.

"Now do you believe me?" I said. They believed me ... we were staying in Calabria *per sempre*.

Elvira showed us to our room for the night, room 5, the room we'd booked for three weeks in June 2009 but now would no longer need. We were staying here at Le Puzelle for just one night and hoped to move into Roberto's mother's house the next day, the following day we were expecting Ian to arrive with our three cubic metres.

My phone rang. It was Ian. He explained that he was ahead of schedule and had already made it to Calabria and would be able to deliver everything the following morning first thing ... he suggested I gave him a call when we were up and he'd be with us in less than half an hour.

While this was good news, we still hadn't seen the house we were moving in to, nor would we have any keys until later the next day.

I spoke to Vincenzo to see if room 8 was occupied, or likely to be so in the next few days. I chose room 8 as it was nearest to the car park and therefore could be used to store our boxes for a day or so. I also offered to pay for the room but Vincenzo would not hear of it.

Before we ate, we drove up into town to see Carlo to make sure that, whatever he'd heard, we *were* here *per sempre*. Carlo owned one of the four bars in Santa Severina's *piazza* and was, I suppose, our closest friend outside Le Puzelle. For three consecutive summers we had sat in the sun at Carlo's tables and watched Santa Severina at work and play. It was from our ringside seat here that we watched someone catch a couple of pigeons by the feet and saw our first Santa Severina wedding. And it was from here that, almost every evening, we observed the intriguing ritual of the *passeggiata*, the leisurely pre-prandial early evening walk when friends and relatives stroll and chat and, sometimes, do a little business; a chance to see and be seen and as much a feature of a large city as it is of a small town or village.

News of my dramatic clarification of our status with the keys had not yet made it as far as the town's *piazza* but by this time we'd learnt that, to get the message across, it was necessary to be emphatic and stress that we had no other house, apartment, caravan, boat, garage, enclosed space anywhere in the known universe; until tomorrow we were homeless.

Later that evening, after another of Salvatore's culinary masterpieces, we drove back up to the town with Vincenzo and Elvira to have a look at 'our' house from the outside. It was smaller than we expected and clearly a modern addition to the locale; it was close to the *centro storico* on a narrow *corso* that was just passable by car but might be difficult for a van. It seemed that dropping our stuff off at Le Puzelle was a better option than expecting Ian to negotiate this part of town.

Monday dawned, our first as Calabrian residents.

After breakfast I called Ian who told me he was making a cup of tea in his van and would be with us soon. I suggested he drive to the edge of town and call; I reminded him that any satellite navigation system based on postcodes wouldn't work here as the whole town had the same postcode.

Half an hour later it was an agitated Ian that called. He had driven up and around the four hairpin bends towards the *centro storico* and, at the top, found himself in the middle of on-going roadworks where it wasn't easy to turn, especially with a trailer. I knew exactly where he was and said I'd be there in five minutes.

Just before the start of the roadworks was the entrance to the castle car park; I could see no van on the road so turned into the car park and had to halt abruptly. I had stopped less than a metre from the front of a UK-registered van and its startled driver.

This was the first time Ian and I had met. The greetings over, he explained how the guys working on the road had unhitched his trailer, wheeled it away while he backed into the car park and then they reunited trailer and van. He said they just saw the problem and immediately helped him solve it; language, he said, wasn't an issue, they just got on with it. This first encounter with Calabrian hospitality had left him almost speechless.

Ian followed me back down to Le Puzelle where we emptied the trailer into room 8. When I say 'we', everyone pitched in and, job done, Ian was soon sitting in the sun eating the breakfast that Giuliano had prepared for him. Once again Ian was marvelling at the generosity of these people.

Giuliano was doing a bit of marvelling of his own. He had been scrutinising Ian's van and trailer when he realised that the steering wheel was on the right. This intrigued him and he quizzed Ian about how easy (or difficult) it was to drive in Italy; he wanted to know everything and particularly how Ian passed other vehicles when he couldn't easily see the oncoming traffic.

Giuliano had recently acquired his first car – almost the first thing he did when we arrived was proudly show off his little red Fiat – and knew that the ability to pass another vehicle (whether you can see the oncoming traffic or not) was an important skill hereabouts.

Ian left Le Puzelle to head north for a pick-up near Milan; his brief experience of Calabria had left him fed, watered and happy that he was leaving us in good hands. Over breakfast he had told us the story of the strange woman whom he moved to France one year and brought back the next ... she had chosen to live in an isolated farmhouse and didn't have a car. He thought it extremely unlikely that he'd be doing the same with us.

(Ian's Italian adventure was not quite over. I later discovered that he never made it to Milan. En route he had an accident on the *autostrada* north of Rome when a wheel from the lorry in front came off and shot into the front of his van. Although he was not badly hurt, the van was undriveable and had to be shipped back to the UK.)

As Ian left Le Puzelle, another car turned into the driveway. It was Angela reporting for her cleaning duties. Angela was a special friend. We were the only clients at Le Puzelle that she had ever really got to know as almost always we were the only ones still there in the morning when she arrived. Unlike most other guests it had not been our style to get up and head for the coast or the hills every morning; there was a pool at Le Puzelle and almost every day we had it to ourselves.

So, sitting under our ancient pool-side olive tree, Angela

gradually became part of our lives and we hers. We had visited her home many times and knew three of her four daughters very well (the fourth was married and lived in the north).

Not surprisingly Angela too needed a little convincing that we were now Calabrian residents and had nowhere else to go ... Giuliano emphasised the point by theatrically re-enacting the key-throwing incident while simultaneously laughing out loud and patting me on the back.

Angela was finally convinced, the more so when she popped her head into room 8 and saw the boxes of evidence for herself ... and immediately offered us the basement of her house to store said boxes should we need to do so.

It was mid-afternoon and, as arranged, we met with Silvana, Vincenzo's ex-wife – Roberto's mother and a classics teacher in Crotone – at her little house in Largo Borrelli ... soon to be our first home in Santa Severina. The plan was to empty the car's contents into the house, sleep there and complete the move the following day by transferring the boxes from Le Puzelle.

This was our first look inside. It was small, two and a half floors: the bottom, the main bedroom and a bathroom; the middle, the kitchen-cum-dining area with another bathroom and, above the kitchen, a sort of mezzanine area with a sofa-bed.

There were two doors to and from the outside world, one off the downstairs bedroom, the other, the main entrance, into the kitchen-cum-diner; there was also a small balcony off the kitchen and a tiny storeroom off the balcony. All-in-all a quirky little house, not suitable for swinging the proverbial cat, that would be fine short-term while we readjusted to life in Calabria.

Silvana waited with us while a wardrobe was delivered and assembled in the bedroom; we paid her the rent up to the end of September and started to unpack the car. Before she left us to our own devices she confirmed what had always been unclear, that we could remain here in the house for as long as we wanted ... she understood that for us it was a springboard, a base for which we were grateful and from where we could begin our search for something more permanent. Somewhere where we could indeed swing that proverbial cat.

By late afternoon, just twenty-four hours after we'd arrived back in Santa Severina, we had emptied the car and had begun to ferry some of the smaller, car-sized, boxes from room 8 at Le Puzelle to Largo Borrelli. We had arranged with Vincenzo that he and Giuliano would help us move what was left the following morning; anything we didn't need immediately or simply hadn't room for at Silvana's house would have a temporary home in Angela's basement.

That evening I had intended to cook our first meal in Calabria as residents ... but time and events got the better of us and instead we took a short trip out of town to Gina's, a small restaurant we'd discovered during the summer when Salvatore had a night off. Gina and her family were more than a little surprised to see us and their welcome was as unexpected as it was effusive; and once again we had to explain that we were here *per sempre*.

So, no, we didn't eat at home as planned but we *did* sleep under our own duvet.

Generally our first twenty-four hours had gone much as we expected.

True, no-one really understood that we were moving here for good, *per sempre*.

It was also a surprise to hear too that somehow it was my fault that Giuliano had overslept on our last day here back in July.

And, yes, Ian did turn up a day earlier than arranged.

And Silvana's house in Largo Borrelli was not really what we were expecting; it was a bit on the small side even for the three cubic metres and Clio-load of our worldly goods.

What was not a surprise were the many kindnesses we were shown that day by Vincenzo, Elvira, Giuliano and Angela at Le Puzelle, and by Silvana and by Gina.

Calabrian generosity was the one thing that we had come to expect.

Two restless nights

It had all happened so fast. Here we were back in Santa Severina in this tiny house, a house that we would try to make a home, albeit a temporary one. And, yes, we were under our own duvet but I recall lying awake that night trying to piece together all the disparate strands that had helped bring us to Italy and to this place.

Odd connections, themselves unconnected and long forgotten, with Italy and Italians wandered round my head, drifted in and out of my consciousness as I desperately sought the release of sleep ...

I pictured the six-year-old me running excitedly along Belfast's Woodstock Road on Sunday afternoons to Fusco's for a large tub of Mr Fusco's wondrous Italian ice-cream. This was our weekend treat and the only time on a Sunday that we were allowed to venture out of the house at this otherwise gloom-ridden time in this part of the city.

In the late fifties there I am again on the hunt for a cornet (which we called a 'poke') of Italian ice-cream, this time on family holidays in the north Antrim coastal resort of Portstewart, the home of Morelli's ice-cream.

The spotty, mid-teen me was enjoying history for the first

time as the genial Eric Howard took us through the story of the 'Re-unification of Italy' and introduced us to the multifarious characters who fought for and against making a nation out of a boot-shaped peninsula. When Kay and I became frequent visitors to Italy bits and pieces of this story emerged from the deep recesses of my memory as I recognised the names of all the protagonists now permanently on display in every city and town as the names of streets, avenues and squares – Garibaldi, Mazzini, Cavour, Crispi, Victor Emmanuel ...

Then there was the less spotty, more confident seventeen-year-old me who decided to spend the ten-week summer holiday working in a jam factory in Germany, one of only three foreigners there ... the other two being young, cocky, good-looking Italian lads. We formed a strange alliance we three, but I was never a part of their plot to sabotage the post-war rebuilding of German industry. I can still see them standing idly, innocently, expectantly, in the corner of the tin-labelling room as, arms folded, they watched the fruits of their nefarious endeavours rattle through the machinery – dozens of tins without a label followed by one or two with dozens of labels shooting off in all directions and the tall, wiry foreman, his slate-blue overall flailing behind as he twisted and turned like a headless chicken screaming "Halt! Halt!". I wished I could recall their names and where they were from but all that is lost forever in the mists of time.

Ten years on, the married me has booked a coach trip from London to Rijeka in what was then Yugoslavia, today's Croatia ... except that something goes wrong with the booking and, at no extra cost, we are flown to Milan and bussed on to Rijeka. It was very late, very dark but, en route to Trieste, I remember stopping for a short toilet-refreshment break at a place called Lido di Jesolo near Venice ... to date the nearest to Venice I have ever been. Only one thing never left me about this forty-year-old adventure – in my mind's eye I could always see the idiosyncratic green and white façade of Milan Airport which, I have recently discovered, has scarcely changed in over forty years .

In the early 1990s the unmarried me is working as a graphic designer for a Manchester-based photographic publishing house and in particular I am working on a book (though not as its designer) with a Scottish-Italian photographer, Owen Logan. The book, *Bloodlines*, documents the cultural relationship between the descendents of Italians who emigrated to Scotland (often as ice-cream makers) and the way of life of the people and places in their Italian homeland. Owen lived with his Italian mother and it is while sitting by their Edinburgh fireside not long before Christmas that I am first introduced to one of the many permutations of the wondrous Panettone cake. Of course these days the Panettone is no stranger to the supermarket shelves but in the UK at this time it was as common as hen's teeth.

Married again, and the next most significant, cataclysmic even, Italian encounter came in the late 1990s when, as I've described in *Stumbling through Italy*, Kay and I happened upon the Capetti brothers' restaurant in Bath.

And here I am, still lying under our very own duvet in Calabria, all these brief Italian encounters jockeying for position in my fading memories ... still fighting off sleep.

Of course the only real catalyst in all of this was when we met Ivano and Vic Capetti and became interested in the land of their forefathers. The rest is mere coincidence and as such unimportant.

I cannot help wonder, however, if those two Italian lads are still around. Like me they'll be pensioners now and, like me, I'm sure that sometimes they think back to that warm adventurous summer by the Rhine where a trio of teenagers began to become men. Perhaps they tell their grandchildren about the quiet, strangely handsome, Irishman they once knew there. Perhaps they went on to design a sophisticated technology for taking the labels *off* tins and bottles without leaving a sticky mess behind. Perhaps one day our paths may yet cross again. Stranger things have happened.

Finally, just before sleep squeezes the form out of these disparate, dispersing memories, I begin to focus on the here and now and what we have to do over these next days and weeks to make ourselves a home in Santa Severina.

*

And now, more than two years on, I'm doing the same thing again ... still under the same duvet, still trying to embrace sleep but unable to stop looking back over these few years in Santa Severina, looking forward (in the literal sense) to how best to describe our experiences. It should be straightforward, one day, one week, one month, one year at a time.

And while the first few weeks can be recounted thus, thereafter there are so many interlacing stories that deserve their independence from our day-to-day lives.

So, with sleep slowly seducing the senses, I decide that, apart from the next chapter, what follows will not be a strictly chronological, blow-by-blow account of life atop this hill but rather a look at aspects of our life in Calabria. Clearly these will begin with a chronological element but are, by definition, destined to go off at tangents as they interweave and overlap.

And perhaps later, when I sense I'm at risk of repeating myself, it might be more appropriate to move forward in a slightly different vein, to weave a broader canvas and concentrate on those areas of our lives that seem important but over a greater timescale.

———————————

Finally, sandwiched between two lines, I decide to conclude each chapter with a related story, a yarn, a snippet, an observation, an incident, a memory that will, I hope, serve to illustrate and emphasise the one constant in our lives here ... that day-to day we have learnt to expect the unexpected.

———————————

Part two

The first year

From our first faltering footsteps as Santa Severina residents to the time we began to walk upright with a modicum of confidence to become part of this Calabrian community.

Settling in

This is not the first book to recount a move to another country, another culture. Nor will it be the last.

But although the essence of the story is not unique, the reality probably, no, almost certainly is.

We did not have family in Italy. Apart from 'meeting, greeting and eating', we did not speak the language. We had not bought a property or land in Italy. We did not move to an area where there were other native English speakers. We did not have a safe haven in England (or anywhere else for that matter). We were, as you must have guessed, not young.

All we brought from our previous lives was that three cubic metres, our little Clio and its bounty and, most importantly, our ability to get on with people. Yes, we had been to Santa Severina before and had unwittingly created a unique little support group of friends who would, we anticipated, come to our rescue as and when required. But that was it.

Many people in England thought we were slightly mad (they didn't necessarily voice this but we could read between the eyes); I suspect many in and around Santa Severina thought the same but they were prepared to play along and lend a helping hand.

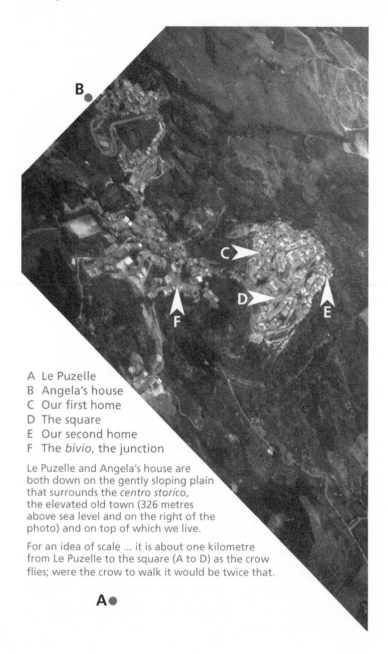

A Le Puzelle
B Angela's house
C Our first home
D The square
E Our second home
F The *bivio*, the junction

Le Puzelle and Angela's house are
both down on the gently sloping plain
that surrounds the *centro storico*,
the elevated old town (326 metres
above sea level and on the right of the
photo) and on top of which we live.

For an idea of scale ... it is about one kilometre
from Le Puzelle to the square (A to D) as the crow
flies; were the crow to walk it would be twice that.

So this story is not about restoring a long-derelict farmhouse, resurrecting an old vineyard, grafting olive trees, tending to the animals, partaking in the ritualistic slaughter of a pig, summer days in the country with family while the grandchildren skipped through the corn or any of the other romantic tales that are generally the stuff of such stories.

Our story is simple ... it is the story of two English-speaking pensioners adapting to a new life as the only English-speakers in a small hilltop town in Calabria. Period.

*

That first morning brought with it a bright Calabrian light trying to force its way through the cracks in the shutters. I woke disorientated, wondering where exactly I was, trying to make sense of the shapes and the light, seeking out the door to the bathroom. Relieved, the reality slowly dawned that this small bedroom, and one and a half times the same space on the floors above, was to be our home for the next few weeks, months perhaps. But in the meantime we had work to do.

Top of our agenda that day was sorting what we needed from room 8 at Le Puzelle (and bringing it up to the house in the *centro storico*), and then taking everything that wouldn't fit or was not a priority across to Angela's house on the outskirts of the town where we could leave it for as long as we needed to. We would get round to unpacking and organising the house itself later in the day.

(There, I've mentioned three locations in quick succession and the only way you'll appreciate what I'm talking about is by referring to the photo opposite ... this is not a Google image but a photo I took from a plane on the approach to Crotone airport. I've had to turn it through 45° to get north in the right place and neither Angela's house nor the Le Puzelle are actually in the shot so I've marked their locations. It's the best I can do.)

I won't bore you with the minutiae of that particular jigsaw puzzle, suffice to say that by lunchtime all our boxes and bits and pieces were in the right place (though sometimes this meant rationalising two or more boxes). And, yes, those destined for Angela's basement had a hair-raising trip in the back of Vincenzo's pick-up in the company of Giuliano who stood up the whole journey holding everything in place as we negotiated the several hairpin bends; Kay and I were in our car behind, sole witnesses to this Calabrian way of relocating.

By early afternoon we were ready to unpack and settle in, ready to personalise these three small spaces, to make something resembling a home out of this little house.

For the first couple of days we were generally house-bound, sorting things out and making lists ... list of things to buy (often things that we'd had in England and never thought to bring or didn't have room for) and lists of things we knew we had brought but were, as Sod's Law would dictate, at the bottom of one of the boxes in Angela's basement.

When we took breaks we familiarised ourselves with all the little side-streets and alleyways on 'our' side of the rock; when we'd been here on holiday it was up in the square we spent our time and not where people, people like us now, actually lived.

It was a five-minute walk to the square, indeed there is hardly anywhere atop the hill that is more than five minutes from the square, so naturally we joined Carlo of an evening for a glass of wine. At first it was a strange feeling ... as visitors we had had a drink *before* we left to dine at Le Puzelle and rarely saw what happened next. Now we were like everyone else and came back out to play after nine, a few sitting at the bars, most plying up and down the square between church and castle, trying to walk off the pasta. For the first time we realised that the *passaggiata* was also a post-prandial ritual, though still one that was generally male dominated. The men had been out and about earlier while the women were cooking and they were out and about again now that the same women were clearing up. A fact of life here but one that was changing as outside influences, brought home via television and movies, slowly infiltrated the Calabrian psyche.

It was mid-September and about eight degrees warmer than in England, for us an extended summer with the luxury of sitting out in the square, glass in hand, on these balmy evenings. At the house there was a small balcony off the kitchen where we generally ate but only a small corner of this ever caught the sun and even then it was for no more than half an hour in the early evening. This we found very frustrating. Of course we weren't here in Santa Severina just for the sun but it would have been good to have been on more than a nodding acquaintance with it ... and even this was only possible when we took it in turns to sit in that cherished corner.

Still there was the *panorama*, a public sitting area and viewing point right on the western edge of the hill, a minute from the house, with dramatic views across the valley to the Sila mountains. And it was to here that we gravitated most days after lunch to read and relax for an hour or so as the sun turned the corner and moved round from south to west. Public it might have been but we never saw anyone else there; it was our own little stone and brick garden in the sun.

One of the first locals to take us under his wing was the retired head of the *Liceo*, Santa Severina's upper or high school, the last stop before university.

On our final evening in the square before we returned to

England back in July I looked up to see this pipe-smoking man heading for our table. Our eyes met momentarily and he thought better of it and abruptly steered a course away from the bar and back into the square itself. About half an hour later he tried again and this time I made sure he didn't know that I had seen him. He made it to our table, stuck out his hand, introduced himself as Severini Franco (surname first) and asked politely if he could join us. *Permesso?*

He had observed us for three years and had been itching to break the ice and practise his English; it was just unfortunate that he chose the evening before we returned to England to do so. But from that first brief encounter we gleaned that he and I had quite a lot in common (apart from our good looks, that is): both ex-headteachers (he retired, I threw the towel in), both with a smattering of German and both dabblers in the dark art of writing. Franco's 'dabbling' was on a slightly higher plain than mine in that he was translating the definitive history of the Kingdom of the Two Sicilies from German to Italian ... I recall how impressed he was that an English-speaking tourist should even have heard of this period in the story of Italy. Truth be known, I surprised myself and quietly thanked the long-dead Eric Howard and his history lessons that I thought I'd forgotten.

So here we were, eleven weeks on and there he is again, a short balding man with a sagacious, ruddy face, pipe in mouth, hand on pipe, striding across the square to renew our brief friendship and, without a single word, just a particular questioning flick of the head, asked, "What the hell are you two doing back here?".

The three of us continued from where we left off in July and for those first few weeks when the evenings still carried the smell of summer we enjoyed many a bottle of wine together.

We renewed another acquaintance early the second evening

when *il sindaco*, the town's mayor Bruno Cortese, asked permission to sit at our table, shook our hands, formally welcomed us to Santa Severina and then relaxed the apparent formality of the occasion by buying us a drink.

We had never actually met before but with a slight nod of the head he had always acknowledged our presence when we were here on holiday and, we were to discover later, we had a number of mutual friends at Le Puzelle which was how he knew we were here to live ... residents and constituents.

I took the opportunity to ask him about ADSL, the broadband telephone-line internet connection that Santa Severina didn't have ... was it imminent, I wanted to know. He assured me it was a priority and that it was fast approaching (he suggested Christmas but omitted to be specific about *which* Christmas) but in the meantime why didn't we invest in a *chiavetta*. We had no idea what he was talking about so, as this was complicated stuff and he had almost no English, he called over a colleague who happened to be passing and who clearly had one of these *chiavetta* things. Nevertheless we still got bogged down in our lack of language, particularly technical language and it was suggested that we pop in to the *Comune*, the Town Hall, the following morning when all would be revealed.

All was revealed ... a *chiavetta* (literally a small key) looks like a memory stick that plugs into the USB socket of any computer but this 'memory stick' can pick up an internet signal like a mobile phone ... and, like a mobile phone, the strength of the signal depends on where the computer happens to be.

We had already set up our respective computers, one on the mezzanine floor and one in the bedroom, but could only use them to record or look over data, we had no connection with the outside world which, for two people for whom such a connection was the normality of life, was unbelievably frustrating. There they sat, two iMacs, sleek white icons of the internet age, symbols of innovative Apple technology, but now more and more like white elephants, trapped, forlorn, in an ADSL-less world ... which, of course, is how it used to be.

Crotone beckoned ... we had our list and second on the list was a *chiavetta*.

We had been aware that the internet could be a problem for us but on holiday had never picked up that the Italians had worked round the problem in such an original way.

Much of southern Italy is remote but even remote areas are home to people who want and need internet access. So the mobile phone companies all adapted their existing technology and came up with the *chiavetta*. It had become a bit like Glasgow's ice-cream wars in the 1980s (without the violence, I hasten to add) with the major rival mobile phone companies coming up with new deals almost daily. And of course while all this was going on Italian Telecom was striving to outflank them all and bring broadband (ADSL) to more and more people.

When *we* bought our *chiavetta*, the best deal was with TIM, if we'd waited a week or two it would have been with WIND and so on, everyone was upping the anti: the download speed, the number of hours available each month, the monthly price and the cost of the hardware, the *chiavetta* itself and eventually even the range of colours available. At the time of writing we can buy the same system, for a third of the monthly fee, for double the hours (perhaps even unlimited time), at much faster speeds ... and the *chiavetta* would be thrown in for free!

But at the time we were happy to return from Crotone with our precious 100-hours-a-month-for-€30, black *chiavetta*, that miraculously put us back in touch with a universe that had obviously missed our company for a little over a week.

It was a very special moment – almost as special as what was at the top of the list when we visited Crotone.

For three years we had been regular visitors to Crotone and each time I could never resist the lure of its fruit and vegetable market, the adjacent fish market and the surrounding purveyors of all sorts of meats, fresh and preserved. Just across the street from the Hotel Concordia – which more than a century earlier provided lodgings for English travel writers Norman Douglas (*Old Calabria*) and George Gissing (*By the Ionian Sea*) – was the colonnaded main entrance and, at long last, I could look, marvel, prod *and* buy.

On display, without the aid of bright colour-enhancing lights, was everything that was in season, almost all grown and produced locally. Here you could actually *smell* tomatoes, onions and mushrooms ... smells of freshness and flavour that I recalled from a distant childhood; aromas almost, but not quite, forgotten.

I was in my element. For almost ten years I had been both seduced and frustrated by Italian markets ... rarely able to buy, only able to dream about what might be concocted with such bounty. And here we were, poised to wander round in search of the plumpest *melanzane* (aubergines), the firmest *cipolle de Tropea* (onions from Tropea), the reddest *pepperone*, the hottest *pepperoncini* and the juiciest of *fichi* (figs).

But first a personal mission. Tucked away in his little unkempt corner cubby-hole, his right foot pounding away rhythmically as the odd spark flew and the large wooden, leather-belted wheel rattled round and round to its own discordant tune, was the diminutive, grey-haired knife grinder whom I'd often watched but never thought I'd ever employ.

I waited till he'd finished the task in hand and then watched his eyes light up as, one by one, I unwrapped my five 'foreign' knives. He examined each carefully (particularly the one with

Keeping the knives of Crotone on edge

its point missing) and said *va bene* as he shooed me away, told me to go and do a bit of shopping and to come back in half an hour.

What a day! A *chiavetta*, the freshest fruits and vegetables this side of the Channel Tunnel and the sharpest knives in Calabria.

We went on to find other markets in Crotone but the one we gravitated to most regularly was the Sunday *Mercato dei Contadine*, the Farmers' Market, where everything was home-cultivated (or collected wild in the countryside) and home-made and nothing (except for preserves) was ever sold out of season. Here we could buy the freshest and cheapest fruit and vegetables, wonderful cooked meats, local cheeses, fresh pasta, honey from Calabrian bees, freshly-made bread, free-range eggs, olive oil and even wine.

At the end of that first week we were shown an extraordinary kindness when, on the Sunday, we were invited to dine with a local character, Avvocato Silvano Cavarretta and his friend Samir. Cavarretta's house was about five minutes walk away in a picturesque cul-de-sac off Corso Aristipo. Samir hailed from Tunisia and, it being mid-Ramadan, he did the cooking but not much of the eating.

It was a strange evening in that we had only just met both and here they were wining and dining us just to welcome us to Santa Severina. We knew that Cavarretta owned several properties in the area and wondered whether he thought we might be in the market for one … if so his selling pitch didn't work as he never mentioned anything along those lines.

――――――――――――― .

Being used to unlimited internet access in the UK we had to make sure we didn't overrun our 100 hours so I devised a chart where we could keep a minute-by-minute record of our (separate) time online ... one *chiavetta*, but two computers. (At this time we hadn't realised we could share the system wirelessly between our two computers.) It was a bit of a surprise therefore when, having clocked up about 20 hours by our reckoning, it stopped functioning. No, it was more than a bit of a surprise, it was a devastating shock, it was like having our candy snatched from us.

Still in shock we jumped into the car and headed for Crotone and the nice man who sold it to us ... he scrutinised our humble chart, visibly taken aback by such fastidiousness, and conceded that we seemed only to have been online about 20 hours. He then called TIM Command Central who said, no, we had used all of our allocated time and, as the agreement stated, it would switch itself off after 100 hours. There was a moment or two of silence as our friend listened intently to a further explanation from the disembodied voice at Command Central. It was not good news.

All three of us learned something that day ... whether we used the internet for 1 second, 59 seconds or 14 minutes 59 seconds ... TIM calculated it as 15 minutes. In reality we didn't have 100 hours, we had 400 sessions of up to 15 minutes (or multiples of 15 minutes) each month. As the guy selling the system didn't appear to know this, Central Command eventually acquiesced and let us start again with a new 'month', a new 100 hours with the same *chiavetta* ... it goes without saying that we still had to fork out another €30. Everyone was happy to lay the blame for the confusion on the fact that we were *straniere*, foreigners!

Back to the drawing board ... a new, improved chart beckoned and we became adept at using the internet for periods of 14 minutes 59 seconds at a time.

The first paper-chase

By the end of our first week we felt fresh enough to start the process of accruing the documents we would need to live and buy things. I mention buying things because we knew that to buy, for example, a television, a computer or a car we would need to have a *codice fiscale*, a number not unlike the US's social security number or the UK's national insurance number, a unique number that identifies the person.

In addition, for day-to-day living we would need a *carta d'identità*, in the short term a passport would suffice but all Italian residents (whether nationals or not) are expected to carry this document at all times; indeed within the European Union it can be used for travelling between countries just like a passport.

The first step in both these processes was a visit to the *Comune*, the town hall, and in particular to the *Anagrafe* office, the registry of births, marriages and deaths.

As I've already mentioned, had we been doing this a year earlier we would have been embarking on the first stages of acquiring a *permesso di soggiorno*, permission to stay, but thanks to European Union legislation this process had been simplified for the citizens of member countries. All *we* needed was a document, issued by the *Anagrafe*, confirming that we had taken up residence in Santa Severina and that we had a verifiable address. It sounded simple enough ... and eventually it was.

We arrived outside the *Anagrafe* office on the top floor of the *Comune* and politely waited our turn. *Il sindaco*, Bruno Cortese, popped his head out of his office to acknowledge our presence. The *Anagrafe* itself, peopled by a man and two women, was a mix of the old and the new. There was a computer on each desk but around the walls there were shelves housing the thick ledgers and registers that had sufficed in a pre-computer age and carried all the records pertaining to this small town and its current compliment of approximately 2350 inhabitants ... soon to be approximately 2352.

We had the feeling we were expected and in tandem with this there was an air of incredulity that two people from England should want to take up residence in Santa Severina. We made the usual noises about having been here on holiday and how much we liked it ... Kay mentioned that the people were very kind and generous (lots of nodding), and that the weather was wonderful (more nodding) and then I threw in that the wine was pretty good too (a lot more nodding and even laughing). We were like a double act and for a time this was to become our standard response when people asked us what we thought of Santa Severina, Calabria or Italy.

So everything seemed to be going swimmingly, the documents we needed were already being processed when the man-in-charge was just making a final check that we didn't need a *permesso di soggiorno* ... he paused, checked again, shook his head and said, no, he'd got it all wrong, we'd have to go to another office in Crotone and fill in a different form and then come back to him with this other document.

We were both dumbfounded and deflated ... the more so because we knew he was completely wrong. We asked him if he was sure, he took another look at his list, cross-referenced with our documents, and confirmed that what he'd just said was authoritative and that was that.

Something told us not to argue. We were absolutely certain he was mistaken but decided to go along with it and return to the square for a coffee and to regroup.

We were sitting in the square no more than five minutes when I noticed said *Anagrafe*-person standing on the steps of the *Comune*, cigarette in hand, looking up and down the square. He started to walk purposefully in our direction and stopped by our table. He told us his list was wrong and that he realised this just after we left the office and, when we'd finished our coffee (and when he'd finished his cigarette), perhaps we could all reconvene back in the *Comune* to finish the paperwork.

We did, and ten fun-filled minutes later, clutching our proof of residency and in the knowledge that our names were duly logged in the huge register on his desk, returned to the square for something a little stronger. Next stop Crotone for our *codice fiscale*.

The *codice fiscale* was the easiest part. Giuliano said he'd come with us as the office was difficult to find and after a short wait at the appropriate counter, we presented our document from the *Anagrafe* and minutes later were duly anointed as Italian residents complete with *codice fiscale*. The sharp-eyed man who did the deed rightly picked up from the paperwork that it was my birthday the following day, proffered his hand and said *Auguri*, in Italian the usual 'congratulations' word for almost all good news.

It actually seemed something of an anti-climax but we knew this was the key to the next two processes ... the *carta d'identità* and qualifying for health care within the Italian health service. Or, as I like to think of them, Catch 22.

The following Monday we duly presented ourselves back at the *Anagrafe* to start the process for the next stage, the identity card. Details of our *codice fiscale* were noted, new forms were completed and then, just the one final question (always a bad sign) ... details of our medical arrangements, either private or state, assuming we qualified for the latter (which we knew we did). They just had to be certain that, as residents, we weren't going to be an illegal burden on the Italian state. Fair enough.

So we explained all about the reciprocal arrangement between EU countries that provided for medical care if one half of the couple were a pensioner. Yes, that was all fine but had we completed that part of the process at the ASL (Aziende Sanitarie Locali) the local administrative centre for such things ... ours was at Mesoraca about 25 kilometres away? Eh, no, we hadn't ... and we should have known because our good doctor, Rocco de Rito, had said as much in an email that Elvira had passed on to us when we were still in England.

So next day we went to Mesoraca and found the grey hospital complex which also housed the ASL offices in a greyer, down-at-heel extremity of the building. On the second floor we eventually tracked down the right office and found ourselves in a smoke-filled room with a strange chain-smoking, ever-sneezing and coughing specimen who looked as though he lived in this little space permanently and hadn't seen the outside world for a decade or two.

Holding our breathe we explained what we needed and showed him that we had all the correct forms from the UK, except that in this case the retired half of the equation, the one in pole-position so-to-speak, was Kay and I, a mere man, was her fortunate and ever-obedient dependent.

He didn't look up ... *Carte d'identità, per favore*, he said. Welcome to Catch 22!

In our inadequate Italian, we explained the problem ... we didn't yet have identity cards and couldn't get them until his part of the paperwork was complete ... we needed the *Tessera Sanitaria* from him *before* we could get our identity cards.

He huffed and puffed (mainly puffed), shook his head, sighed, raised his hands in abject resignation and huffed a bit more until he realised we were still standing there and were not inclined to leave until we had the documentation we were entitled to.

Still huffing between puffing and sneezing, he opened a drawer and took out two green cards, the green medical cards that would be our passport to the identity cards as well as legitimising us as part of the Italian healthcare system. He started to complete them.

Simultaneously (and upside-down) Kay and I realised he was still not on the right wavelength ... he could not get his head round the fact that Kay was the 'lead' pensioner and I was *her* dependent, even though this was clear on the reciprocal forms we had brought from England and we had explained it several times. Also, it was his job to know such things ... he alone dealt with the medical regulations pertaining to *straniere* like us for the whole area. He tore up the first two cards, lit another cigarette and started again ... and started to repeat the same mistakes. This time we were more aggressive and kept him on his toes until, with just a few amendments, just a little crossing out here and there, the deed was done. Finally, we each had our own germ-ridden *Tessera Sanitaria*.

Never was fresh air more welcoming; never was a simple bit of form-filling more complicated. Not because of the forms, just the person filling out the forms. How much easier would this process have been if instead we had been able to deal with our friend Franco Barone at Santa Severina's own ASL:

Back again at the *Anagrafe* we were finally on the last lap

... or so we thought. There was, we were informed after the details of our *Tessera Sanitaria* were duly noted, just one other process to complete ... the *Vigile Urbane* (the local cop – there were two in Santa Severina) would call at our house at some random time, just to check that we were actually living where we said we were. Not a problem, we could see the logic of that ... we'd probably invite him in for a cuppa.

And so it was that for the next week or so we were virtually house-bound, ever anticipating the knock on the door that would be the local bobby just checking up on us. It never happened.

Up in the square one evening I was explaining this inconvenient predicament to Franco Severini when he said ... don't worry, that's all sorted ... we had a word with them, we told them they were wasting their time when everybody knows who you are and where you live. And that was that, though I never did find out who the 'we' were. A day or two later a television show was being filmed in the square and among the crowds we happened to bump into our man from the *Anagrafe* who told us to pop into his office the following day when everything could be finalised.

We did. It was. But not quite ...

When we returned there was a demob-happy atmosphere in the knowledge that we'd nearly got to the end of the road. One of the *Vigile Urbane* even offered us a few sweets from the bowl in the cupboard normally reserved for children to keep them quiet while mum or dad did the paperwork. We handed over our photos and our money (€7.50), we were measured, our eye colour was noted as was the colour of our hair ... I tried unsuccessfully to maintain that I was blonde and not white.

We arranged to come back early the follow week to collect the cards, "But not Monday, Monday's always a difficult day." On Tuesday I was formally presented with my identity card in its little plastic folder ... Kay got her's too but, amid all the smiles and handshakes, I noticed a mistake. I didn't want to be a party-pooper, but I had to point out that Kay was not Irish, she was British ... I had (as I usually do) stressed my Irishness and someone had made the assumption that Kay must also be Irish. Just a few weeks in Santa Severina and she was already branded as *irlandese*!

It took another few days for Kay's second *carta d'identità* to be processed, though this time we didn't get any of those scrumptious sweeties.

The process worked, but the few spanners that were thrown into the works were actually our mistakes and in particular the British disregard for how others see the name of our country and/or our nationality.

Like other passports the British passport is emblazoned with its country of origin – the long-winded 'United Kingdom of Great Britain and Northern Ireland'. But, as we all know, this is rarely used, normally we say we are from Great Britain or the UK, or England, Scotland or Wales or, in my case, Northern Ireland. (Those born in Northern Ireland can claim dual nationality and can carry, as I do, an Irish passport alongside their UK one.)

So the 'mistake' that our friend from the *Anagrafe* made on our very first visit was probably not his fault ... he was trying to equate our last address in England with his list of qualifying countries which may have included *Gran Bretagna* or *Regno Unito*, both of which are regularly used in Italy. Even if we had said we were from *Gran Bretagna*, it's conceivable that his list said *Regno Unito*; or vise-versa.

There is, I sometimes feel, an arrogance by the good citizens of the United Kingdom of Great Britain and Northern Ireland that everyone in Europe and beyond should be *au fait* with all the names we give ourselves ... British, English, Irish, Welsh, Scottish and all the places we say we are from. I wonder would a citizen of, for example, Sicily who would undoubtedly describe him- or herself as Sicilian rather than Italian, have the same problem in the UK (sorry Great Britain, sorry England). There is no doubt that Sicily would not appear on any UK list of European countries.

I wonder too how many of those forums that jolly ex-pats use to complain about Johnny Foreigner's bureaucracy and/ or lack of common sense are the result of something as basic as understanding where *they* come from. Not what they call themselves, not the label they prefer but their country of citizenship as viewed from the outside. For citizens of the United Kingdom of Great Britain and Northern Ireland this is an unexpected and unique minefield.

But then it's not my problem, I'm Irish ... well, almost.

Concurrent with the identity card paper-chase we were trying to open a bank account. A simple enough task you might think and indeed we were led to believe it would be straightforward. So one morning we arranged to meet Vincenzo's son Roberto in Crotone so that we could open our account at his local branch.

But it didn't go according to plan for, though we could produce our passports and evidence of regular income (our pensions), even our *codice fiscale*, that morning we were dealing with Signor Unhelpful, Signor Unsmiling, Signor Downright Rude and Signor Pain-in-the-Ass, all carefully moulded into Signor Bloody Obnoxious. He just didn't want us as customers of his bank and kept throwing up all sorts of obstacles ... including, if my Italian served me well, the notion that we could even be international money launderers cleverly disguised as pensioners who had spent the last three years befriending everyone at Le Puzelle with nefarious intent. Basically, as far as Signor Bloody Obnoxious was concerned, we were *persona non grata* and that was all there was to it.

Even Roberto emerged shaken, perplexed and angry and wondering whether he might change banks himself.

But all was not lost and when we told Carlo of our experience, he rummaged in his wallet, wrote a number on a piece of paper and told us to give this guy a call. I took the easy way out and asked Carlo to ring him and set up a meeting whenever it was convenient.

The week we moved house we met up with our so-called Family Banker, Vincenzo Geraldi – a name that rang a bell but at the time I couldn't quite place it.

The aforementioned television programme that was being recorded in the square was part of a cooking series with a typical Italian twist and an unnatural, wispy red-haired presenter who clearly had been round too many corners at excessive speed for his own good, and his hair's.

The premise of the *Cuochi senza Frontiere*, normally based in small towns like Santa Severina, was that a local person known for his or her cooking prowess would cook a meal (outside and in front of the castle and most of the town) while a local *straniere*, a foreigner living in the same town, would cook a typical dish from his or her home country. Someone in a silly medieval costume would be the adjudicator.

Have you guessed where this is going?

One afternoon there was a knock on the door ... itself unusual at this time of day as having a nap was more the order of things.

There were two people standing on the doorstep. One a

thirty-something man whom we didn't recognise, the other a local character, a sprightly widow-woman in her mid-70s. We knew Maruzza to be a member of what we profanely called the 'God Squad', a small band of 'groupies' who often hung out with the local priest. I immediately assumed that these two were on a missionary mission and that we were going to be sold eternal salvation.

So, not unreasonably given the evidence to hand, I made it clear that we didn't want any, we weren't Catholic (nor likely to become so) and tried to shut the door, the old how-to-get-rid-of-Jehovah's-Witnesses routine. Kay, on the other hand, was actually listening to what they were saying ... which was that they had heard of my culinary prowess (I am usually the household cook rather than Kay) and would I be willing to participate in a television programme, the producer of which was said thirty-something.

I declined this offer to star in my own show for two reasons. First of all it was already abundantly clear that I didn't have enough Italian to pull this off in front of cameras, my fellow Santa Severinese, and a wider audience beyond. So in faltering Italian I got this self-evident point across and Maruzza and friend left in search of a Romanian.

My second thought was – what the hell is a typical English (or Irish) dish? How often, in any other part of Europe or America, do you come across an English restaurant serving typical or traditional English dishes? Along with the rest of the UK, England itself is bursting with a myriad of non-English restaurants and I can only think of one in the area we used to live in that only served so-called English fayre. Indeed a number of years back it was suggested by a government minister that, based on its popularity, Chicken Tikka Massala was "now a true British national dish". I am inclined to agree.

House-hunting

We could not have made the move to Calabria without somewhere to live, somewhere, in the short term at least, to call home. For that we were, and remain, grateful to Roberto and his mother Silvana.

However we knew quite soon that this little house was not for us and that, sooner or later, we would be on the move. Again we were looking for somewhere to rent, if we were ever in a position to buy, we wanted to be sure we had made the right choice in moving to this town.

So, after a couple of weeks in Santa Severina, we put the word out that we were house-hunting and that we were looking for something with at least two bedrooms. We were not specific about buying or renting as sometimes people have places to sell but will consider renting if asked.

Not so the first place we saw. It was not far from where we lived and was a typical Calabrian house, a bit on the gloomy side inside but it didn't matter, according to his representative the German owner definitely wanted to sell and that was that. Our enthusiasm at finally getting this process under way turned to despair. It wasn't a good start.

It got worse. Our route back home took us past the home of

a genial elderly couple with whom we had become friendly. With a beaming smile Vincenzo, who was not good on his feet, would continually chastise me for walking everywhere too fast. *Piano, piano*, he would say as he gestured with his hand for me to slow down.

When we told them we had been house-hunting we were all but frog-marched into *their* house while Rosa phoned their niece, Elena, who worked at the *Comune* and who definitely had an apartment to rent ... right next door ... almost certainly got two bedrooms. We were plied with coffee while we waited for Elena to arrive but when she did it was only to confirm that her apartment had just the one bedroom. Still, it's the thought that counts.

Another well-meaning friend told us that her aunt had a place just round the corner, definitely only for rent. We tried to control our enthusiasm and arranged a viewing.

It was like taking a step back in time. The tiny, two-storey house was in need of radical renovation but the impression given was that we could rent it as seen; there was no mention of refurbishment, a coat of paint, the odd kitchen unit. In reality it was only a few steps away from being an up-market stable, complete with a wooden trap-door hiding a dodgy staircase that linked the two floors. I couldn't quite see it ... Kay moving table aside to open hole in the floor to nip downstairs to make a coffee. Politely we thanked everyone for their time and patience and said we'd think about it.

So when Vincenzo at Le Puzelle said he knew of an apartment to rent we tried to be cool about it and not get too excited. He and Elvira met us by the *bivio*, the junction off the main road that, via four hairpin bends, leads up to Santa Severina's *centro storico*.

As the point of contact between the lower town and the road up to the *centro storico*, the *bivio* is an important Santa

Severina landmark. People talk about it as if it is a place in its own right with its own small community and its own name. This particular *bivio* once had a name, *Bivio Piedi Galluccio*, but these days it is simply *il bivio* and in Santa Severina it is generally the key word when people give directions.

We should have been more trusting of Vincenzo; after all he was one of only a few people in Santa Severina who was still called 'Don', as in Don Vincenzo, a mark of respect dating back to the time of Spanish rule in southern Italy.

There were actually two apartments, on the second and top floors, both modern, well-appointed and furnished with the basics ... and reasonably priced. We preferred the one on the second floor and actually *did* need to think about it this time.

There were two issues, the first of which was something we would have to decide upon wherever we looked: did we want to be up in the *centro storico* or did we want to be able to *see* the *centro storico* from below? This was something we never really resolved and continued to look at places both up above and down below. I think we resigned ourselves to the fact that when we found it, wherever it was, we'd know.

The second snag with this particular apartment was the communal staircase, it was just unrendered concrete with bannisters that were no more than bits of wood clumsily nailed to the wall. Inside the front door was fine, pristine even, it was just that unfinished staircase.

This was a phenomenon we'd experienced elsewhere in Calabria, where the home is deemed to begin at the front door to the house or apartment and not the door to the building. It is not unusual for an apartment's approach to resemble a building site and for it to be a veritable palace on the other side of that door.

We did return to have another look and though we really liked the apartment we still found the approach off-putting.

So it went on the back burner ... it was good, excellent even, but we had time to look around ... though not a lot as we were beginning to find our little house claustrophobic, a base for eating and sleeping rather than a place for living.

Later that same evening we had an unexpected visitor. He introduced himself as Dino, spoke fairly good English and said he understood we might be in the market for a property. Dino, an architect, was a native of Cyprus but had married a local woman, also an architect. He went on to explain that we had been chatting with his daughter in the square a few days earlier and that she had mentioned that we were on the lookout for somewhere ... the local grapevine did the rest and here he was.

We accompanied Dino to his home to view the apartment above it (which at the time included his studio); it was truly magnificent with a rooftop terrace that would have been to die for in the summer months but, even had we intended to buy, it was way beyond our means. Over a glass of his mother-in-law's exquisite *limoncello* we were straight with him and his wife Rosalba. We liked it very, very much but, unless we were to win the lottery, it was not for us. We knew that for someone, some time, it would become a beautiful home.

They were fine with this and we chatted on for a while and, as we were leaving, I asked him to let us know if he ever heard of anything else. We were still no further on but at least we had made another contact ... and one in the right business.

Silvana, our landlady, was having a steel grill fitted in front of the air-conditioning unit outside her/our house and we got chatting with the local *fabbro* (ironworker), Giuseppe. Whether he already knew we were looking for something or was just chancing his arm, we shall never know but somehow he dropped into the conversation that he had an apartment to rent above his workshop. It was on the road halfway between the *bivio* and Le Puzelle and we thought we'd take a look.

Our first attempt at dropping in was thwarted when I recognised Silvana's car parked outside and we decided it might be imprudent to arrive at that particular moment. We tried again the next day and were shown round a veritable palace (complete with marble staircase up to the first floor and beyond) with wonderful views up to Santa Severina itself and across the valley to nearby Scandale.

It was partly furnished but needed kitchen units and a bed and wardrobes. It was very tempting. We wanted a second opinion and arranged to meet Elvira there the next day.

That afternoon we bumped into Dino's wife Rosalba who was chatting with her friend Antonietta who in turn mentioned that her sister would be moving soon and that maybe she would want to rent out her old house. Rosalba told us that Dino had also wondered about this particular house and promised to remind him. It was all very nebulous but Dino did call us to confirm that this 'mystery' house might be available and that he'd try to set up a meeting with the owners. He told us what part of the town it was in but that was all we knew.

As it happened this was the one part of the town we had never explored. It was originally known as the Greek quarter, a name retained by the main thoroughfare Via Grecia, and boasted slightly more modern housing than today's *centro storico* though, like the *centro storico,* it is at the top of the hill. The housing is newer because this area was the original town centre until the earthquake of 1783 (the last in a series of five that spring in Calabria) when a large chunk of the eastern side of the town and its buildings fell away.

We were curious and spent a fruitless hour wandering in

and out of the streets and alleyways off Via Grecia looking for some sort of clue that might point us in the right direction. Nothing ... but at least now we had discovered this part of town and knew that it was another option for us.

As arranged we returned to have another look at Giuseppe's apartment with Elvira but still couldn't make up our minds. The rent was reasonable, the only snags were the kitchen and the bedroom. I suggested to Giuseppe that if he bought the bedroom we would buy the kitchen. He agreed and we told him we would make up our minds early the following week.

It was Monday, four weeks to the day since we moved in and it seemed that this house was getting smaller and smaller. We really did need to move. Nothing new had materialised and we hadn't heard back from Dino.

That evening we decided to go to the furniture store on the main road, the *Strada Statali*, that everyone else from Santa Severina seemed to frequent, to get us out of the house and to price a kitchen ... and, embarrassingly, bumped into Giuseppe and his wife and daughter who were doing exactly the same thing ... except that, surprise, surprise, they were looking at bedrooms. After the embarrassed camaraderie and laughter had died down, we said we were close to deciding and agreed to call him the next day; we had, we said hopefully, one more place to see.

On Tuesday afternoon Dino finally called and we arranged to meet him in the square at noon on the Wednesday. I called Giuseppe and apologised for this further delay and said we needed just one more day.

At five past noon on Wednesday we were once again walking along Via Grecia, though this time with slightly more purposeful intent. Dino explained how he had designed a new house for this couple and their children, just in front of their old one, the one we were going to see, right on the eastern edge of the hill.

We turned right near the end of Via Grecia ... Dino pointed to the yellow house at the bottom ... "That's it", he said. He rang the bell.

The door was opened by a young auburn-haired woman whom he introduced as Silvana Gerardi and who in turn introduced us to her husband Raffaele Vizza. (In Italy husbands and wives normally retain their family surnames and the children take the father's name; coincidentally Kay and I had always done the same.)

We spent a little over half an hour with Silvana and Raffaele but both of us knew within a few moments of entering this house that we had finally found what we were looking for ... if pushed we could not have said what that actually was, we just recognised it when we saw it. We also knew how fortunate we were that we'd waited that extra day.

Before we left and after being introduced to most of the neighbours, we had agreed a monthly rent, a provisional date for moving in, the first of November, and exchanged telephone numbers. We couldn't wait and went home invigorated, excited and ready, eager even, to start packing once again.

But first things first, I had to make that difficult call to Giuseppe to explain that, much as we liked his apartment, we had decided to opt for somewhere nearer the *centro storico*. I rehearsed my speech several times and was more than a little relieved when I got his answering machine and didn't have to explain myself any more than I needed to. He did get back to me later that day and I could sense that he was not best pleased ... I just hoped he hadn't ordered that bedroom.

So what was it about this particular house? Why were we so

sure that this house was for us? There is no single answer.

In statistical terms, it was three times the space for less than sixty percent of the rent.

In practical terms we could see it was a house that had been looked after and it was one that would be easy to maintain; there were also radiators *in situ* in readiness for a gas central heating system ... only problem being that gas, *metano*, wouldn't arrive in Santa Severina till the following spring.

In emotive terms this house already felt like a home. Indeed for the next couple of weeks it would be exactly that, a home to Silvana, Raffaele and their children, Francesco and Alessia.

And finally, we were somehow aware that this family would not pass on their marital home lightly; there was a very real feeling that they also chose us to look after it for them and that they were confident *they* had made the right choice.

We were so excited that we phoned a day or two later and arranged to go round and have another look. We took Elvira with us, not only because we respected her opinion but also because we wanted to share this house with someone. Elvira approved.

If you feel you need a description, then here it is; if not then skip the next two paragraphs and fast-forward a couple of pages, to the photographic version.

The 'block' has four floors; Silvana's brother and family live on the top two, we have the bottom two. Our two floors are linked by a spiral staircase. On the top floor, off a wide hallway, are a large living/dining room, a large bedroom, a small office-cum-studio (originally a bedroom), a bathroom, a small living area and, off it, an under-stairs storage space (which also houses the washing machine); a spiral staircase goes down to a large kitchen/dining area, a small bedroom complete with Lion King mural (created by Raffaele for the children), a utility area which also has a shower unit and toilet and, at the back, a very narrow (no more than a metre wide) underground pantry-cum-cantina.

There is a front door at the upper level and a back door at the lower. The main bedroom and smaller living area are linked outside by a balcony from which, on the left, you can see the sea at Strongoli and, on the right, the valley below Santa Severina and the hills beyond as far as Scandale, San Máuro and Cutro. In the middle, between these two extremes, is Silvana and Raffaele's beautiful new home, less than five metres away. Beyond their small back garden is a sheer drop, the very edge of the cliff.

––––––––––

At first we found it strange that some of the apartments we saw didn't have the full compliment of furniture, particularly the kitchen.

The reason for this is that kitchens and bedrooms have a more flexible element here in Calabria than elsewhere. For a start, the kitchen is generally called a 'kitchen corner' and may take up one or two walls of a larger room also used for dining ... in some houses you'll even find there's car in there too! It is flexible in that people often take it with them when they move for it usually includes a built-in fridge/freezer, an oven and hob, a dishwasher and, of course, a sink and fittings.

At the furniture store you choose the style and the colour, the accessories required and the total length and a few weeks later a couple of guys come and put it all together for you in a morning ... and all this can be bought at a very reasonable price (or of course at a more unreasonable one if you prefer). And when you move, you just take it all with you ... assuming you still like it, that is.

––––––––––

The top of the spiral staircase, the Lion King room and one end of the kitchen

People and places

When we arrived to live in Santa Severina, our 'support group' was based in and around Le Puzelle. Up in the *centro storico* we were, apart from Carlo at the bar and Franco Severini, on our own.

But gradually our circle of acquaintances grew. Locally we already knew the elderly couple Rosa and Vincenzo and it was while chatting to them one day about the imminent arrival of *metano*, gas, that a woman came out of a nearby house and asked us if we were the English friends of Roberto, Roberto Sculco.

Momentarily this threw us because we knew that Roberto, the first person we ever met at Le Puzelle, had died in February 2007. He had been a great friend and we loved him dearly and here we were back in Santa Severina ... and talking to his sister. When we told her that, yes, we knew Roberto well, she wept openly and hugged us both; she said that Roberto often talked of us. We were invited in for a coffee and a cry.

What Vittoria didn't know at the time was that Kay and I had taken a number of photos of Roberto which we'd never got round to showing him. So when, a day or two later, we turned up at her house with a small selection of these, two or three copies of each, she was once again overcome with emotion. Wiping away the tears she explained that the only recent photos of Roberto that the family had were very formal, head and shoulder shots.

Roberto's ailing mother was there too and more emotional scenes followed when Vittoria showed her the photos and I promised to print up some more for the rest of the family. Roberto was, as I've said elsewhere, a much-loved, generous man with a great sense of fun that he often shared with us. Like many others, we still miss him.

We often used to have a morning coffee with Franco Severini and his pipe and on one particular morning we avoided Carlo's and headed for the bar in the far corner of the square near the church – the castle end of the square was teeming with schoolchildren from nearby Mesoraca, in town for a week-long project.

One of the accompanying teachers, understandably weary of his charges, abandoned them and his colleagues temporarily and, recognising Franco, sloped off and joined us for a coffee.

Franco introduced us to Stumpo, Domenico Francesco Stumpo, Maestro Stumpo, gifted musician and composer, quirky, intellectual individual, occasional wearer of eccentric hats and, before the week was out and thereafter, very dear friend.

Stumpo hailed from nearby Cotronei in the foothills of the Sila mountains; he taught in Mesoraca but had recently moved to Santa Severina with his wife Francesca Loria and their daughter Carmen. Both Stumpo and Francesca were talented musicians (Carmen, on the other hand, hated music) and they had moved to Santa Severina because at the time the town had gained, thanks to the mayor, a well-deserved reputation as a cultural centre.

Through Stumpo and Francesca we were eventually to meet many other local musicians and in particular Enzo Ziparo and family; Enzo also happened to be architect Dino's brother-in-law. We both enjoy music but are, ourselves, completely unmusical until, that is, I reinvented myself as a Grand Master and internationally known exponent of the rare, four-sided, wooden Irish triangle. At the time of writing, Stumpo and I are well-advanced in our plans to make one just to assuage all the doubters.

As I've already suggested we increasingly found the need to get out of the house so soon came to be on *buongiorno* or *buona sera* terms with almost everybody in the town. We sometimes walked further afield, down to the *pasticceria* at the *bivio*, for example, or to Le Puzelle and back or even out into the nearby countryside.

People often found this strange and would offer us lifts and didn't always understand why we declined and preferred to go places *a piedi*, on foot, when we clearly had a car.

We were, of course, killing time; even before we found our house on Via Grecia, we knew our days were numbered at the first house. We were treading water, unsettled, restless, eager to find and be somewhere different, somewhere we could make and call home.

The day before we first saw our new home-to-be, Carlo said he would like to take us on the 'Tigano' tour of Santa Severina. Tigano was Carlo's surname and Tuesday was his day off. Coincidentally we started at the other end of Via Grecia where he and his *fidanzata* Anna Maria had just bought a house in need of considerable remodelling and renovation.

Carlo and Anna Maria would marry the following September and he took advantage of our guided tour to ask us to the wedding. We first met Anna Maria back in June when they told us about their plan to marry in 2009 and even then I was pretty sure that somehow we would be at their wedding. Imperceptibly over the years he had become that sort of friend and now he was the one person we would see almost every day.

Back to the guided tour ... we began at Carlo's matrimonial-home-to-be and proceeded up Via Grecia to say hello to some of the Pino side of the family; Pino owned the other bar at the castle-end of the square and was Carlo's cousin – a real cousin, not the sort of cousin who was really just a family friend or with whom there was some long-forgotten or uncertain familial connection. We also stopped to chat to the mother-in-law of Carlo's brother Ricardo whom we had also met in the summer.

From there we headed for the house of another of Carlo's brothers, Mario, at the end of Via dei Bizantini ... and in so doing must have passed within fifty metres of our home-to-be though of course we didn't realise it at the time. Mario wasn't in; as usual he was busy at his shop near the square where he sold almost everything imaginable that wasn't edible, a veritable Aladdin's cave.

Nevertheless Carlo insisted that we climb up onto a nearby wall (as you do) so that we could look down into Mario's walled garden, *un giardino particolare*. In reality it was only unique because Calabrians don't normally 'do' gardens in the sense that we understand them ... vegetable plots for food, yes, but gardens for pleasure and as a place to relax such as this, rarely, though increasingly so these days.

From Mario's we headed further along Via dei Bizantini to Carlo's family home where he still lived with his parents and two sisters, Anastasia and Antonietta. We went in and met his mother who was busy preparing olives, not for oil (that particular harvest would begin in November) but to preserve in jars. Like almost every woman in Santa Severina she was adept at conserving a glut of this, a glut of that, whatever happened to be in season, week in, week out; year in, year out.

Everywhere we went that morning there was the pervading, almost intoxicating, aroma of fermenting grapes for the *vendemmia*, the grape harvest, had just finished and behind almost every garage-like door (in truth not garages, most will never have seen a car, but small storage areas and workshops, *magazzini* they are called locally) the process was under way to keep the town's tables well stocked with wine (usually red wine) for the forthcoming year and beyond.

You probably guessed that Kay and I enjoy a glass or three of the red wine but only ever bought a few supermarket bottles the first week we arrived. Thereafter we were given wine or bought it as all the locals did, in 5-litre demijohns. So, though we arrived in Santa Severina while the *vendemmia* and its heady, aromatic aftermath was on-going, we were soon in the market for whatever was left of last year's vintage.

We found our first source through Giuliano and one evening we went together to Carmine's house down in the lower town beyond the *bivio*; clutching our two empty demijohns (which we were originally given full) we watched as Carmine drained ten litres of the glorious red nectar from a large stainless-steel vat. He warned us it was good and it was very strong and that he didn't have much left ... and then insisted that we go up into his house meet his wife Maria and try a glass. He was right, it was indeed a wonderfully full-bodied, smooth red wine and we managed to acquire another ten litres before supplies dried up.

Our circle of friends suddenly exploded through a chance encounter that Kay had in the dentist's waiting room. Actually he wasn't a dentist, or rather he was but not at that particular moment ...

I'll start at the beginning ...

Yet again, I had lost my bridge, that stuck-on tooth, newly repaired in England with 'sophisticated laser technology that guaranteed a stronger bond', just broke off. I was directed to the dentist *studio* near the *centro storico*.

The *studio* was the domain of two brothers, both doctors one of whom was also a dentist and, as luck would have it, I turned up to have my bridge repaired the morning the dentist, who was also a doctor, was being a doctor. In the afternoon he would become a dentist. It was all very confusing but meant that I had to come back some time after four.

I told him I was a friend of Vincenzo but it only occurred to me later that he probably assumed I was on holiday at Le Puzelle which may explain why the tooth fell off again about a week later ... perhaps he only did a temporary repair on the (mistaken) assumption I would be at home soon. He was right ... but what he didn't know was that home just happened to be Santa Severina. When I returned still clutching said tooth, he apologised and had another go and didn't charge me.

It seemed better this time and lasted a full fortnight before it fell out ... on Strongoli beach. Have you ever tried looking for a tooth on a sandy beach? It's not easy but we did actually find it.

Back in Santa Severina I discovered there was another dentist so thought I'd give him a go and see if his glue was any stronger. He was straight with me and said that I needed to see a specialist, possibly even invest in a new bridge, but that he would do his best, free of charge, as he wasn't confident it would work.

It did work but only for about three weeks by which time I had found out about Calabrodental, an impressive state-of the-art dental clinic on the outskirts of Crotone and made an appointment (more of Calabrodental later).

So let's go back to the waiting room of the first dentist who was being a doctor at the time ... it was here that a woman spoke to Kay in English and said something like "You're not from these 'ere parts, are you?" The woman was Lina and we arranged to have an *aperitivo* at Carlo's with her that evening ... and several other evenings thereafter. (I have a theory that an *aperitivo* is just a name the Italians give for having a drink at a time of day when people don't normally do so. Sounds more plausible if you say you're having an *aperitivo*.)

Lina was born in Santa Severina but migrated north before going to London in her late teens where she met a Dutchman whom she later married. She settled in Holland and now had three grown-up children. She spoke Italian, Dutch and English – no prizes for guessing which language we conversed in.

Lina had returned to Santa Severina for a few months to look after her elderly aunt and only ever got out in the evenings. She had two other aunts and an uncle in Santa Severina so when we did meet up our table soon became two or three to accommodate her extended family, particularly Agata, Vittorio and Anna Clara whom we already 'knew' though, until then, not by name.

In early October Lina was joined by her husband, Barend, their two daughters and Naseer, the Afghan husband of one of her daughters. When in Santa Severina, Barend, it seemed, focused on two things – finding good sources of olive oil and red wine. And it was on this latter crusade that found a unique international foursome – Barend, Naseer, Ciccio (Lina's uncle) and me – blazing a trail along the lanes between Santa Severina and Strongoli ... on the same morning Kay and I were supposed to collect our identity cards from the *Comune*.

Ciccio knew of two *cantine* that sold good wine at the right price (the price was very important to Barend) and so his car's boot was full of demijohns, including four that I'd managed to scrape together. This was to be my first experience of buying wine the Calabrian way, of just turning up at a *cantina* and asking to try it ... *rosso*, *rosato* or *bianco* and, if it was good, of filling up the demijohns. It was also my first experience of *rosato*, a lighter red that people generally drank in the summer but not at all like the rosé that you buy in a supermarket.

At the first *cantina* near Strongoli we hit gold both on price and taste but Barend decided not to fill up all his demijohns ... there was just a chance that our next port of call might be cheaper and/or better. It was in fact a little dearer but possibly better quality so all the remaining demijohns were filled ... and somehow I had acquired a fifth.

We arrived back in Santa Severina slightly flushed and just before the *Comune* shut for the *siesta*.

There are two Strongolis; there is the old hilltop town about seven or eight kilometers inland and there is Marina di Strongoli its seafront offshoot. Both are at the southern extremity of the Cirò wine region, centred in the town of Cirò, and well-known in Calabria and in Italy, less so internationally.

This was my first time in the Cirò (other than passing through) but it is a part of Calabria that, later, we often gravitated to, particularly to Torre Melissa and Cirò itself, in search of wine and sometimes too for an out-of-season walk along the beach at Strongoli. Finally, but after almost two years of dedicated research (somebody had to do it) and a nod from Stumpo, we did find a source of wonderful red wine to which we have remained loyal ... and share (the source, not the wine) with nobody. The price? Approximately \$2 or £1.30 a litre. Extortionate I call it.

Barend and family returned to Holland, laden with Calabrian goodies, leaving us to keep Lina sane ... she was staying on till the new year. As well as looking after her aunt Lina was charged with finding a house or apartment for the family to rent for a month the following summer. One evening she told us she'd heard about a house just off Via Grecia and had called round only to find that someone else had just pipped her to the post ... Kay and I.

Throughout this time we had constantly been on the lookout for the good doctor's surgery, Rocco De Rito's *studio*. We had found the surgeries of two other doctors in the town (one of whom was also a dentist!) but it was becoming more important that I found Rocco's as the supply of blood pressure tablets that I'd brought with me from England would soon run out.

Coincidentally Elvira mentioned in passing that she had bumped into Rocco and that he was looking forward to meeting us again soon, his two newest patients ... perhaps at his surgery, his *studio* ... not in Santa Severina as we expected but in nearby Roccabernarda, ten kilometres away!

We had always met Rocco at Le Puzelle and had therefore assumed that he was a doctor in Santa Severina. It had simply never occurred to us that his *studio* might be in another town. It looked like we might have to change doctors but in the meantime, I needed those tablets. So, clutching our newly acquired *Tessera Sanitaria* (which already included his name as our doctor), we went to see him in Roccabernarda, to formally sign up as his patients and to get my first prescription.

He remains our doctor, The Good Doctor as I call him. Because that's what he is.

On my first visit to Calabrodental my bridge was once more stuck back in place and, as before, I was advised that it would not last ... as sure as the Pope is Catholic, I would be forced to consider a more radical (and costly) solution to the problem. Of course they were right but they gave it a couple more shots before I realised the game was up and we went down that more costly route ... and, for the record, I cannot praise their skill and professionalism enough.

It was after my first few visits to Calabrodental that I began to notice something about people's teeth in the area generally, but more specifically and more often in Santa Severina itself. Many teenagers and adults alike seemed to be missing a tooth, the same tooth, and generally they did nothing about it. It was always on the top, just round the corner from the front and the first tooth (or the first space) you see when someone begins to smile. Most often on the left jaw but sometimes the right; occasionally both sides.

I have asked people about it but nobody has come up with a reasonable explanation, usually because they had never noticed it before ... until I raised the subject, that is. Age doesn't seem to be a factor, of course it is most noticeable in the young, the age group you might reasonably expect not to have such gaps or to be more conscious of them.

I have wondered whether it was something dietary, the curse of the over-cooked pizza crust perhaps or the rock-hard local *fresa*, a circular, whole-wheat frisbee with a hole in the middle (Carlo once told me the hole was the best bit!). Or maybe something genetic, something in the heredity water.

My subtle sleuthing has drawn a blank so I am resigned to the notion that I am exaggerating its prevalence or that is no more than mere coincidence. Perhaps I am barking up the wrong tree and what I am really aware of is that so few people appear to do anything about it – having a gap in their smile is not such a big deal. I was more conscious of my gap, the scourge of that enigmatic smile, and such vanity cost me thousands.

Moving

It was Tuesday 28 October. As planned we woke at five, had a quick breakfast and got ready for the five-thirty knock on the door. It was Giuliano and I could see from his face, and the drizzle that framed it, that the day's adventure was off. We wouldn't be going with him and Salvatore on a hunting trip into the Sila mountains ... to hunt for mushrooms, *porcini*, that is. Salvatore had called him to say that if it was drizzling in Santa Severina then it would be worse in the Sila ... Salvatore knew about these things for his father was a professional *porcini* hunter.

Crestfallen we undressed and went back to bed but I couldn't settle and decided to go out for a walk. The rain had petered out so, after a coffee in the square, I deliberately wandered in the general direction of Via Grecia (as had become our custom) in the hope that I might just bump into either Silvana or Raffaele who had still not been able to give us a definite date for moving.

(The only real contact we had had since our second visit was to pass on details of my *codice fiscale* so that an account could be set up with the local supplier of electricity; most other services were paid through the Comune.)

All thoughts of what might have been in the Sila were

interrupted by the sound of a horn and I looked round. It was Silvana on her way to school and, with that ingrained Calabrian indifference to any other traffic, she just stopped in the middle of the road, wound down the window and said the words that we were so desperate to hear: "We're moving into the new house tomorrow ... you can move in on Thursday if you like." *"If you like ...?"* If she hadn't been in a car I would have hugged her ... instead I ran back to the house to break the news to Kay.

A day that had dawned as a disappointment had taken on a bright, exhilarating, new lease of life; and Thursday couldn't come soon enough. Apart from the things we used day-to-day, we were packed up, ready and waiting ... all we had to do was drive into Crotone and pick up our new washing machine and buy a few plants.

And soon enough Thursday did dawn, bright, warm, ordinary and we started to shuttle our worldly goods, car-load by car-load, from the western side of the hill round to the eastern side, no more than a five-minute drive, less by foot. That said the nearest we could get the car to the front door was about fifty metres.

Raffaele solved this particular problem by borrowing his brother-in-law's versatile *Ape*, one of those wondrous three-wheeled workhorses that I was dying to have a ride in and that day I fulfilled that ambition many times. We also had to visit Angela's basement and retrieve everything we'd left with her six weeks earlier.

By late afternoon our three cubic metres and the contents of the Clio had moved once again and, along with our new washing machine, were safely tucked away in Via Grecia. All we had to do was sort it all out and make a real home here in Santa Severina.

Apart from returning to our little west-side ex-house to clean it from top to bottom, we spent the weekend virtually house-bound as, finally, we were to find permanent homes for all our possessions.

Paintings, pictures and mirrors went up on the walls; books, CDs and DVDs adorned the bookcases; we each had a wardrobe; demijohns of red wine had a fresh, dark place to hide; the toolbox finally left the car now that there was space indoors; ornaments found places to show themselves off; the breadmaker and coffee machine had permanent homes; computers, printer and desks changed the small bedroom upstairs into our 'office' (for the moment we could live with the foot-wide strip of Disney characters that went right round the wall).

There were plants on the balcony and indoors; and the garlic that Kay had lovingly cultivated and braided in England had pride of place in the pantry.

From the balcony and its scattering of plants we renewed our acquaintance with the big yellow ball in the sky and at long last had our morning coffee in the sun.

And, I almost forgot ... we had a loaf of bread. Gino one of the town's two bakers had cleverly used this moving period, when he rightly guessed we would not be making our own bread, to drop off a loaf of his freshly baked bread for us to try. The unspoken message was "there's more where this came from". To this day we only ever buy Gino's bread.

Of course what we didn't have was a pool or a reclaimed vineyard or an ageing olive grove or a mature fruit orchard or a long, winding track to the longer, winding track to the house – not that I begrudge anyone such accessories – but we were content, we had the beginnings of a life in this small town twixt mountains and sea; we had a home and we had friends. What more could you need?

The answer of course is obvious ... a really good source of excellent red wine at a reasonable price, the hunt for which, at this time, was on-going.

A bank account would also have helped and to that end our first visitor was Vincenzo Geraldi who was making a pitch for being our friendly Family Banker. He got off to a good start when he told us we knew his father and eventually the penny dropped and we recalled the man who, when we lived in the other house, had a *magazzino* at the back and had always been very friendly towards us.

We had done a bit of research ourselves and knew that 'his' bank's first claim to fame was dealing with many southern Italians' predisposition for using the 'under-the-mattress' system of banking. They did this by pioneering teletext banking; everyone, they reasoned, had a television so why not use this to create a personal banking system.

These days they use the internet, it was in fact an internet-only bank, with a Family Banker a phonecall or email away, and that suited us as we were used to such things.

He won us over. We signed up and a few days later he returned with all the paperwork and the cards and we were online ... he even set up the payment of our bi-monthly electricity bill.

Up yours Signor Bloody Obnoxious of Crotone!

That week was a watershed. We were settled into our new home where we could accommodate friends and family and invite people round to eat with us. We had a bank account and all the right documents and numbers to verify our status as residents of Santa Severina and of Italy. We had friends and neighbours.

We were getting used to seeing the sun again and to the fact that it was much warmer on this side of the hill. Silvana told us that, in the winter, the local teachers could tell where pupils lived by what they wore coming to school as those from the western side were always well wrapped up (west to east five minutes on foot, possibly longer by car).

We also had daily refuse collections. We had just moved from a country where the trend was from weekly to fortnightly collections and here they were doing away with the large local refuse wagons and bringing in daily collections based on type of recyclable rubbish. Everyone was given different coloured bags for paper, glass and plastic & tin and biodegradable bags for organic matter ... you left out a green bag (glass), they left you another green bag. On Fridays you left out anything and everything that did not fall into any of the other categories.

But most of all we had the Gerardi family itself, the family of Silvana. We were not aware of it at the time but, to coin a phrase, we had landed on our feet. For all sorts of reasons this house, this little corner of Santa Severina and this family were to shape much of what we were to count as important and special in the months and years to come.

———————

We first met the father of our Family-Banker-to-be a few days after we moved to Santa Severina. He had just arrived in his *Ape* and was opening up his *magazzino* as we were walking past; he thrust forth a welcoming hand and said just one word "Geraldi". Introductions over he got on with his work and we left him to unload the empty plastic *cassette* from the back of his *Ape* ... a sure sign (though we did not recognise it as such at the time) that he had just finished his *vendemmia*, the grape harvest.

About a week later we saw Signor Geraldi again but this time we were invited into the holy of holies to see the fruits of his and his wife's labours. Like every *magazzino* it was bursting with all sorts of home-grown goodies, all preserved lovingly: shelves packed with jars of tomatoes, olives, artichokes, beans, peppers and chillies, demijohns of wine, *salsicci* (spicy sausages, more akin to salami) and bunches of herbs hanging from the ceiling, a veritable Aladdin's cave of homage to hard work and traditions handed down, one generation to another.

I thought I should show him our equivalent and left Kay to wonder as I ran back to the house and returned with one of her braided strings of garlic that we'd brought from England. I held it up proudly. "Ah", said Geraldi, "little ones", as he pushed aside the bunches of oregano hanging from the ceiling to reveal strings of the largest garlic bulbs I have ever seen. He was too polite to say it but I'm sure he was thinking something like "This, now *this* is garlic." As we clearly didn't need garlic, we left with a tidy bunch of the most used herb locally, oregano.

———————————

Autumn entertainment

Summer officially ended on September 21 so, by the time we moved to Via Grecia, we were almost halfway into autumn, though generally the days remained warm, around 20 degrees. Local people seemed to take the change of season quite literally ... we could sense an expectation that September 22 would somehow feel different to the day before.

Once a week we drove out of town to Gina's, the small restaurant in the countryside that we liked. For the first couple of weeks we were able to sit outside but by October the diminishing light and the cooler evenings brought us inside. Gina and her husband Franco were from Santa Severina so, although it was off the beaten track many of their customers were people we knew, if not by name then certainly to see.

It was strange how soon we felt we were part of the fabric of this place and how quickly people accepted us as such. There were other *straniere* locally, a Russian woman, some Romanians (including our friend Giuliano and his mother), a couple of Moroccans, a Tunisian man, a Polish woman and her family; all those that were married, were married to or lived with locals. Apart from the Moroccan carers, we were the only couple with no direct or marital connection to Santa Severina.

This did, I suppose make us unique, make people wonder about our sanity and what had brought us here. Ostensibly all the other *straniere* had left a poorer country for a richer one; we, on the other hand, appeared to have done the opposite.

This is the only way I can explain the speed with which we were assimilated into the day-to-day life of Santa Severina. We had made a decision to come here from somewhere that many will have considered to be a better place, certainly a more affluent place. People appeared to respect the fact that we had chosen their town; sometimes they thought we were slightly mad but they respected our choice and in turn it made *them* feel good about their town and about Calabria. And it worked both ways, it also made us feel good about Santa Severina.

We had been shown so many kindnesses it would be difficult to quantify them but now that we were settled it was pay-back time. At long last we had space to cook and space for people to sit but decided to start modestly and invited Giuliano round for dinner.

He had become a close friend and, being Romanian, had experience of some of the ins and outs of getting the paperwork together; he had always been there for us and our friendship belied the age difference (not far off forty years).

With Giuliano fed and watered and seemingly none the worse for the experience it was time to think big ... so we invited everyone from Le Puzelle, including the long-suffering Giuliano, and then realised that we would have to do this in two shifts, not just because of the numbers but also people's availability.

They all knew that I did the cooking so there was an element of curiosity and we had a one hundred percent attendance despite the fact that the first 'shift' during the last week in November coincided with a particularly vicious *temporale*, a storm that was so bad that Raffaele called round to see if we were alright ... and was surprised to find a roomful of people eating, drinking and laughing.

But Raffaele didn't just turn up because of the wind and the rain, it was the fact that we kept losing power and he rightly surmised that this was our first experience of such conditions. Every ten or fifteen minutes the lights would go out (as did the oven) and the emergency light would come on in the kitchen where we were eating. After the first time we had gathered together as many candles and night lights as we could find and distributed them round the room.

Somehow we muddled through and Raffaele braved the elements again a little later and dropped in a bottle of wine as his contribution to our candlelit party.

Italian meals have an element of elasticity: they are of indeterminate length both in time and number of courses, though a minimum of five courses is normal. I decided to go the whole hog and stick to the traditional Italian format using typical Italian ingredients. One thing I had learnt about the local eating habits was that southern Italians are very conservative when it comes to food ... they don't generally like to try anything new.

So after the *aperitivo* I had prepared a selection of antipasti, a mushroom-based pasta dish, a chicken-based meat dish, a pudding and finished off with liqueurs and coffee. I knew I had one fussy eater to contend with who ate neither onions nor mushrooms so prepared his dishes separately. He was so pleased and several times made a point of showing off his empty plate and making sure everyone, particularly his wife, took note that he had eaten everything.

One thing I decided to take a chance with was the bread. Whatever the occasion, there is always bread on a Calabrian table; so, just to see what happened, I decided to make my own and served up three different types, none of which was normal fare in Calabria. They ate the lot.

The next day it was clear that the word was out and by mid-morning a full report on the minutiae of the evening's menu had already reached Carlo who jokingly reminded me that the real test would be cooking for Salvatore, Le Puzelle's renowned chef, who was down for the next shift in a couple of week's time

In the meantime we had two other engagements. The first of these was a four-hour drive to Brindisi in Apulia to collect Kay's daughter and her fiancé who would be staying a week but (thank goodness) leaving from the much nearer Lamezia Airport the day after flights to and from the UK resumed.

This was the first time we'd shared our space here with others and it was a strange feeling; we wondered whether or not they saw things the way we did, if they could understand why we liked this place. Whether they liked it or not, we spent much of the time showing off the people and places, both in Santa Severina and the surrounding countryside, that were special to us. Both Silvana and Angela insisted that we drop in with our visitors for a coffee and these two whistle-stop tours have since become a regular feature of all such visits, as has Le Puzelle.

Our second engagement was when we asked Silvana and Raffaele to eat with us at Le Puzelle, we simply wanted to thank them for all their kindnesses to us when and since we moved in, at so many levels we wanted to show our appreciation.

The arrangement was that they would knock the door at eight and we'd go together. They did, and standing behind them on the doorstep were their kids, Francesco and Alessia. We had been expecting the four of us to go in the one car but now that we were six, two cars it was. I made sure that I was in front and when we arrived at Le Puzelle, Kay ran in to break the news to the waiter Martino about the increase in numbers and, by the time Raffaele and family arrived, the table for four had become a table for six. Nobody was any the wiser.

At first this unexpected turn of events threw us, it had simply never occurred to us that Silvana and Raffaele would arrive with their children. But then this is southern Italy and the notion of family is very strong and people always try to do things together *as* a family, no matter what the age range may be. For us it wasn't a problem that Francesco and Alessia would be eating with us ... the fact that it never occurred to us was more of a worry. The more so when it happened again four days later and we clearly hadn't learnt anything from the first experience.

It was the evening when the remainder of our friends from Le Puzelle ate with us. The table was set for six, a smaller gathering than the first one, but when one of Gabriella's children and both of Salvatore's turned up it ended just the same and I had to rustle up some more child-friendly food. Nevertheless it seemed to go well and Salvatore unwittingly paid me a compliment when the two dishes that he seemed to relish the most (going by the amount he ate and the fact that he asked about the ingredients) were the two that I had concocted for the occasion.

In many Italian homes the sound of the television is a constant background noise. Even when people visit the house it is generally left on even if nobody is actually watching it. When Salvatore arrived to eat with us that night he instinctively lifted the tele-commando and switched on *our* television but neither he nor anyone else even looked at it.

Nor did anyone notice when I took every opportunity to subtly reduce the volume. It was like having an extra family member in the room, some ancient, deaf, chair-bound relative that everyone was accustomed to being there but who was generally ignored.

We had two televisions, one we had bought to keep us sane in the first house and one that we inherited from Silvana and Raffaele. We had decided not to invest in anything more sophisticated like a satellite system, where we could watch in English, for at least two years. We wanted to come to grips with the language first and so only watched Italian television and programmes in Italian.

We watched three programmes regularly; all were towards the rubbish end of the spectrum but we watched them knowing this but also with a purpose – we knew they would help us with the language.

The first was the Italian incarnation of *Who wants to be a Millionaire?*. Apart from the general chit-chat between contestants and host Gerry Scotti there were was the bonus of hearing the question, seeing it in writing *and* trying to answer it. We became quite adept at this and often used to get the right answers far quicker that the contestants who seemed to revel in rattling on for ever and ever about the minutiae of how they arrived at their decision before actually telling anybody what it was. The long-suffering Gerry Scotti sometimes looked as if he was about to nod off.

The second was another quiz show, the Italian equivalent of *Wheel of Fortune*. Again this involved words and phrases though this time there was a cryptic clue to unravel; apparently this show also featured the presenter's leggy blonde assistant but I can't recall noticing her ... just the words and phrases.

Finally on our list of must-sees there was a soap opera, *Tempesta d'Amore*, set in an up-market hotel in the Bavarian countryside and each 'season' focussing on one unlikely love-affair while all sorts of other unconvincing shenanigans went on in the background ... we loved it! (Made us wonder why *Crossroads*, that English attempt at a hotel-based soap set near a motorway junction in the heart of the UK's industrial heartland didn't work?)

As the location would suggest, this was a German-made programme which had been dubbed into Italian and curiously it was this that made it easier for us to understand and was why (and only why) we watched it. We began to realise that dubbed programmes are generally translated into a form of language that is clear and universal as opposed to regional dialects or complicated constructions. Once we got over the lack of voice-to-mouth synchronisation then such programmes were much easier for us to understand.

Italian television channels were and are bloated with imported (often American) programmes that are dubbed; indeed dubbing to a very high standard is almost an artform in itself in Italy and one that Italians are particularly proud of.

There was one other programme at the other end of the intellectual spectrum that we often delved into of a weekend, a broad-based arts programme called *Che tempo che fa*. It was often difficult to follow but it had an innovative format and a presenter unfazed at doing a live interview with Oasis's Noel Gallagher where a form of dubbing made the interview linguistically seamless. Given Noel Gallagher's history of unpredictability on such occasions, this was no mean feat.

Everything was going well. If there had a been a plan then everything was going according to plan: we were enjoying the extended summer even if it was called autumn; our new house was beginning to become a home where we were falling into domestic and social routines; we had an internet connection of sorts; we had successfully seen off the first round of paperwork; we were starting to come to terms with the things that were different ... well almost.

The main thing that was different, apart from eating habits and family conventions, was the language. And despite the fact that we coped and had the company of Gerry Scotti and his friends every evening, it remained (and remains) a struggle.

———————

Our friend Stumpo spoke some English and from time to time enjoyed practising it on us ... until, that is, he was told off.

Early one evening, before the clocks went back, we were partaking of an *aperitivo* with Stumpo at Carlo's bar; Stumpo was trying to explain something and, not for the first time, both Kay and I were floundering with the language, so he finally got the gist of his message across in English. Unfortunately for Stumpo, Carlo overheard and gave Stumpo a moderate telling off, reminding him that it did us no good if he kept speaking to us in English ... we had to learn to understand the Italian.

It seemed a trifle harsh on poor, well-meaning Stumpo but of course Carlo was right ... we needed to hear Italian, we heard enough English when we spoke to one another.

Stumpo, it has to be said, took the telling off to heart and from that moment has rarely uttered a word of English in our presence.

———————

Living in a foreign language

We had had expectations. In our naivety we had expected that, living in the country, we would assimilate the language reasonably quickly. We were so, so wrong.

The main stumbling block was, of course, our age. Children and young adults absorb and learn languages quickly – I recall the extent to which my German improved after just ten weeks in Bad Honnef when I was seventeen. After ten weeks in Santa Severina our Italian had moved on a bit but was basically no more than it had been at the beginning ... we were reasonably adept at the language for meeting, greeting and eating.

We had two different approaches to the problem: Kay, a natural mimic, went down the copy and learn route; I also did this to the best of my ability, but I was neither a natural mimic nor able to shrug off my northern Irish accent, – 'sledgehammer' Italian as it has been called elsewhere – so I also tried to teach myself the basics of the grammar. In addition I had a further self-inflicted disadvantage in that in general I needed to see a word written before I could assimilate it and use it. In time this turned into an advantage in that it enabled me to text people on our Italian mobile phone and also to send emails in Italian.

Added to these general considerations is the fact that Italian grammar is complicated and has far more verb tenses than English, including a much-used subjunctive form (virtually non-existent in English these days) which itself has three tenses.

Kay's excellence came to the fore with all the everyday chit-chat that people use ... the how-are-you-today—the-weather-is-awful-isn't-it—that-wind-is-so-cold—and-what-about-that-rain-last-night—and-hasn't-the-*bambina*-shot-up sort of thing. Having worked for myself at home for fourteen years, commenting on the weather on a daily basis did not come naturally to me in English let alone Italian.

So while on the whole I copped out of finding fault with the weather, from time to time I found ways of commenting instead on the fact everyone seemed to be dissatisfied with the weather whatever it was doing. One small step that helped me participate in what did not come naturally.

Like most Calabrian towns, Santa Severina has its own language, its *dialetto*. Mesoraca, Angela's home town, has its *dialetto*; as does Stumpo's home town, Cotronei, likewise The Good Doctor's home, Roccabernarda; everywhere has its *dialetto*. Of course these days, thanks to Gerry Scotti and the levelling that is part and parcel of today's media-led technological society, everyone understands Italian; but generally most people, particularly those over fifty, often slip into their local tongue when they converse.

Of course the majority usually spoke to us in Italian and most made allowances for our lack of language by speaking that little bit more clearly and more slowly ... arguably they were treating us a bit like children but, hey, linguistically we *were* children. Indeed one child in particular, Stumpo's razor-sharp daughter Carmen, very quickly caught on to our deficiencies and ever-so-slightly changed her way of speaking so that we were more likely to understand her ... oh that a few more adults had done the same.

One group seldom made any allowances – the elderly. For those seventy and over, their local dialect *was* the mother tongue, and they made few concessions to our inadequacy – they just got on with it, teeth or no teeth, they spoke as they'd always spoken and assumed we'd get the gist of whatever point they were making.

In one sense we were out on a limb in that we were the only *straniere* couple who both spoke the same language – everyone else either worked with or for Italians or was married to an Italian which meant that, unlike us, the non-Italian partner was obliged to assimilate the language, there was no escape. And for some, particularly Romanians such as Giuliano, learning Italian was relatively straightforward as the two languages have a common linguistic source.

Having just painted a rather bleak picture of our linguistic skills I realise it was probably not as bad as it sounds. We complemented each other; Kay had the accent and the conversation skills, I did any texting and most emails.

And of course we did make headway but unfortunately just not at the rate we had hoped. I recall saying to a heavily pregnant neighbour that when her unborn child was two or three years old he would be speaking better Italian than us. At the time I knew this to be a sad fact of life; worse still, it has already come to pass.

And there was another personal aspect to learning and speaking the language that puzzled me ... indeed sometimes still does: there are some people I find it easy to converse with in Italian and others I find difficult. This is not about how *they* speak to me, it's something to do with how confident they make me feel when *I'm* talking to them. I used to think this was a male-female thing in that I generally found it easier to talk with women but then I found the same happened with some men too. Having rejected the male-female scenario I looked for other clues that might explain this phenomenon.

Could it be that I felt easier around Juventus supporters rather than followers of Inter Milan (everyone in Santa Severina seemed to be one or the other)? Perhaps it was fans of the bewildering Silvio Berlosconi on the one hand and those that saw him as the devil incarnate on the other? Those who ate the crusts of their pizza and those who didn't? The devout Catholics or those who were generally indifferent to the church ... whom our friend Franco maintained were by far the majority in Calabria?

There is one elderly man whom I suspect isn't interested in football, is certainly indifferent to Berlosconi, doubt if he's ever willingly eaten a pizza, would consider himself a devout Catholic but not overtly so. He generally speaks in dialect and, paradoxically, I normally get the gist of what he's saying and we have a reasonable conversation, even about the weather. I just find it easy to talk to him. And yet there are others, more articulate and with a full set of teeth, and I flounder. It's not an intellectual thing, not that I feel inhibited with those who are more articulate ... I have no problem with Stumpo for example.

Having discounted football, religion, pizza crusts, Berlosconi and number of teeth, I came to the conclusion it was something to do with whether or not I sensed, rightly or wrongly, that people were being judgemental about to what extent I was butchering their beautiful language; whether or not I observed that cringe, that wrinkling of the nose, that screwing up of the eyes, real or imagined, when I started to speak.

There is a uniquely Italian word, *simpatico*. Look it up in a dictionary and it is generally no more than 'nice'. But in Italy it has more subtle undertones ... of being a good person, being likeable, sympathetic even; being somebody worthy of friendship, someone you can trust. I have wondered whether my ability to speak reasonably coherently to some and to stammer and stutter lamentably with others has been directly proportional to some *simpatico* rating I was giving *them*?

Then again it might simply have had something to do with the amount of wine I may or may not have consumed at the time. The mathematic rationale goes something like this: more wine = more coherent = less butchering.

We soon discovered that there was another, almost foolproof, way of communicating in Italian that didn't involve speaking at all.

The Italian language has a strong non-verbal side – there are books and articles galore about the infamous Italian hand gestures and their meanings. Sometimes the gesture says it all; sometimes a few words or a movement of the head accompany the gesture to convey a wealth of meaning. There are also, it has to be said, a few that are less than polite so, should you decide to delve into any of the explanatory videos on the internet, you do so at your own risk.

Something else that works in our favour is the ever-increasing acceptance into Italian parlance of English (and American) words and phrases, particularly in advertising in all its incarnations: *il weekend*, *lo shopping*, *il western*, *lo stress*, *la star*, *trendy*, *OK* and, of course, almost every word to do with computer technology. It helped, but for our purposes it wasn't happening fast enough and we also had to contend with a backlash from Italian language purists!

But then, somewhere along this tortuous linguistic minefield, I found I had one unexpected asset ... sometimes I could make people laugh in Italian.

When I found that making fun of the weather – and the fact that in November I was still wearing shirts with short sleeves while everyone else was wrapped up for the winter – it was a turning point. When people looked at my bare arms and asked wasn't I cold, I'd say how hot it was today and that I was off to the seaside (people always want to know where you're going – or where you've been); they would have a good laugh and probably not notice if I'd said *alla mare* and not *al mare*.

When Silvana and others noticed a little framed napkin on the kitchen wall that had drawings of three types of cheese and the caption 'Cheeses of Nazereth', it didn't stop me trying to translate the joke ... even a joke that relied on the similarly of two words in *English*, cheeses and Jesus, and had a built-in element of religious mockery. But they got it.

When I noticed that one of (mobile phone network) Wind's television adverts made much of the phrase *Passa a Wind*, I couldn't resist telling someone, with sound effects, what this sounded like to English-listening ears ... and was surprised when, a few weeks later, Stumpo told me the same story, unaware that I was the source.

For some reason I found it easier to explain something as linguistically complicated as the Cheeses of Nazereth story than explaining to Raffaele that a tap was leaking.

And there was always one ready-made joke at hand to assist me ... septuagenarian Silvio Berlosconi, he with the penchant for sleek, dark-dyed hair and, it is reported, 17-year-old girls. I think it's fair to say that a majority of Santa Severenese saw the then country's Prime Minister as a figure of fun so, when I suggested that I might vote for my fellow oldie as I liked his implied virility, people got the joke and, I guess, were impressed that I was taking an interest in national Italian politics. Most Italians had still not got over the embarrassment of the time he referred to Barack Obama as being *bronzato*, sunburnt!

At the time of writing Silvio has just exited the political scene – whether this is temporary or permanent remains to be seen. But with his departure I had an excuse for learning and using the words and phrases that implied being upset at someone's parting or missing somebody or having a real sense of loss ... but only with those whom I knew couldn't stand the man and who felt absolutely no sense of loss.

Of course Santa Severina had its small cabal of Berlosconi faithful so sometimes the bars would resound to the raised voices of political debate as viewpoints polarised – I would have loved to participate but knew that, while I might get away with the jokes, I would flounder with the polemic.

And then there was Nek. Nek is a singer and musician, one of many Italian superstars in this field. He came to our attention when we saw him perform on, I think, *Che tempo che fa* one evening and what we liked about him was that we understood most of the words.

Unlike English it is easy to rhyme words in Italian. For example the first person plural form of all Italian verbs, in most tenses, has the same ending; in the present tense this would be *-iamo*. So 'we love', *amiamo* rhymes with 'we hate' *odiamo* and so on. How difficult can it be to write songs in Italian? Back to Nek.

We found Nek worth listening to for three reasons: firstly we liked the sound and rhythm of his music, secondly his songs were never over-complicated and thirdly he sang, to our ears anyway, clearly and distinctly which was a useful tool in coming to grips with the language. Despite the raised eyebrows from some of our more esoteric musical friends, we became Nek fans and soon had a collection of his music on our iPods. At the time, of course, we had no idea whether or not we fitted the normal profile for a Nek fan. Nor did we care.

––––––––––––

There was one other curious historical (as opposed to hysterical) aspect to coming to grips with day-to-day Italian in Santa Severina: many older men insisted on speaking to us, to me in particular, in German.

I suspect it's my colouring (fair-skinned, white hair) and the fact that I speak Italian with that delicate 'sledgehammer' propensity that I mentioned – being from the north of Ireland such an accent is part of my guttural inheritance and the reason I found German relatively easy when I was young. I suppose too the fact that I was able to respond to them in German helped cement this belief. Even when I would insist that we were English-speaking they still wanted to speak to me in German and in so-doing show off *their* linguistic repertoire.

As teenagers many of Santa Severina's finest left the land and headed north to work in Germany's burgeoning post-war car industry and it was here that they learnt their German. Many went separately and alone, worked and lived in a foreign language for up to a decade, returning home only once or twice a year ... one told us how, when he came back to Santa Severina to visit his family, his children would ask their mother who he was.

So Santa Severina has this sub-culture of men in their seventies and eighties who speak some German and who liked to speak to us in either German or a mixture of German and the local dialect. One man in particular always begins and ends every conversation with the same German phrase ... *alles klar?* he asks. This is German for 'is everything clear?' and must surely have been the phrase he heard most often from his German colleagues when they were explaining things to him at work. We still do not know his real name, to us he is, and always will be, Alles Klar.

There is another who normally speaks to us in Italian when we meet in the street but when he is in the company of others he always talks in German and invariably with an impish glint in his eye ... unashamedly he is showing everyone that he can still hack it!

Many of these men bought land when they finally returned to Calabria and most still receive a monthly pension from their erstwhile German employer. To a man they are proud men who embarked on a difficult life-journey through economic necessity and now, in the twilight of their lives, there is nothing they like more than telling anyone who will listen about their German adventure.

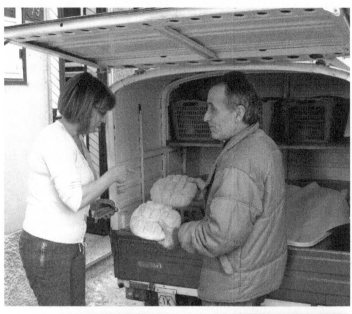

Gino and Andrea doing their rounds

Celebrating the ordinary

A friend in England once asked me what we did at weekends ... the answer was simple, the weekend was like any other part of the week or the month and the only discernible difference was that here in Santa Severina there were fewer shopping opportunities on a Sunday.

True, the town's few shops – three small supermarkets, a newsagent, a butcher, a post office, a florist, a ladies clothes shop, a couple of hairdressers/barbers, a gift shop – all closed on a Sunday but I was referring to another local phenomenon ... the number of things actually available on the doorstep.

There were, we soon discovered, two bakers, three or four men selling vegetable and fruit, a fish man, a cheese man, people selling pots and pans, clothes, bedding, carpets and rugs, households goods; indeed almost everything imaginable for the essentials to life. Their vans and *ape*s covered every road and street in the town, some every day, some on specific days ... basically, apart from price considerations, people could survive without ever leaving the house.

Some of those who lived on first- and second-floor apartments took this concept to extremes and had set up a little pulley on the balcony and a basket at the end of a rope and when, for example, Gino turned up with his freshly-baked bread, they would lower the basket down to him and up would come *una mezzaluna* or *un triangalo*. This same system was used for fruit and veg, fish, cheese and even dry cleaning; and of course in the winter a larger basket might be used to bring up wood for the *caminetto*. Still more sophisticated were the balconies that had an electrically-powered pulley suitable for larger logs and even furniture.

And like many other small towns there was a mouth-watering bonus – the *pasticceria*, an Italian cake shop with the seductive name of Le Antiche Delizie, literally 'antique delights'. Here, every day of the week courtesy of the Quaranta brothers, there were wonderful cream and almond confections such as Weight Watchers never dreamed of.

So we found Santa Severina to be pretty much self-contained. Our baker of choice was Gino (except Thursdays), we generally bought vegetables and fruit from Andrea (except Mondays), sometimes we bought cheese from the van on Thursdays, occasionally we left dry cleaning with the man who turned up every Friday. An ordered world it was.

And we soon found we had a place in that order. Even though we had only been in Santa Severina a few months, still less in Via Grecia, we realised we had been accepted into the normality of life locally and that somehow we had become an integral part of the fabric of the place. And much of this was due to the fact that we were, in an increasingly real sense, part of the Gerardi family, an ordinary, yet extraordinary, Calabrian family.

The man I mentioned at the end of the last chapter, the one with the glint in his eye when he speaks to us in German is Silvana's father Mario, the head of the family. His anonymity didn't last long!

Mario is no ordinary man. At the end of the war when, in

the wake of Mussolini's death, Italy was engulfed in something akin to civil war, he was captured and imprisoned near Genova on Italy's north eastern coast. Being Mario he escaped and walked home to Santa Severina; it took him a month.

He went on to work for Volkswagon in Germany and to father five children with his wife Emelia: Antonietta who lives fifty metres from us in the apartment above her parents; Sergio who lives in Abruzzo; Anna Maria who lives outside Rome; Aurelio who lives above us; and Silvana who lives five metres away. All are married, all have two children (except Sergio who has one) and, at the time of writing, Mario and Emelia have one great-grandson.

Mario built all the houses and apartments (including the one in which we now live) with money he earned in Germany, he also bought land in the countryside and built a small house there too; that land is now divided up among his five children, the sons share the house.

None of this we knew when we moved into Silvana's house, but it wasn't long before we were taken to meet Mario and Emelia and it was while I was studying a forty-year-old family portrait in their hallway that Mario and I cemented a unique bond. He pointed to each of his five children in turn, named them and then punched me on the shoulder and said *e solo con una moglie*, and with only one wife. Clearly news of my past misdemeanours had reached his ears and he couldn't resist making a point about, as he saw it, his family values.

Of course he had that twinkle in his eye when he said this and it was not meant in any pejorative way. Mario was proud of his life, of his wife and of his five children, all of whom had done well for themselves in their chosen careers, and he didn't mind who knew it. I'm not sure why this should have been something that became an anchor in our relationship but it developed into a sort of two-way catchphrase. If I can get a

The Gerardi family in the '70s, Silvana is the youngest; Silvana and *her* family today

word in before him (not easy), I thump *him* on the shoulder and say *e con solo cinque moglie*, and with only *five* wives ... not true of course, but he likes to think it is and, as a reprisal, grits his teeth as he threatens to hit me over the head with his walking stick, calls me *cattivo*, naughty ... and then has a good laugh at the very thought of it.

Silvana is proud of her father and what he achieved in his life and told us once that when (as happened again recently) Italy is knocked out of some international event like football's World Cup, then the Gerardi family always gives its support to Germany. For them it's a way of saying 'thank you' for helping to pay for their education.

In November when we moved into Silvana's house we were just beginning to learn about her extended family as unwittingly we started to become a part of it. Even those whom we had not yet met, Sergio and Anna Maria and their respective spouses, Angela and Attilio, were people we knew of and knew we were going to meet soon when they returned to Santa Severina between Christmas (*Natale*) and New Year (*Capodanno*).

I had also got to know Raffaele's parents for he and I made several trips to their home at the bottom of the hill when we moved a bedroom in his brother-in-law Aurelio's *ape*.

Kay and I decided we'd like to invest in our own bedroom and returned to the furniture store where we'd looked at kitchens a month or so earlier. We ordered a bedroom and then moved all our bedroom furniture down to the guest room, the Lion King room, having first moved bedroom furniture already there into the adjacent utility room. There was nothing wrong with these wardrobes and the adjoining 'bridge' of cupboards that spanned the bed but, as it was originally for children, and therefore lower, we anticipated that any adult guests would soon get a headache when they sat up in bed of a morning.

So, when Raffaele finally got over the shock that we two oldies had done all this dismantling and shifting ourselves, we loaded it into the *ape* and took it down to his parents' house where it would become a guest room for *their* grandchildren ... the same children whose bedroom furniture it once was! We made three trips and each time had a break and a glass of wine by the open fire in the kitchen with Raffaele's mother. He took me into the family *magazzino* where he kept his off-the-road Alfa Romeo and all sorts of other cherished possessions ... Aladdin never had a cave of such delights ... the most memorable for me (apart from the Alfa Romeo and the old, pristine Vespa) being the beautiful old wooden cot that Raffaele slept in as a baby.

So we had acquired two extended families, the Geraldis at the top and the Vizzas at the bottom but, for obvious reasons, we saw more of Silvana's and began to feel a particular affinity with her family, both immediate and extended, on the very edge of the rock.

One of the things I liked about the time we spent Christmas at Sciacca in Sicily a few years before (see *Stumbling through Italy*) was the extent to which the feverish commercialism associated with that time of year seemed to be less obvious, muted even. And that's how we found it in Santa Severina and in Crotone. It was December before we realised that Christmas was just around the corner ... in the UK we were used to the Christmas rush kicking in sometime around late September, early October. Refreshing it certainly was.

We had no specific plans for this time until we were invited to join Elvira and Vincenzo at their home (next to Le Puzelle) to eat on 24 December. In Italy it is the twenty-fourth rather than the twenty-fifth that is the day associated with Christmas gluttony, and in particular with a meal traditionally consisting of thirteen fish courses.

Thankfully Elvira didn't go the whole hog and I also made a modest contribution and we ate and drank well before exchanging presents. It was a low-key affair which suited all four of us just fine; we also booked ourselves in to spend *Capodanno* eating and dancing at Le Puzelle ... a really good party we were led to believe. But somebody threw a small spanner into the works.

Kay's younger daughter sent me a clandestine email to explain that she and her boyfriend were going to fly into Lamezia on 3 January as a surprise for Kay ... though just what excuse I was going to make at eight in the evening for driving to Lamezia I wasn't quite sure.

Eventually Amber agreed that I would have to tell Kay and, as we knew we would want to take her and Tom to eat at Le Puzelle, we decided to bow out of the festivities there for *Capodanno* and instead the four of us would eat there a few days later. I happened to mention this change of plan to Silvana who immediately said that we were to spend *Capodanno* at their house with the rest of the family ... and could she borrow a few chairs!

For me that evening in Silvana's house was a watershed.

I freely admit that I am not the world's greatest celebrator. Some things are worth celebrating others, by far the majority, are mere tokens to the whims of others and, as such, are generally empty, ritualistic or meaningless and usually belittle *real* celebrations.

Christmas and associated extravagances, as you will have gathered, generally leave me yearning for the twenty-sixth of December to dawn. New Year didn't generally do anything for me as I couldn't get my head round how that second hand being to the right of midnight was going to make any difference to anything. Ironically we watched that happen in New Orleans as 2004 became 2005; eight months later and life had certainly changed there in the aftermath of hurricane Katrina. The place where we had stood was no more.

Birthdays that end in a zero are something else I don't really get ... now two zeros, that might be different. We shall see.

As a republican, royal jubilees, weddings and associated flag-waving I consider a waste of time and a misuse of somebody else's money. Better the celebration to remember an end to power and influence (and associated riches) just because of an accident of birth; a celebration of democracy.

There *are* things worth celebrating ... recovery from a serious illness or not having that gene that has bedevilled other family members; I like the concept of the 'wake', a party to reflect on and celebrate someone's life rather than bemoaning the inevitable, their death.

Some achievements of a few sportsmen and women are worth celebrating, like the perseverance and determination of marathon runner Paula Radcliffe or the four unknown Scottish housewives who won Olympic gold for curling ... as opposed to the illiterate, egotistical thuggery of some of the UK's over-paid, so-called soccer 'stars'. (Can you tell, I'm enjoying this?)

Marriages can be worth celebrating ... or not as the case may be. In the last five years I have attended five in four different countries. In my opinion (at the time) not all were worth celebrating, though of course I was too polite to say so. So far one has gone the way I suspected it might.

So celebrating *Capodanno* with the Gerardi family was clearly going to be a personal challenge ... would I survive until midnight, I wondered?

There were eighteen of us round the table; sixteen family, Kay and I. The family consisted of Mario and Emelia, all five of their children and their respective spouses and four of their ten grandchildren – the others being grown up and with their own lives to lead.

Mario sat at the head with Emelia next to him; we were at their end of the table with Anna Maria (and husband Attilio) and Sergio (and wife Angela) all of whom we were meeting for the first time. Each of the women had contributed to the preparation of the food which made me feel guilty for not having done the same ... something which I now always do on such occasions.

I lost count of the number of courses we ate that night.

At one point I went up to see Mario in response to that flick-of-the-head summons which he does so well; I knelt down to talk to him. He asked me to look round the table at everyone laughing, drinking and eating. He took his wife's hand and said, "All of this we created together."

Momentarily I felt very humble, very honoured to be here and to be allowed to share this with him, with Emelia and with this family. I should have guessed what would happen next ... he thumped me on the shoulder and said "And with only one wife". Then he shook my hand and laughed.

After the food, Mario and Emelia slipped off home while everyone pitched in to clear the room for part two of *Capodanno* Calabrian-style ... the dancing.

This was fast, furious, letting-one's-hair-down dancing that seemed to act as a sort of release (particularly for the women) from the stress and strain of the holiday 'season'; of the year perhaps. Most of the men gyrated modestly in the background (and occasionally sloped off into the garden for a cigarette), leaving little old me as the only truly 'active' male participant with young Mario (Aurelio's son) as my only competitor.

Midnight came and went with the aid of a muted clock on the television; everyone exchanged the Italian double kiss and proclaimed *buon anno* before going outside into the relative warmth of the evening to have a look at the free firework displays courtesy of the towns across the valley, Scandale, San Máuro and Rocca di Neto. A few glasses of *fragolino frizzante* were clinked and a few liqueurs downed, including some Irish whiskey I remembered to bring, before finishing off the evening with some less frenetic dancing. I loved every single minute of it.

There was one other essentially Calabrian element that dominated the festivities, an absent friend in the shape of Rino Gaetano.

Rino Gaetano was born in Crotone and died in Rome in 1981; for the Gerardi boys and girls in their formative years he was an idol, a star like no other, a man who died in his prime, aged just 31. Gaetano left behind one song in particular, an anthem that had lasted the distance and, almost thirty years after his death, is remembered and cherished by those who continued to dance the night away to his music.

And this night was our first experience of *Ma il cielo è sempre più blu*, the Gaetano anthem that means so much to Calabrians of all ages. *But the sky is always bluer* is no more than a musical list of all the ordinary things that happen to people or that people do ... but whatever happens, whoever you are, *ma il cielo è sempre più blu*.

That *Capodanno*, we had our first taste of this essentially Calabrian anthem ... and the second taste whenever someone else dropped in to wish everyone *buon anno* ... and the third ... and the fourth. Whenever a new face appeared, the miraculously music changed and everyone danced and sang (again) to the music and lyrics of Rino Gaetano.

It was addictive but more than that it was a celebration of being Calabrian, a celebration of a young man, a local boy, that all the adults remembered and revered with unashamed passion ... and they were going to make sure that the next generation would never forget Rino Gaetano.

Should you get the chance, find and play this song and you will understand.

That first *Capodanno* we had experienced a family at play, a family that for the first time had invited two almost complete strangers to share in their simple festivities. Later, when we thanked Silvana for allowing us to be a part of this occasion with her extended family, she embraced us both and said, *d'ora in poi sarà sempre così*. Silvana was not being polite, she meant every word ... from now on this is how it will always be.

For the second time that evening I felt humbled.

Afterwards something else occurred to us ... this was the first time we'd seen Mario and Emelia for some time and we'd noticed that there were other people of a similar age who had fallen off the radar. The answer was simple – many of the elderly simply stayed indoors for much of the winter as they believed themselves to be prone to a number of winter illnesses, most notably *la cervicale*. This has no English translation other than 'relating to the neck'. It is, I suspect, something that has the same medical authority as not going out with wet hair for fear of getting one's 'death of cold' ... in other words nonsense.

Nevertheless the elderly clearly ventured out less at this time and when they did they often held a scarf over their mouth in a protective way for if they didn't already have *la cervicale* then the next worst thing was a *colpo d'aria*, a hit of air, which seemingly could do almost as much damage.

If you have read my *Keeping up with the Lawrences*, then I apologise for repeating the same story here.

On one occasion I was passing the Town Hall when I saw Mario carefully negotiating the steps down from the *Comune* to the level *piazza* with the help of his two aluminium sticks. As ever, his upper body walked purposefully, wishing those sticks away, willing them to be invisible. He saw me and paused, recognising the question in my eyes and the related twist of my head which asked him what he had been doing in the *Comune*?

He stopped, adjusted his balance, slowly turned to look back at the building, pointed with one of his sticks and, with a twinkle in eyes that deserved a younger body, said, *Just checking whether I was alive or dead*. He shrugged his shoulders, flicked his chin with a finger, then off he strode, not unaware of the irony in those few words.

The second paper-chase

Given our lack of language, we had done quite well with getting all our personal documentation in order in a matter of weeks. Now that we had a permanent home, it was time to concentrate our energies in another direction and chase the car-related paperwork.

Once again ex-pat websites were full of gloom and doom about doing this in Italy and included wildly differing estimates as to how much time and money the process might take. From the small print it was often obvious that many of these gripes were years out of date and, I suspect, many had no foundation even when they *were* in date. It seemed like a veritable minefield but, if past experiences were anything to go by, then I guessed that ninety percent of the various horror stories were probably self-inflicted and, as such, said more about the people themselves than the process.

There were three elements to what we had to do, the first two of which were more car specific, registration and insurance; the third was acquiring an Italian driving licence, *la patenta*.

The law of the land allowed for a externally registered car to remain in the country for a maximum of six months after which it would have to return to its country of registration (in our case, England) before being re-imported. In a nutshell we had until mid-March, six months from 13 September.

As the only one who drove, I had the same timescale within which to change my driving licence.

Now I fully admit that some might find the details of this particular paper-chase a tad boring ... particularly those who don't drive and have no interest in four-wheeled transport. I have included it for two reasons: first it may help someone who has to do the same and second it does throw some light on how the Italian bureaucracy works and, in particular, that if you work with it, it works with you ... even if, as in our case, you understand less than fifty percent of what's happening.

The process began with a visit to the *Motorizzazione Civile* on the outskirts of Crotone to pick up the various forms. With hindsight I could also have picked up the driving licence forms for the two counters were next to each other. It would have been straightforward to have had both processes running concurrently. But, as dear old Vincenzo would say, *piano, piano* ... slowly does it.

The sandy-haired man behind the counter was incredibly helpful and even threw in a few words of English just because he could; he was even more intrigued when he found out that we hailed from his home town, Santa Severina. Thereafter, with Antonio's sporadic linguistic help, his courtesy, his humour and his colourful sweaters, we hit few snags.

Before we could proceed and because, having been born in Naples, our car had Italian ancestry, we had to visit another office on the other side of Crotone, the *Automobile Club d'Italia*, the body ultimately responsible for the registration of motor vehicles. Here its original Italian *targa*, the licence plate number, was fed into the national computer and we discovered that, though the car had had a GB licence plate since early September, the paperwork relating to this had only filtered through to Italy the previous week ... up until that time it still existed as an Italian car. To this day, I remain unsure as to whether, if we'd started the process a couple of weeks earlier, it would have made things any different

What was important was that there was no impediment to changing the *targa* from English to Italian; apart from the fact that it was left-hand drive, it was as if it had never been Italian. What was even more important was that I had kept the original Italian licence document that was part of the paperwork when I bought it, which meant that I didn't have to get its British equivalent translated.

When we returned to Antonio with the completed forms, the process truly got under way and we were passed upstairs to his colleague Signor Grimaldi and his wondrous moustache. Signor Grimaldi sent us on our way again with three payment slips to take to the Post Office; we were to return with the receipted evidence to show that these parts of the process had been paid for.

The next stage was to arrange for (and pay for) a *revisione*, a test of the car's roadworthyness, the Italian equivalent to the UK's MOT though in Italy cars are checked every two years. In our case there would also be a check that its engine and chassis numbers corresponded to the relevant documentation – in other words that, as well as being international money launderers, we weren't importing dodgy cars on behalf of the English underworld.

Again Signor Grimaldi pointed us in the right direction and, as the holiday season was fast approaching, I let things lapse for a couple of weeks and booked it in for Saturday 3 January in Crotone.

What we didn't realise until we turned up in January for the test was that it was to be in two parts, one at the Crotone site and the other somewhere in the countryside. The first part completed, it soon became clear that we had absolutely no idea where to go next, despite several attempts at using a form of prehistoric satellite navigation and drawing maps on the ground with a stick, until one of the testers went for the easy option and jumped into his car and suggested we follow him. Eight kilometres later, down roads and tracks we never knew existed, we arrived at the second site.

Here we joined the queue for the final part of the test and were surprised to see that ours, and only ours, was personally conducted by Signor Grimaldi whose responsibility it clearly was to check all the aforementioned numbers. Job done, we took the papers to the office, paid for the test and were told we could collect our new *targa* on Monday morning at the *Motorizzazione Civile*.

On the Monday we were personally handed our new number-plates by our friend Antonio; we had both wrongly assumed that the new licence number would have been no more than an official piece of paper ... it was indeed that but along with it came the actual number-plates, front and back.

Unfortunately there were two more hurdles to overcome before I could attach them to the car.

The first was to return with all the paperwork to the *Automobile Club d'Italia* in order to get the car's new registration document, the bit of paper that, in the eyes of the police, made everything legal. And of course, we paid for that too when we returned a day or two later to collect the actual document. In total the whole process took about six weeks (though could have taken much less if we'd been in a hurry) and cost around four hundred euro. And still I couldn't attach those damn plates to the car ... not until I could find Italian insurance cover.

In anticipation I had already started this process by visiting

Santa Severina's Unipol insurance agent. At this stage I had the new licence number (I even took the plates with me as a visual aid) but the agent, or rather his Head Office, could not come to grips with the difference between the UK's no-claims bonus system and Italy's bonus/malus way of assessing past driving history. It was clear I was going to be financially penalised despite the fact that I had over forty years of accident-free motoring.

Unipol Head Office didn't want to know and that was basically that ... until the agent spotted the AXA logo on my UK insurance and suggested I pay the local Crotone branch a visit. Until then I hadn't realised that AXA (with whom I had only been insured since September) had an Italian offshoot; he gave me the address and directions.

There now followed the most bizarre series of events in my experience of the insurance business.

It was Friday. I turned up at said address but could not find AXA. The building housed a couple of other insurance companies and so I thought, hell, I've got this far, no harm in trying.

By this time I had all the required documentation for the car but I also brought my AXA paperwork and everything relating to my pre-AXA insurance. I was ushered into an office where a friendly young man told me that AXA had moved to another part of town. I explained the situation, the problem, as best I could and spread the paperwork out on the desk. He took a look, nodded, tut-tutted, turned it this way and that and told me that his company couldn't really help and that I really should go to AXA. He tried to give me directions, but soon saw that he was dealing with a cretin when it came to Crotone's back streets, gave up, changed tack and asked if he could photocopy certain documents.

When he returned with his copies he told me to come back

on Wednesday morning and we'd go together to the AXA office.

Wednesday morning sees my new-found friend Pino and I driving across a drizzling Crotone (in his car). He double parks in Via Torino and we enter the dowdy apartment block that also houses AXA. We climb the stairs to their first-floor offices and enter the domain of Maria who shakes my hand and asks me to sit.

Pino (remember this guy works for a *rival* insurance company) produces a memory stick on which he has created an analysis of my insurance history and how it might translate to the Italian system and Maria plugs it into her computer. (Maria turns out to be his cousin ... though in Italy that can just mean anything from long-standing family friend to having gone to school together.) He explains a few more of the details to cousin Maria and a quarter of an hour later the deed is done, the car is finally insured and I have paid the first of two six-monthly instalments.

Only one technicality remains ... I need to discontinue the car's UK insurance and remind the broker that I am due a six-month rebate.

It is just over two weeks since I got the number-plates and, drizzle or no drizzle, I am going to fix them to the car.

Proudly I stepped back to look at our little Clio, the little Clio that got us this far: it had been born in Naples as BR208YS, for a short time it was British-registered as X147KTF and now, back in Italy, it was DM294VS ... and looked the better for it.

More than a few passers-by stopped to watch as I worked, came over to shake hands and say *auguri*, Italian for congratulations, because, rightly, they realised this was a significant stage in our relationship with the people of Santa

Severina; it said something about us and it also said something about what we thought of them and their town. It said we were not just passing through and that we were here to stay.

It also made us less visible.

By comparison, changing my driving licence was less public and more straightforward. I was now used to the forms and having to pay for different aspects of the process at the post office. The only bit that threw me initially was the sight test ... until I realised that in the UK the only such test I took was a part of my original driving test forty-plus years earlier. In Italy a sight test is compulsory every five years ... quite a sensible idea methinks.

Eighty euro well spent in my book as it automatically erased the few penalty points I'd picked up in the UK for exceeding the speed limit.

_____

When we arrived at the *revisione* centre in the countryside for the second part of the test to check the car's credentials and roadworthiness, we parked the car in the queue (it didn't open for another quarter of an hour) and headed for the handy on-site coffee bar.

Here we each had a coffee for which I attempted to pay. The bartender shook his head and finger and explained that it was free, just a part of the service so, jokingly, I said that in that case I'd have a shot of *grappa* in mine, a so-called *caffè corretto*. He turned, lifted a bottle of *grappa* from the shelf and it was all I could do to stop him topping up my coffee.

What was odd about this little episode was that, by definition, the people who made use of this particular bar were all driving cars, vans or trucks. It just seemed incongruous to find this little bar, with its shelf well-stocked with spirits and liqueurs, supplying *caffè corretto* free to its customers.

I slept on that last paragraph and wondered whether or not there was any evidence of an increase in alcohol-related accidents following the biennial *revisione*. I reasoned that, statistically, it would be fairly easy to assess and somebody surely would have made the connection ... assuming there was a connection to be made.

Autumn into winter, outside and in

We had arrived in Santa Severina around the time of the *vendemmia*, the grape harvest, one of many local seasonal events related to and governed by the time of year and the resulting natural bounty of the surrounding countryside.

The grape harvest had of course only one outcome, lots and lots of the local red wine. Each year's vintage is generally 'tasted' on 11 November, the day of San Martino, and naturally it is generally pronounced *molto buono* (pretty damn good, perhaps even the best ever) and well on its way to maturity.

In November there is also the olive harvest and that first November we were invited to lend a hand at Le Puzelle where there were a mere two hundred trees to be harvested, and all by hand ... which is why Le Puzelle was normally closed at this time of year.

To say it was hard work would be an understatement and bear in mind *we* only worked the one day. That said, it wasn't all about beating the trees with long sticks and gathering the fallen olives in nets and loading the boxes onto the truck; there was also the camaraderie, the fun of working together, the lunchtime break with lots of bread, cheese, pasta and wine and a sense of partaking in a traditional process that results

Giuliano taking a break from beating the olives ... sunglasses in November?

in that thick green oil that for Calabrians is as important as bread and wine.

Not all the olives were for oil; those from a few designated trees, black and smaller than the others, were stored and preserved separately and would be a part of the Le Puzelle's table for months to come.

Up in the square there were more *ape*s than usual as those with surpluses from their plots, their *orti*, in the countryside sold their vegetables for next to nothing. Late October through November was the season for brassicas – cauliflower, broccoli and rape – and there was an abundance.

Also at this time we discovered *cachi* (the persimmon or sharon fruit), a plump orange fruit with the texture of an over-ripe plum and its own unique taste *and* the bonus of having no stone in the middle. Silvana turned up one day with some and, embarrassingly, we had to ask her what to do with them.

As November slid into December it was time for the sweet, bright orange *mandarini* to grace every table. You could buy them by the kilo if you wanted, but much better by the *cassetta* ... not only cheaper but they might even take you through to Christmas.

The orange, pith-less, peel of the *mandarini* has another use – as the main ingredient, along with sugar and neat alcohol, of *liquore di mandarini*, mandarin liqueur. Unlike the UK, ninety-six percent proof alcohol is available from most Italian supermarkets; it is, after all, the main ingredient of *liquore di mandarini*, *limoncello* and other liqueurs. It's sale is illegal in the UK for one simple reason ... there are some people there who would just drink it straight from the bottle. Yes, they drink it in Italy but not before doing something constructive with it by adding the natural colours and flavours of the countryside and some sugar.

So, as you might expect, the first thing we did when we bought our first box of mandarins was to make *liquore di mandarini* and within a few days, just after Silvana turned up with a bagful of lemons from the tree in her back garden, we made some *limoncello*.

While much of the local produce was cultivated, there was an abundance of fine fare available free of charge in the surrounding countryside At this time of year there were some astonishingly colourful mushrooms to be found at small roadside stalls or from car boots ... of course you could collect them yourself but exact locations of such delicacies are usually well-kept secrets.

Walnuts and chestnut were everywhere and, though the former were generally cultivated, we soon learnt to always carry a bag or two in the car just in case we passed a little copse of chestnut trees that someone else had missed or even a tree of dark, late-season figs overhanging the road.

There is nothing more satisfying than returning home to a warm, cosy house with a bagful of free ill-gotten gains, just from having gone for a trip into the nearby countryside. The problem with this idyllic scenario was that we soon discovered the 'warm, cosy house' part to be an illusion for our first winter at least.

As I've noted elsewhere Calabrian houses were generally built to keep the sun at bay so that in the winter it is often colder inside than it is outside. At one time Silvana and Raffaele's upstairs kitchen had a *cammineto*, a wood-burning fire that was both a focal point and a source of heat for a radiator-based central heating system. But in anticipation of the imminent arrival of *metano*, gas, and because it created a lot of dust and ash, it was removed, though the radiators remained. In its place they put the spiral staircase and extended their home downwards to create a new, larger kitchen, a utility area and the Lion King bedroom in what had once been a *maggazino*.

Unfortunately for them (and for us) the availability of *metano* had taken on an element of elasticity (not uncommon in Italy) and though all of Santa Severina now had piped gas as far as the door, the system had not yet been tested and inaugurated. During our first winter, therefore, it was simply not an option. The latest proposed time for testing the system was early in 2009 with the aim of being on stream by the following summer.

At that time the only source of heat available to us was additional clothing and/or electric heaters – oil-filled, halogen or convector. We tried them all.

Nothing really did the trick for, even if we could have afforded the cost of the electricity we were using just to keep warm, there was another unexpected genie in the bottle. All Calabrian houses have a default three megawatt limit on the power available at any given time. This was definitely something we hadn't reckoned on ... indeed something we hadn't heard of until the lights went out.

And they did go out – frequently – as we juggled with the needs of hot water, heating, cooking (a bottled gas hob but an electric oven) and the washing machine to keep within that three kilowatts. We could have paid a fixed sum and doubled the potential output available but this would only have meant that we would have spent much more and still not have made the house very much warmer.

This was the essence of the problem, the electric heating was not adequate; even with a bottomless cash pit and six megawatts we probably could not have heated the house sufficiently and certainly not to the level we were used to in the UK. That said, I think it's safe to say that full-blast UK-style central heating is not overly healthy and that both Kay and I were brought up in non-centrally-heated houses and seem to be none the worse for the experience. Cooler would have been fine; cold was not what we were expecting.

There I was at the end of the last chapter, out in the late-January drizzle, fixing those coveted new numberplates to the car, exchanging pleasantries with the locals and acknowledging their good wishes ... but not really looking forward to going back indoors where it was a tad on the cooler side.

Of course we survived by wrapping up well, spending a lot of time outdoors rather than in the house (no bad thing) and grasping at any positive signs that there would definitely be *metano* by the following winter.

Unknown to Silvana and Raffaele, much as we loved them, their family and this house, we had already discussed the unthinkable and decided that, should there be no *metano* the following year, then we would reluctantly have to consider moving on.

The limoncello we made was good, very good some have said. But when I first started asking people about the recipe, and in particular the length of time the lemon rind has to sit in the alcohol before being discarded and the sugar added, I found that there were as many recipes as people I asked. On one occasion my simple question even started an argument between two friends.

We found Calabrians generally to be both very passionate about how to make or cook their favourite drink or dish and very conservative about what it is they eat and drink. This latter trait came to the fore once when we entertained a Calabrian friend who quickly made us aware that there was no bread on the table in such a way that we felt obliged to rectify this misdemeanour at once. As you've probably guessed, she never ate any.

Women, aware that I do the cooking, would often ask me what we would be eating that evening (I think this was often a test to see if I really *did* do the cooking) and when I described, say, an adaption of an Italian dish, the response was generally something along the lines of, "but that's not a Calabrian dish" as if it were only possible to eat something intrinsically Calabrian while in Calabria.

But then what is a typical Calabrian dish? The answer of course is *pasta al forno*, pasta cooked in the oven. But even though there is, I imagine, a basic recipe somewhere in the Calabrian psyche, get three Calabrian women in a room to discuss the finer points of this dish and they'll be arguing about it for hours. In this town there are at least as many recipes for *pasta al forno* as there are families in Santa Severina.

I recall how, when I was asked to list the ingredients for a particular salad dressing (that people had just eaten and seemed to like) and got to the last one, honey, there was a distinct intake of breath; I might just as well have said arsenic ... I think maybe next time I'll try that.

Of course all of the above are a mix of individual incidents and generalisations ... I should also add that, on at least two occasions, I have been specifically asked to cook something oriental as our guests *wanted* to try something different. Indeed one person invited himself back with his new girlfriend so that she could share the same experience as his ex-girlfriend.

Amber discovers that oranges grow on trees; Neff discovers Calabrian snow

Comings and goings

January and February was a busy time. Early in the new year, in the space of a few days, we welcomed and bade farewell to Amber and Tom ... their fleeting 'surprise' visit was all too short but it did afford us the opportunity to demonstrate to Amber that oranges did really grow on trees and not just supermarket shelves.

At the end of the month our first non-family guests were expected, two friends from England. Vanessa was an ex-client from my graphic designer days but it was her partner Jon who made the big impression in Santa Severina ... he was, after all, an accomplished musician.

When Stumpo and other local musicians heard they were to have a fellow muso in their midst it was only a matter of time before they rustled up a guitar and found an opportunity for a jam session. The 'opportunity' they exploited was the dinner for dignitaries following a musical performed in Santa Severina that somehow we four got invited to. Stumpo had written the lyrics and score for the show; he also performed with others and alongside his wife Francesca. Francesca played the violin but it was her voice that took us by surprise ... it was the most beautiful singing voice I'd ever heard and to say it took my breathe away is no exaggeration.

So the post-show dinner got under way and, tucked away in the corner there was Stumpo, some fellow musicians and four gate-crashers, one of whom was busily tuning his newly acquired guitar. That evening Jon became an honorary Calabrian and embraced the music of his hosts effortlessly and with great skill. Still there are people who talk about that evening and the Englishman who could play the *taranatella*.

It was while taking Vanessa and Jon back to Lamezia Airport that our beloved little Clio started to misbehave. It was all of a-splutter and there was a red warning light flickering menacingly, clearly trying to tell us something. We stopped for a few moments to consult the handbook, found reference to the offending light but did not understand a word for of course the handbook, the car's original, was in Italian. We had no way of knowing how serious the problem was or whether or not we'd make the airport in time for the flight.

Regardless, we did what Italians would have done, we shrugged our shoulders and pressed on. A car overtook us and out of the corner of my eye I thought I saw the driver wave to us; Kay thought I was clutching at straws and seeing things. The car was now out of sight but I was still convinced that it was a car I should have recognised ... I decided it was not unlike Roberto's car, (Roberto, the son of Vincenzo), so I stopped and called him to ask if he'd just overtaken us. He had and he had already stopped at a bar in the never-ending Botricello for a coffee ... about five kilometres up ahead.

When we caught up with him, Roberto, whose English was pretty good, read the part in the car's manual about our disconcerting warning light. He attempted a translation then took a shot in the dark and said he didn't think it was serious and that we should definitely make it to the airport ... he also reminded us that he wasn't very technically-minded. In short, although his unfounded optimism seemed to reassure our passengers, I realised it was no more just that – unfounded optimism. I kept my thoughts to myself.

We pressed on and, just as Roberto had predicted, eventually staggered into Lamezia Airport and deposited our two agitated friends outside ... just in time to make their flight. We of course had to do it all over again; we limped home while the car continued to indulge in its random stop-start antics.

Finally back in Santa Severina I consulted with Raffaele about local mechanics. He told me there were two but that naturally it would make sense if I went to Enzo. He recognised the 'why?' in my expression and told me that Enzo drove exactly the same car as us and would clearly know what the problem was. He was right.

Despite language difficulties and my embarrassing attempts at mimicking the sounds the car had been making, it took Enzo less than five minutes to diagnose that we needed a new set of plugs, a new distributor cap and adjoining leads; he told us it would be ready by the evening. He was as good as his word.

Later the same week we returned to Lamezia to collect our next visitors – Vanessa's son Joe and his then girlfriend, Harriet. The car behaved itself impeccably there and back twice within four days.

This was the problem with Lamezia, it was about one hour, forty minutes drive away and it wasn't the easiest of drives ... there was a short stretch of about twenty minutes of fast dual carriageway but the rest was a mixture of winding country lanes and stop-start built-up areas along the Ionian coast and around Calabria's administrative capital, Catanzaro.

There was another airport much closer, just south of Crotone but, at the time, it only operated in the summer and even then the few routes it offered were of no help to anyone coming from England. For the moment Lamezia was the only option though it did have one thing in its favour ... a few kilometres away there was one of Calabria's largest *Centro Commerciale*, a shopping centre, what Americans would call a mall. Every time we went to Lamezia a little bit of retail therapy became compulsory.

Within ten days of returning Joe and Harriet to Lamezia we were back there again to pick up my nephew Graham.

Graham and I had history: we were wont to go off and do things together, things that fathers and sons sometimes don't get round to, things uncles and nephews do much better. Once we met up in Chicago and set off on an American road trip down to Atlanta through the heart of bourbon country, Kentucky and Tennessee ... not that we remember much about it. We had contrived on another occasion to 'accidentally' meet up in Chicago as a surprise for Kay; more of a shock really. We had turned up in Belfast together when his father, my brother, was just expecting to collect *him* from the airport. Kay and I also turned up unexpectedly at his wedding in Las Vegas ... he knew we were coming but neither his sister nor his father did ... nor did the bride.

When he went to live in America he bequeathed me his whisky collection, one bottle of which was a rare Bushmills whiskey (Irish, hence the 'e' in whiskey) that I was only allowed to drink when we were together. That was the rule ... and for Neff and Unc (or nicknames for each other) that time had now arrived.

Apart from finishing off the Bushmills, we visited all the places where we had taken all our other guests, the places that had become part of our guided tour – Crotone, Le Castella, Carlo's bar, Angela's house, Silvana's house and Le Puzelle. But Neff was staying longer than others and would be with us for a week so one day we decided to go further afield and visit Elvira at her workplace in Cosenza.

We were about halfway there, at the highest point of the main road, the *Strada Statali*, when we decided to take a short detour south to Lorica and lake Arvo, into the heart of the Sila mountains. Just as we reached the lake we were forced to make a hasty retreat as the weather changed so quickly and we just made it back to the *Strada Statali*, before the snow made all side-roads impassable. It was a white-out, the likes of which none of us had ever experienced. Such a rapid change in conditions was, of course, something we should have anticipated: the *Strada Statali* linking Crotone and Cosenza traverses the Sila mountains where, at this time of year, there are several busy ski resorts. Calabria was a place we had come to associate with sun rather than snow and such carelessness could have been more costly.

Back on the *Strada Statali* we considered returning east to the Crotone side but Kay was out-voted and we finally decided to press on to Cosenza where we arrived forty minutes later to a bright spring-like day.

At the end of the week we returned with Neff to Lamezia Airport ... the only difference being that all three of us were on the same flight to London. Kay was heading for London itself and I was flying on to Ireland to see family. We would meet up again later in the week in England at a wedding and then return to Santa Severina the following day. This was to be our first trip away from Santa Severina in over five months.

For me it felt very strange. Of course it was good to see family and catch up with things, especially with my grandson Rhys. But it was strange being away from Santa Severina. I actually missed it much more than I expected to. Indeed, after only a few days away, I was longing to return.

This was something I was to experience every time I left Santa Severina; for me a totally new phenomenon; it was/is, I suppose, a form of homesickness. But when it first happened it was puzzling and caused me to wonder what it was about this place and these people that had such a pull. I still have not found one defining answer ... perhaps as this story unweaves, it may become clearer, perhaps I'll return to these thoughts.

Our return to Santa Severina had an element of the surreal. I swear I saw a tear in Silvana's eye as she hugged us warmly to welcome us back. *Bentornati* she said and then added that she had been worried that we might never come back – it had only been eight days!

I often wonder what we did to deserve such friends, such generous, giving people, people who are exactly as they seem. Like Francesca's voice, it sometimes takes my breath away.

We soon learnt too that there were rituals and conventions around coming and going. When Giuliano went to Romania that January he came to say goodbye to us ... but not just us, he made a point of saying goodbye to all the people that were important to him. We realised that we should do the same when we went to England and, now that we were back, it was just as important to re-present ourselves to those same people, to confirm that we had indeed returned safely.

Before we left we had also said goodbye to Santa Severina's *sindaco*, the mayor Bruno Cortese, who had asked us to try and do something for him on our travels. As mayor, Bruno knew that there was to be an advertising campaign on London taxis that February to entice people to visit Calabria; a thousand taxis would each carry an image of a castle alongside an internationally-renowned and respected Calabrian footballer, Gennaro Gattuso, whose wife happened to be Scottish.

There had been two striking castles on the short-list to represent the region, Santa Severina and Le Castella, but it was the latter that was finally chosen. No matter, Bruno wanted to see a photo of a London cab advertising Calabria.

Fortunately, outside London's Liverpool Street Station, we came across a gaggle of such cabs and got our photographs. In the process a curious taxi driver asked me why I kept taking photos of his cab and was more than a little surprised when I told him that I lived there and pleased when I suggested that a photo of his cab might well end up on the mayoral wall in a small Calabrian town.

_____

When we returned to collect our car from Enzo *mecannico*, as opposed to Enzo *chitarrista* or Enzo *idraulico* – we had learnt that attaching a characteristic helped when trying to pinpoint exactly which Enzo – he took us into the house adjacent to his garage and introduced us to his mother, Sara. A quarter of an hour later we left with a car that worked and a jar of Sara's *carciofi* (artichokes) preserved in oil.

When I returned the next morning with the cash – yes, he let me, more or less a complete stranger, vacate the premises without paying – Sara gave me half a dozen eggs. Such was the way of things in this town.

Thereafter we became good friends with Enzo and his extended family but, in particular, his mother. We had a puncture a few weeks later and while I watched as Enzo repaired the tyre, Kay sat in the house with Sara and, as before, we didn't leave empty-handed.

We were getting used to such generosity so it did not phase Kay when I returned one morning, after having been out of the house for no more than five minutes, with five litres of wine. Or when people give us some of their extra home-grown aubergines, broccoli or chillies; or when a neighbour turns up at the door with a bag of *mandarini*; or when someone thinks you'd like a bottle of their olive oil or a jar of *passata*; or someone pays for your cup of coffee at Carlo's; or when Gino *panettiere* throws in an extra small loaf of bread and says *questo è per la signora*, this is for your wife; or when Stumpo and Carmen pop in with a loaf of bread from Mesoraca, better than your average bread they maintain; or when Silvana drops off a plateful of home-made *lasagna* or some *sussamele* (a Calabrian biscuit available only at Christmas). All these and so much more became almost normal in our day-to-day lives.

It was such occasions that reinforced what we had already begun to realise ... that every day we should learn to expect the unexpected.

Winter into spring

At the end of March the clocks went forward one hour; there was more light in the evenings and Santa Severina was warming again. Spring was in the air and summer just around the corner. From time to time there was the faint whiff of gas around the town as the system was being tested.

It was at this time of year that Kay in particular got restless; hitherto in late March she would be itching to get out into the garden sorting out the flower beds and preparing the vegetable patch for a new season. All we had at Santa Severina was a balcony, albeit a balcony that she had made into mini haven for all sorts of plants. But it wasn't the same.

I had a word with Silvana and asked if she knew of anywhere where we could grow a few vegetables, our very own *orticello*, little plot. *In campagna*, she said, local shorthand for 'at my/ our land in the country' and then added *fra i ulivi*, between the olive trees. She went on to say that we could go with them to have a look and if it was what we had in mind then she'd give us a key. Of course at this point there was no 'we' ... I hadn't mentioned it to Kay yet.

But when I did all was well and a few days later we went with Raffaele, Silvana and Alessia to have a look. We were shown how the land was divided between the five Gerardi children – Silvana and Antonietta had olive groves, Sergio and Anna Maria (the two that lived away) had the walnut trees and Aurelio worked the vines. There was also a house (technically half Aurelio's and half Sergio's but used by everyone) and a couple of outhouses which Aurelio in particular used as he was the one who spent more of his time looking after it all.

Just below the house was Silvana's olive grove and she said we could use as much as we wanted between the lines of trees … about four metres wide for as far as the eye could see and bigger than any garden we'd ever had in England. She said we could use water from the house until the really hot weather began, thereafter we would have to pump water up from the well at the bottom beyond the walnut trees. Apparently Aurelio was the well-expert and he would show us how to use the petrol-driven pump which fed a network of underground tubes and stand-pipes. Raffaele also showed us where he kept his small rotovator which we could use whenever we wanted but he suggested we wait for a week or two by which time Aurelio, with his man-sized tractor and rotovator, would have turned over the soil for us. Once again the unconditional generosity of this family took us by surprise.

On our way back to Santa Severina itself we took a short detour as Raffaele was on the look-out for wild asparagus, *asparagi selvataci*, which was just coming into season. When we told him how we'd once collected *asparagi* in Sardinia (see *Stumbling through Italy*) he was most impressed and wrongly assumed that we still remembered what the plant looked like. In total we found two stalks that afternoon … I say 'we' but it was Raffaele who found them (they were on his side of the car) and neither Kay nor I was any the wiser about what to look for.

But, after many false starts, we did become experts and over the few weeks that took March into April became quite skilful when it came to finding *asparagi selvataci*. We would drive down into the countryside, park up and walk for hours up and down tracks and lanes in search of the little spiky plant and its bounty. Normally we would keep to public areas such as the roadside itself or open land but more than once people invited us onto their land to take what we could find. In such cases what we normally found was that someone else had beaten us to it (probably without permission) and that any asparagus had already been harvested. In total we collected around three kilos over those few weeks and enjoyed many a meal courtesy of mother nature ... we just had to put up with that distinctive asparagus urine odour.

Almost subconsciously we were assimilating other things: we could look at a track or piece of land and know with certainty whether or not we were likely to find asparagus there; we also noticed how there was rarely (if ever) asparagus plants on both sides of the same road at the same place; and that whenever a road curved, the asparagus would often change sides, probably something to do with how the light changed.

We enjoyed this time immensely. But gradually it became the 'B' movie as the only show in town for us was the fact that finally we had our own key to the Gerardi land and Aurelio had just finished rotavating between Silvana's olive trees.

In southern Italy full-blown garden centres as we know it are few and far between; the nearest equivalent is a DIY store or supermarket for the tools and a *vivaio*, a nursery, for plants and seeds.

Increasingly we took time off from asparagus hunting and did the rounds of them all and finally found that the best place to buy seedlings for most vegetables and packets of seeds for a few others, was right on our doorstep in Santa Severina itself. On our travels we bought a rake, a couple of trowels, some string, gardening gloves and other bits and pieces that we'd had in England but that we never thought we'd ever need again. The only things we couldn't find were kneelers, compacted foam pads that would help Kay in particular when we got round to weeding; we solved this by asking a friend in England to buy them for us and stick them in the post

We did some internet research on the best times to plant out in southern Italy and Kay decked out almost every available level surface with little white plastic cups filled with potting compost and runner bean seeds.

It was Friday 10 April, the beginning of the Easter weekend, and at long last we were measuring up our paths and beds in preparation for those seedlings that continued to pop up everywhere around the house.

I know we'd come to Santa Severina to retire but we were incredibly excited at the prospect of growing things again. Word of our insanity spread quickly and thereafter everyone would talk to us about the progress, or lack of it, of our plot; many even came to see it, sometimes with, sometimes without our knowledge. We only found out about this latter group when we talked to people who had clearly been there to have a look at how the 'English' did things ... we suspected that Aurelio was running private tours from the town.

Naturally enough there was a mountain of advice available about how to do this and that; when to plant, when not to plant; how much to water, how little to water; when to water, when not to water ... trouble was that it was often contradictory so we decided to learn by our own mistakes ... of which there were many.

If 'gay abandon' means what I think it means, then that is what we started with. At our *orticello*, in Aurelio's outhouse, there was a good selection of tools, including a *zappa*, the Italian version of a spade, more akin to a large hoe, but far more effective and economical (in terms of energy) than its English equivalent. And in Italian the word is also onomatopoeic: the verb *zappare* means to zap the earth with a *zappa*. A great tool and an even greater word.

By the end of April we had planted three types of tomato, peppers, chillies, lettuce, spinach, aubergines, beetroot, courgettes, runner beans, cucumbers and marrow. Everything, except the spinach, beetroot and beans had been acquired locally as seedlings, a strip of seven in individual polystyrene 'pots' for fifty *centesimi*, half a euro.

The cucumbers and marrows had been given to us by a friend who had, unwittingly, mixed up which was which. We discovered this mistake much later when we realised that the climbing frame I'd made for the cucumbers was supporting marrows instead ... meanwhile the cucumbers were barely surviving in the marrow patch.

The smell of *metano* had gone, the delicate odour of *asparagi* urine was no more; only the fresh, colourful scents of spring filled our lungs and in particular the wonderful aroma of tomato plants heading upwards toward the sun.

At first we went to the *orto* in the mornings and whenever we wanted a break or felt our embryonic plants could survive and grow unwatched, we headed deeper into the surrounding countryside just to amble and drink in the abundance of wild flowers such as we'd never seen before.

In Calabria, we found, if you ask someone the name of a roadside flower the conversation goes something like this: *Come si chiamo questa fiora azzurra? Ah, queste fiore qui, queste fiore si chiamano le fiore azzurre.* Asking someone to name that blue flower usually generates the response, "We call them the blue flowers." Only once did someone who made such a response see the funny side. Maybe we just asked the wrong people.

The *orto* in the making

And even if someone did have a name for 'that blue flower', it would almost certainly have been a local name, a name that would probably mean nothing to someone from Roccabernarda or Cotronei, as likely as not a name with no obvious botanical origin.

Anal to a fault, we needed to know the name of those blue flowers, *and* of all the others, so we invested in a couple of books about wild flowers and Kay soon became on first-name terms with many that we happened upon: there was the bright yellow of the daisy-like *crepide*; the deep red of the tiny pea-like *ginistrino purpureo*; the deeper red of the *sulla comune*; the blue-purple of the upright *cipollaccio*; and of course the delicate blues of the *giaggiola del poveretti* and the *cicoria*, two of Calabria's many blue flowers. There were some easier to recognise – and pronounce – like crocuses, poppies, thistles, borage and wild sweet peas and endless fields rampant with almost every colour imaginable.

All these and many more were our constant companions throughout this time and many were also edible – one of our books was half 'flora' and half recipes. No such thing as 'don't pick the wild flowers' here … for centuries in times of hardship, endemic in the south through many generations and even within living memory, such natural bounty kept people alive and, momentarily, brought colour to a grey existence. It was not unusual to see people, usually men, out in the fields gathering something, we knew not what, that would either feed their family directly or, by default, through their animals.

We also took to walking alongside the river Neto which ran close to and parallel to the Crotone to Cosenza *Strada Statali*.

In the spring its waters receded to reveal a ramshackle path that had started with good intentions before the river took over and chewed away at its route making it almost impossible to find, let alone follow. So we just followed our instincts as the Neto sparkled and gurgled alongside, tumbling over large smooth mini boulders on its way to the sea at Strongoli.

We collected bits of wood, interesting pebbles and some of the larger stones, grey, black, yellow, red and white; we sought out those that had one flattish side which made excellent doorstops and bookends.

Our surprise at never seeing any other human walking by the river was countered by the surprise in people's faces when we said that's where we had been.

We rarely saw any birds by the Neto, the odd heron and that was it. Indeed on all our walks birds were few and far between, a few jays, some crows and occasionally, if we were lucky, a close encounter with what we thought were kestrels, but Calabrians called them *falcone*.

In our *asparagi* collecting days it was not unusual to round a bend and disturb one sitting lazily on a telegraph pole or a gate-post, unaware till then that humans could walk as well as drive. Then of it'd go, slowly at first, that large expanse of wing taking it ever higher up into a tree or higher still to catch a thermal to start another circular descent in search of food.

Often we would watch the *falcone* from our balcony as they circled effortlessly, sometimes in pairs, in search of whatever moved down there in that beautiful expansive valley between Santa Severina and neighbouring Scandale. Occasionally we had visitors closer to home when a robin, a tit or a sparrow would flit along the balcony picking at titbits.

But by far the most prolific bird hereabouts arrived in the early spring, stayed about two months and then was gone. We never tired of watching their antics as they swooped and darted hither and thither between the houses, over the roofs, around the washing ... the chatter of the swifts was a welcome addition around our balcony, particularly as their favourite pastime was scooping up all those insects that bite people.

In early May Kay returned to England for a week by herself and I was left in sole charge of the *orto* and the balcony, mainly watering at this stage.

This was the first time I had been in Santa Severina left to my own devices. But I had work to do and in particular trying to get back into something called *Stumbling through Italy* that I had started a few years earlier but not touched for almost a year.

As people knew that, cooking-wise at least, I could look after myself I was not inundated with dinner dates. I only ever told a few people that Kay was in England but because people were so used to seeing us together, they (mainly women) couldn't stop themselves from asking *E la moglie?* And, it has to be said that when I replied *In Inghilterra*, I did notice one or two raised eyebrows.

It was strange being in this place and this house without Kay. This whole adventure was something we'd done together and generally every step of the way we had literally been side by side. Unsolicited and unpaid by me, people (mostly men) later told Kay that I hardly left the house and that when I did I looked incredibly down. One went as far as saying that he thought he saw a tear in my eye up in the square. Naturally I agreed with this observation ... but then ruined it by saying they were tears of joy.

I don't want to give the impression that all Santa Severina's males are just old romantics at heart; it's just as likely they said what they said so that I might do the same for them sometime. One, who shall remain nameless, confessed to me that he was jealous that my wife was away for a week.

Mario, he of the two aluminium sticks, the twinkling eyes and a penchant for slapping me on the shoulder, didn't take long to work out when and how often we went to the *orto* ... it was, after all, *his* land.

It was while Kay was in England that he asked if he could go with me *in campagna* and of course I obliged; the same thing happened a day or two later, then every day I, and then 'we' when Kay got back, went to the *orto*. When he got to the land he would spend anything up to two and a half hours working on the vines, tying them in with grass and discarding any unwanted shoots, or doing all sorts of other odd jobs about the place.

He was having a great time and always looked at us as if we were some sort of weaklings when we'd had enough and wanted to get back home. As May was heading towards June and we felt more comfortable working in the afternoon, so Mario changed *his* work schedule and almost every day accompanied us there after his afternoon *siesta*. This worked better for all of us as his son, Aurelio, normally stopped by later in the afternoon and so he could take Mario back up to Santa Severina.

Here was a man, well into his eighties, who had found a new lease of life; he was enjoying himself immensely and it was all our fault. But there was a down side.

Mario didn't know when to stop; he loved his land and all that he had achieved there and, though Aurelio was his natural successor, Mario still wanted to be involved, wanted to show these not-so-young whippersnappers that he could still hack it. But the family was getting worried.

Aurelio and Attilio (who was back home for a few days) took Kay and I aside and asked us not to take him any more. They felt that Mario didn't know when enough was enough and were worried that he could have an accident or illness somewhere on the land unseen by us. We agreed but asked that they should tell him that it wasn't our idea. We knew that we had created a unique bond with Mario, we knew that if he ever asked if he could come with us it would be hard to say no. He never did ask us again ... and we missed him.

By early May it was clear that *metano* was definitely going to be online for the following winter. The first part of the process that affected us was when we were told that work would begin soon on hooking up the pipes that controlled the radiators to a unit, a *termosifone*, that would it turn be attached to the main source of hot water, a *caldaia*, in plain man's language a gas-fired central heating boiler.

The work got under way and soon everything was almost ready for the boiler ... an alcove had been cut into the outside wall of the balcony awaiting its arrival.

I was standing outside with Silvana watching the work in progress and asked her about the next stage, the boiler. Quite unexpectedly she seemed overwhelmed with emotion and drew me aside. Composing herself she explained that there were two types of boiler, one that was adequate, not particularly efficient but cheap and another that was more efficient, more than adequate but more expensive ... by the time they had paid for all the preparatory work, she and Raffaele could only afford the cheaper one. I could see that telling me this was hurting.

I took her into the kitchen to join Kay and explained that we had already discussed this eventuality and had decided that we would share the costs with them ... and our half would be the better boiler. Kay nodded in agreement.

Silvana hugged us and said that she knew the previous winter had been difficult for us (though we had never said so) and that they didn't want us to leave ... and of course if we ever did we could take the boiler with us!

I was lying of course, we had not discussed it but I knew it was what we should do and that Kay would agree.

———————————

It was time for us to do something unexpected.

Kay's birthday was in late March and, ever the romantic, I

gave her ... a postcard. She didn't really understand it at first.

The card was homemade and had a date on one side superimposed over a photo of Nek and a map of Lecce in Puglia on the other. Nek was on a much-publicised Italian tour and would be *in concerto* at Lecce at the end of April ... and, whatever our musician friends thought, we two oldies were going to be there. I had already booked online.

Lecce and this part of Puglia, known as *Il Salento* by Italians and the heel by everyone else, was a part of Italy we knew well, a part of Italy we loved dearly. And though we would have liked to have stayed longer and visit people and places in the area, we were in the middle of our *orto-entusiasmo* and so decided to just stay the one night.

It was nearly a five-hour drive to Lecce. We arrived early afternoon and checked into the bed & breakfast we'd booked just round the corner from the *Teatro Politeama Greca*, one of Lecce's oldest theatres and, in its present form, dating from the early 20th century.

We spent the late afternoon and early evening wandering round the city's beautiful *centro storico* and hoping we would find the workshop of the woman from whom we bought some glass a few years earlier. We did ... but she wasn't there. All too soon it was time to find somewhere to eat ready for the nine o'clock concert.

For a short time we were the only two in the restaurant – it was only seven-thirty and unusual to find a restaurant open this early – until a group of about a dozen twenty- and thirty-somethings joined us; they were Nek's backing band and crew, though of the Great Man Himself there was no sign.

Later I had a moment of panic as we negotiated the queue to enter the theatre ... I noticed that I was the only person with a paper ticket, a page I'd printed off from the internet when I booked. I wondered if I'd missed out a stage, perhaps should have gone to the theatre's box office and had my paper converted to a real ticket ... there did seem to be a queue at the box office as well.

No, I was right first time ... the oldest, probably the only *straniere* in the building, appeared also to be the only person who'd used the internet to book.

We enjoyed the concert immensely.

The *Teatro Politeama Greca* was outstandingly beautiful, a truly stunning setting, an *objet d'art* in itself and as such not a venue you might associate with such a concert. But it worked.

We were at least forty to fifty years older than most of the audience, at least fifteen years older than the next oldest; but we didn't care nor, do I believe, did anyone even notice.

Like everyone else we hooted, we cheered, we clapped, we stood up, we danced in the aisles, we even took illegal photographs. (There was a woman patrolling the central aisle chastising anyone who took photos and threatening them with eviction ... she could tell who they were by the flash from their camera or phone. I didn't use flash.)

We had a ball. And later, after a nightcap at a local bar, walking in the warmth of the late evening we bumped into the band's drummer and told him how much we had enjoyed ourselves. He shook our hands and thanked us.

I wonder did he ever tell the Great Man Himself about his oldest fans ... and foreign too?

There are still people in Santa Severina who find it hard to believe we went all the way to Lecce to see Nek *in concerto* ... were the photos legal, I could of course prove it.

Neto and Nek

Neff and other nicknames

Neff's American wife Jo was in the UK for a few weeks and he decided to bring her over to see us in Calabria. He was the first person to revisit and the first also not to need picking up at the airport ... he hired a car and drove here.

When we first came to live in Calabria I wrote a turn-by-turn guide for would-be drivers from Lamezia Airport to Santa Severina in the misguided assumption that that's how they'd get here. I had (and have) never used it ... and the one person who did realise he could drive himself was the one person who didn't need it, the one person who, like his uncle, could usually remember a route having done it once.

We met in Carlo's bar in the square ... in fact Neff and Jo got there first and were already downing their first beer when we arrived. It was to be a short visit, three days, but three days of better weather than the snow Neff had experienced in February in the Sila. Also Attilio Pugliese was in town.

Before Christmas Silvana had told me that Attilio, her brother-in-law, was really looking forward to meeting us; *she* thought we'd get on well together. When we did meet up for the first time at *Capodanno*, we did indeed seem to hit it off – I suspect the seating arrangements were no accident – and now, in late May, he and Anna Maria were back in town ... both were Santa Severenese but lived south of Rome.

May was also the time of year that the Gerardi family reopened their summer quarters to the fresh air at their holiday homes at *Villaggio Il Tucano*, on the coast near Le Castella. Such holiday villages are popular in Calabria but we didn't realise until then that three of the Gerardi family, the three daughters, each had an apartment at *Il Tucano* ... nor that we four (Kay and I, Neff and Jo) would get invited to pop in for the afternoon as each couple, aided and abetted by Silvana's brother, Aurelio, and his wife Rosanna, opened the shutters, blew the winter cobwebs away and did a few odd jobs in preparation for the season.

We were given the guided tour of the village and had to imagine this eight-hundred-apartments teeming with thousands of bronzed bodies in the blistering heat of summer. That day was hot enough, like a warm summer's day in England, and bikini-clad Silvana told us that they didn't normally use their apartment on a regular basis till the end of June and that we could come and stay whenever we liked. From June until the end of August the family would live there.

In the meantime this late spring sun was too good to miss so, the guided tour complete, we returned to Antonietta's apartment, sat out on the patio, opened some wine and relaxed like true Calabrians.

Holiday villages are not for us, at least holiday villages in the summer holiday season are not our cup of tea. Our afternoon there was pleasant enough, we enjoyed ourselves precisely because we were by the sea *without* the hordes. For Silvana and Raffaele it was different; as hard-working teachers this was a place they could relax for the summer and a safe, self-contained village where Francesco and Alessia could do their own thing with their friends.

We decided we probably wouldn't take them up on their offer just yet but that it would be good to drop in some time during the summer if only to see whether or not our imaginary picture was near the mark.

As well as being with Neff and Jo, I seemed to spend quite a bit of time that day bonding with Attilio. I took him back to a conversation we'd had at *Capodanno* when he tried to describe his father to me, he said he thought we knew each other. From his description – wiry, a good head of hair, strong as an ox and fit as a fiddle – I had suggested the name Francesco? No, he said emphatically, Pugliese, his name is Pugliese. I didn't know anyone of that name so gave up, I couldn't work out who he was talking about.

Now, nearly five months on, I had solved the puzzle ... actually with the help of Carlo, Attilio's cousin, I had solved it in January but this was my first opportunity to tell Attilio. I reminded him that he had said his father's name was Pugliese. He nodded. Ciccio Pugliese? I asked. He nodded again. Francesco ... Ciccio? I ventured.

Ciccio was the *diminutivo*, the shortened name, for most people called Francesco; sometimes it's shortened even further to Chic'. We had been talking about the same person all along, even if we weren't speaking the same language. Attilio probably had never heard anyone ever call his father Francesco (the name I knew him by); for Attilio he was *papà* but he would have heard others calling him Ciccio or, more likely, Pugliese (in the same way as we talked about Stumpo).

I was just about to explain why Neff was called Neff when his name was actually Graham ... and thought better of it.

Diminutivi are part of the Italian psyche. Most common names have at least one *diminutivo* but in places like Santa Severina, where everybody knows everybody, variations on the *diminutivi* themselves make identification easier. We have, for example, four friends called Nino, Anton, Tonino and Toto; we have a fifth called Antonio. In fact all five are called Antonio, the first four are just shortened variations, *diminutivi*.

Some *diminutivi* go a stage further and, to the outsider, are almost unrecognisable from the original, like Gino for Luigi, Pino for Giuseppe and Turuzzo for Salvatore.

There is, for many, a stage even further when it comes to names; some people are given nicknames, *soprannomi*. The aforementioned (and late) Ciccio Pugliese was known to some as *Serpa*. *Serpa* is local dialect for 'serpent' and the nickname referred to the idiosyncratic manner in which he drove his three-wheeled Ape. Ciccio was the Michael Schumacher of Ape-drivers and, even in his eighties, would screech round bends with a panache and swagger that belied his years. Some swear that they had seen him negotiate one bend out of the square at such speed that there were only two wheels on the ground.

Giovanni is *il professore*, which reflects his accumulated knowledge and is not any academic title he may have acquired at university. It was while delivering a package with a friend to a family in Roccabernarda in the mid-seventies, and subsequently lunching with them, that his host first called him *il professore*. The next time he called into a bar in Santa Severina, people had already heard the story and his *soprannome* lives on today.

Today that same bar is owned by Pino Tigano or *Ignaz* as people call him after the slighty cheeky and mischievous Ignatz Mouse in the *Krazy Kat* cartoons.

Ignaz' family name, Tigano, itself has a *soprannome*, the whole family are known as *da Foderara* because several generations ago it was the Tigano family who were known for making *la fodera*, the lining for wine casks.

Kay and I have also begun to follow this example for, because there are so many people who share the same name, we have begun to add a characteristic to pinpoint which one we are talking about: for us Gino *Pane* is the Gino who makes bread; Enzo *Meccanico* is the Enzo who repairs cars.

For me one of the most unusual stories of all is how one family acquired the name *i Napolitani*, the Neapolitans. It began several generations ago when a woman from Santa Severina decided to emigrate to America. She therefore travelled to Naples, the port of embarkation for would-be emigrants, and it was while she was in Naples that she changed her mind and returned to Santa Severina. Since then the family has been known as *i Napolitani*.

Nicknames reflect a characteristic that others see in someone and, initially at least, are not always known by those to whom the name is directed – particularly those *soprannomi* which are a little 'naughty' and reflect a trait that others see but about which the recipient remains blissfully unaware. There are many such in Santa Severina but it would be inappropriate to go into any more detail.

As I mentioned in *Stumbling through Italy*, I too had acquired an Italian name which, for a number of years, remained a well-kept secret. When I did find out I was told that its source was Roberto and for a year or two believed this to be Roberto, the son of Vincenzo Bisceglia whom, by the way, I have never heard referred to as Enzo, his obvious *diminutivo*.

A chance meeting with a new face in Santa Severina led me to another Roberto. The new face was Domenico Faragò, a bright young man in his twenties who had lived and worked in the financial world in Milan and London for some years and was now back in his home town for a while. He spoke excellent English and we became good friends ... especially when we realised he was the nephew of our dear departed friend, Roberto Sculco.

Domenico had been very close to his uncle and was pleased to put a face to my nickname and went on to remind me that it was his uncle Roberto who first coined it. I realised then that somewhere in this sordid tale of intrigue I had simply jumped to the wrong conclusion and got my Robertos mixed up. I was happy to discover that Roberto Sculco was the source for I knew it would have been meant kindly ... not that the same wouldn't have been the case with the other Roberto.

You have to realise that nobody actually called me by my *soprannome* to my face ... it was the name some people used when they talked *about* me in my absence and a step up from being known as *gli inglese* even when, of course, I was actually *l'irlandese*.

So there I was, my *soprannome* unchanged, only its source. But the story doesn't finish there.

We were having an *aperitivo* with Domenico Farago at Carlo's early one evening and I went inside to pay and happened to mention to Carlo the story of how I got my two Robertos mixed up and that I now knew that Roberto Sculco was the source of my *soprannome*. Carlo raised an eyebrow and asked me who'd told me that ... I pointed to Domenico who was sitting outside. Carlo smiled a knowing smile and a few moments later came out and joined us at our table.

He asked Domenico why it was he thought that the name originated with his uncle Roberto. Domenico replied reasonably that he first heard it from his uncle and so assumed he had thought it up. Carlo laughed and shook his head ...

"And who do you think first mentioned it to Roberto?" he asked.

Three pennies dropped at the same time, given further

credence by the broad grin (or was it smug look?) on Carlo's face.

Carlo was the source and proud of it. He it was who, during our first couple of weeks on holiday at Le Puzelle back in 2006, when we sat outside his bar almost every evening, decided that I reminded him of someone, someone from every Italian's childhood stories. Carlo mentioned it to Roberto who passed it on to his family and his colleagues at Le Puzelle, including the other Roberto.

*

All too soon Neff's visit was over. Having been in Santa Severina twice he'd made his mark, particularly with Carlo to whom, of course, he was Graham. And as ever, as he'd done with our names *and* our surnames, Carlo tried and succeeded in getting his tongue round a name that was not easy for an Italian to pronounce.

Our own names were also fraught with difficulties for Italians but they were of different natures. Kay was purely a linguistic problem in that it is pronounced exactly like a very common Italian word *che*. Unfortunately it's most common usage as a single word, the Italian equivalent of 'what'. So, when Kay was asked her name and said what sounded like *che* to an Italian, they would repeat the question. It often led to comical situations, reminiscent of a Marx Brothers movie, with everybody saying *che* or Kay in turn and getting nowhere.

I found the easiest way to explain it was to spell it, *kappa-a-ipsilon*, Kay. This too has its difficulties in that this seemingly straightforward three-letter word contained two letters not normally part of the Italian alphabet, *kappa* and *ipsilon*.

(The Italian alphabet has twenty-one letters, though there is an extended alphabet that probably reflects the power of global advertising in English. The additional letters are: j, k, w, x and y; there's even an Italian car called the Ypsilon.)

Niall, on the other hand, has recognisable letters but, to the Italian ear, the sounds do not match the letters; nor is it an easy word to pronounce. An Italian would want to say something like the word 'knee' with 'al' at the end, knee-al. It was the 'i' that was the problem, it is not a natural Italian sound when it is pronounced like the English word 'eye'.

So I got (and get) all sorts of variations: the above 'knee-al' being the most common, while the most bizarre sounds like 'oil' with an 'n' at the beginning, 'n-oil'. I have only recently discovered that, if I spell my name incorrectly 'Naill' instead of 'Niall', people will pronounce it almost perfectly.

It has to be said that Carlo was not the only person to try until he got it right, many others have done the same; it is, I suppose, a sign of respect when people make such an effort.

Ah yes, I nearly forgot ... my *soprannome*, the one that Carlo first coined in 2006 ... when he named me after the white-wigged, slightly off-beat, woodcarver in Carlo Collodi's *Pinocchio*. For Carlo I was the 'father' of the colourful Pinocchio, I was Mastro Geppetto.

———————

As you will recall, I had given someone a nickname of my own: The Good Doctor. It reflected how I saw our friend and doctor Rocco de Rito, he with the *studio* in nearby Roccabernarda. (Two years later he introduced me to another of his patients, an American woman, Vicky. Vicky too had a nickname for him ... she called him The Good Doctor!)

On one of my regular visits to The Good Doctor to renew my prescription he told me that the particular drug I was taking had been removed from the list of prescription drugs (at a fixed price of three euro); he could still prescribe it but I would have to pay sixteen euro each time at *la farmacia*. He could, of course, still prescribe other similar drugs that did much the same thing and would keep me alive and that were on 'the list'. I chose to go down the latter route.

So I started taking my new drug, having first checked its credentials with my pharmacist son, Kieron, in Northern Ireland. A few days later I started having hot flushes almost every evening and, as this was something I'd never experienced before, I put it down to my new blood pressure pill. I thought it might wear off but when it didn't I asked Kieron if this was a likely side-effect. It was.

Back to The Good Doctor. He prescribed me yet another drug and I gave it a few days to kick into my system and, sure enough, there were no more hot flushes. It was worse, much worse, worse than I could ever have imagined ... I had become allergic to red wine! I couldn't believe it at first, just a mouthful made me feel nauseous; it was probably the same with all alcohol but, as I normally only ever drank red wine, that's all that was important.

The Good Doctor was surprised to see me again so soon and when I told him about my little local difficulty with the red nectar he was like a man on a mission. I knew that he too enjoyed a glass of red wine and that my predicament was one that he would have understood.

"We can't have that" he said waving his finger from side to side in that essentially Italian way, "not red wine, you have to have your red wine" ... at the same time The Good Doctor's mouse-hand was working overtime as he scoured his computer until he found what he was looking for ... "I think this will do the trick", he said optimistically but with feigned certainty.

So, armed with my third prescription in almost as many weeks, I presented myself back at *la farmacia* in Santa Severina where *il farmacista* was more than a little surprised to see me again so soon. I told him my tale of woe and got exactly the same reaction ... it was as if an allergy to this vegetable or that fruit was fine, but *not* to red wine, that could not be allowed to happen, it wasn't natural.

It never happened again; The Good Doctor had worked his magic.

Turning up the heat

Before Attilio returned to Rome we met up one afternoon at the *orto* to get the benefit of his experience.

He told us three important things: that we weren't watering enough, not in terms of frequency or time of day, but in terms of amount; we had planted the wrong way, we should have followed the natural lie of the land to that the water could drain from plant to plant; and that some of our rows were too close together.

He hadn't spotted one other thing ... we had decided to stake up our tomatoes after the seedlings showed evidence of progress skywards but by that time the ground was far too hard and we couldn't get the canes to go down far enough; we should have done it at the planting stage when the earth was wetter, softer.

The watering was hard work as it was now early June, the time of year we were normally in Santa Severina on holiday only this year instead of sitting in the sun we were, by choice, working in it instead.

I remember thinking back to those other idyllic years at Le Puzelle where we sat day in, day out, under that ancient olive tree by the pool and did nothing for three weeks except chat to friends, read, drink and eat. We had come a long way: in October I had helped Guiliano cover that same pool for the winter and the following month we had helped to bring in the olive harvest, even from that old tree that still had something to offer.

What made the watering such hard work was using the *pozzo romano*, the 'Roman' well.

For the three summer months water in Santa Severina was at a premium, and several days each week supplies to the town would be cut off for anything up to eight hours.

People got round this by installing a *serbatoio*, a tank that filled itself at night and, when there was no mains water, was automatically triggered to pump its water into the system. So, when a tap was turned on and the running water was accompanied by the sound of an electric pump, then the mains water was off; and when there was no such pumping sound all was normal.

A simple and efficient way of making people water conscious though it did depend on people installing their own *serbatoio*. The options were straightforward: install a *serbatoio* or do without and rely on buckets, pans and bottles filled manually for washing and cooking and bottled water for drinking. Our big blue *serbatoio* behind the curtain in the utility room held 500 litres and I think we have only ever needed to use about one third of it ... but then for a couple of years in the eighties Kay and I had lived on a narrowboat where conserving water became second-nature.

The *pozzo romano* at the bottom of the Gerardi land was the answer to their and our water problem at the *orto*. Mario had sunk the well years before and it had never run dry. The water was brought to the surface using a petrol-driven pump located in a small half-buried stone shack next to the well.

Each day when it was time to water our plants I would walk the hundred and fifty metres to the well, go down into what I thought of as subterranean hell, pull the engine's pull-cord and hope that it would start first time (it rarely did) and when eventually the motor was pumping I knew that water was on its way to the several stand-pipes dotted around the land.

Each stand-pipe had an outlet and a large on/off lever and there was a long hose that fitted on to the outlet nozzle; this was normally attached to the stand-pipe nearest our plot but sometimes others would move it to other locations.

It was a basic system but it worked and was much better than what many others had, if they had water at all. That said, I hated it, mainly because increasingly I found the process debilitating in the heat. I walked each way twice to start the motor and twice to cut it off; also the 'subterranean hell' was unpleasant ... not spooky or anything so ridiculous, I just knew that all those pesky insects flitting around were eyeing me up as food. And yes, I did get bitten many, many times.

Even in the late afternoon, when the hottest part of the day was long gone it was still hotter than would have been in an English garden (no surprise there) but we wouldn't have tried to work in such heat in England. It made me realise just why we spent so much time under that olive tree at Le Puzelle.

That was the downside. There was also a lot of fun and a lot of pleasure and, of course, eventually the fruits of our labours began to show themselves. I still remember Kay calling out "We've got a tomato .. no, two tomatoes."

The only things that did not do particularly well were things grown from seeds that we'd brought from England. All the seedlings we'd bought in Santa Severina flourished and we had more courgettes and tomatoes than we knew what to do with. Like native Calabrians we eventually had to turn our hand to making *passata* and *sugo* with our excess tomatoes, the ones that we couldn't give away. And of course we froze as much as we could. People joked that they could see us next year trawling the streets in our very own *Ape*, selling our wares just like all the others. Once, when I momentarily went along with this scenario, someone even offered to 'find' me an *Ape*.

At home things were changing. It was only three months since we were in 'keep-the-heat-in' mode now we were noticeably heading towards the other extreme, we were making sure the house was always cool.

This proved easier to do, particularly so downstairs. But, as yet, even upstairs, which got more of the sun and had more windows, it was wonderful to feel the warm air, particularly when accompanied by a cooling breeze. When we pulled up the east-facing shutters in the morning a bright piercing light entered each room ... it had been the same throughout the winter but this early-summer light was brighter, more penetrating and brought with it an intoxicating, enveloping warmth such as we had never before experienced.

We knew this would not last and that as the summer progressed this light and this heat would intensify to levels we could only imagine. Fortunately we both could generally cope with the heat.

Silvana and Raffaele were spending every free day at *Il Tucano* and we were watering their garden and indoor plants; I did all the plants in the garden and the grass (where, unusually, Raffaele had installed sprinklers, though they were manually operated); Kay looked after the plants on their three balconies. We knew that soon they would be off for two months and this would become our daily early evening routine for the duration. It was never a chore, just something we did for friends and, if we had to miss an evening for some reason, we knew everything would survive.

As you will have gleaned, sitting on beaches accumulating sand in every orifice, cheek by jowl with hordes of people seemingly enjoying themselves in this granular garden ... is not for us. However, just to be sure, we did take Silvana and Raffaele up on an invitation to join them for the day at their apartment.

We arrived mid-morning and found them on the smaller beach that they preferred and that they hoped they'd 'get' for the incoming season. There were two beaches and together they supported eight hundred families, each of which would have its 'patch' centred on a large umbrella. Each umbrella-patch was numbered and these were to be allocated for the season on a first-come, first-served basis, the following morning. Those that turned up could chose their patch, those that didn't, by far the majority, would have a number, and an umbrella-patch, allocated to them.

It was still off-season so there were very few people about and we really did enjoy ourselves that morning, just relaxing, chatting and playing with Francesco and Alessia. Even I, a born-again non-swimmer, ventured into the Ionian Sea and baptised my whole body therein ... much to the delight of the kids and the shock of Kay.

Silvana disappeared back to the apartment a short time before everyone else ... she was off to prepare lunch for the six of us. Lunch was, as we had come to expect, a true Calabrian feast, eaten alfresco on the patio.

The Calabrian male is generally not enlightened when it comes to helping out around the house. This is changing and one of the men in the vanguard of this change is Raffaele; we know that it's not his way to leave everything to Silvana.

So what happened after we'd had our lunch was, for a short time, puzzling.

The kids had gone for a lie down, Kay and I were clearing the table and Silvana was preparing to wash up; we knew that normally Raffaele would pitch in but instead he gave me a nod, indicating that I should follow him. We two then sloped off down towards the larger beach which hitherto I'd only seen from a distance.

On the beach there were different zones all named with letters and in the middle there was a table where the people who owned and ran the complex were putting the finishing touches to their number system in preparation for the following day's allocation.

I was introduced to the main man and we talked a little about New York where he had a son and where we'd both been many times. Raffaele was chatting to his colleague about the allocation. It was clear throughout that both men had a lot of respect for Raffaele who was one of the longest-standing residents at *Il Tucano*, one of the first to buy an apartment; also, unlike most others, Raffaele and Silvana *never* rented it out, it was, and remained, a sanctuary for them and their family.

Even with my limited Italian I soon realised what Raffaele was doing here ... he didn't really want to get up early the next morning to start queueing at seven, nor did he want to leave things to chance. Both he and Silvana wanted the same umbrella-patch as last year (and probably the year before) and he was doing his best, using his 'history' and his charm (and me as an amiable diversion) to circumvent the system. I think he probably succeeded.

In Santa Severina itself, things were warming up in an altogether different way.

At the beginning of June a large stage was erected in

front of the castle and this would become the focus for the forthcoming summer entertainment which would carry on through the summer and into September.

Much of the entertainment would be musical but everything got underway in mid-June when the pupils from Santa Severina's dance school gave one of half a dozen performances ... other performances would take place in the home towns of all the other dancers. If there were a couple of girls from Scandale, then there would be a performance in Scandale.

I said 'girls' for they were mostly girls and Alessia was one of them so we were duty-bound to attend ... of course we would have anyway. For Silvana and Raffaele this was an exhausting time ... they were still teaching (she in the *Scuola Media* at nearby San Máuro, he in the Santa Severina's *Scuola Elementare*) and over a two-week period every other evening they would have to take Alessia to a different venue and sit through the same performance; and of course Francesco usually had to tag along too.

Other events followed, at first generally, but not only, at weekends; all of it free. Sometimes the square was simply a mass of bodies, walking, watching, talking; seats and tables at Carlo's and all the other bars were at a premium as they almost met in the middle of the square.

It was the most extraordinary summer I had ever experienced and more than once we wished that we could have shared it with others, other friends or family; we knew to try and describe it was futile, you had to experience it.

I think people were put off from coming to Calabria by their preconceptions of how hot it might become – a number did actually voice such concerns. Of course they were right.

During that summer we got to know a retired teacher who,

it seemed, only made his way up to the square during the warmer months. He overheard us talking one morning as we had a cup of coffee at Carlos's and was quick to let us know that he spoke some English.

At first we didn't know his name but we eventually recognised a stouter version of him from a calendar which featured photographs of classes from the *Scuola Elementare* going back as far as the fifties. He was Francesco Miranti and from what we heard from some of his grown-up ex-pupils, a teacher the children feared like no other.

Now in his eighties there was little to fear for it was clear he was not a well man; one day in response to our *come va?*, how are you?, he rested both hands atop his cane and looked roughly in our direction and with, a hint of melancholy in his voice, coined a phrase in English that we never forgot: "I'm stone blind, lamb in one leg and the diabetes has got me". Kay's response was equally memorable ... "But life is good, no?" He nodded unconvincingly.

His mixed metaphor, 'stone blind' illustrated the complexities of *our* language but it was his description of his lameness that endeared us to him and gave him his English *soprannome* ... thereafter to us he was always, affectionately, Lamb-In-One-Leg.

Back to school

Santa Severina had a language school that operated from May through to September. It was the brainchild of *il sindaco*, Bruno Cortese, and it brought the youth of the world to Santa Severina for periods of up to a month to learn Italian and experience Calabrian culture and hospitality. The bars loved it.

This much we knew from what others had told us but we didn't even know where the school was, let alone that it might be something we could take advantage of. When the wife of a friend asked us why other *stranieri* found Italian easier to grasp than we seemed to (age might have occurred to her I thought to myself) and then went on to ask why we hadn't gone to LALEO (*Libera Accademia delle Lingue Europee ed Oriental*), it seemed time to make some further enquires.

LALEO was easy to find, it was right next to the *carabiniere* headquarters; once inside, it proved harder to find a human to talk to. Lessons were in progress but the office was empty so we had a wander round its cloistered courtyard which had the feel of an erstwhile convent; we sat in the sun until we heard voices emanating from the office area.

Having re-established human contact we introduced ourselves and asked if we could join one of the groups. We explained that we had been residents of Santa Severina for about eight months. Surprisingly, the young woman, Daniella, said she'd never seen us before and had never realised there were any English speakers in Santa Severina. She added that it was an unusual request and that the school didn't normally take in residents. She gave us details of the fees, which included room and board, which we wouldn't require, took our number and said that she would talk to *il sindaco*, Bruno Cortese. We heard nothing for a month.

In mid-June we finally heard from Daniella that *il sindaco* had said we could join the July course; she went on to say that we should attend the school on the first Friday in July to take a test with our fellow students to determine our respective levels. The course would begin the following Monday.

To my query on the cost, she simply said *niente. Il sindaco*, she went on, didn't expect us to pay.

Irrespective of the heat factor, we already knew that July was going to be a difficult month for us.

We were watering and harvesting at the *orto* nearly every day in the late afternoon; we were watering our own wall and balcony plants as well as Silvana's, inside and out; it was getting increasingly hotter, so much so that we decided (as Silvana had suggested) to migrate at night down to the Lion King room to sleep where it was much cooler; and of course we wanted to be up in the square most evenings when there was entertainment.

Now, every morning we would be at LALEO from nine-thirty till one trying to improve our Italian. We did actually think about pulling out, particularly when, after the test, we found we were to be in different groups.

The test itself was a strange affair, there were in total that month between sixty and seventy students. Some, like us, had

Italian to varying degrees, others zero. Many of those in the latter group simply wrote their name on the test paper and then got up and walked out, handing their blank paper to one of the teachers as they did so.

At the end of the time allocated there were two left: me and a bearded man who was, apart from me, the oldest student, probably in his early forties. Was it that, being older, he and I wrote slower, had killed off too many brain cells or thought more?

At the weekend we bumped into the school's administrator Georgio (who was from Georgia) who told us we would be in different groups but that he could arrange for us to be together if we preferred. This was a difficult decision for we could see that being together might help but the same could be said of the other option.

We decided to leave things as they were and see what happened.

Monday morning dawned and there we were two sixty-somethings turning up at school; two ex-teachers, one an ex-headteacher. There was something surreal about it all.

Kay was in one of the two larger groups of around twenty-eight students, I was in the third group of a dozen or so. When we finally sat down in our room with our teacher Mima, who only spoke to us in Italian, we were asked one-by-one to introduce ourselves ... in Italian, of course.

I was sitting next to Dragon from Montenegro and opposite Dragona, also from Montenegro. Also in our class there was another Montenegrin, an Egyptian, two Russians, two Ukrainians, two Argentines and an Algerian; forty-five years separated the youngest from the oldest.

Linguistically I was not the weakest (I would say I was about fourth from the bottom) but there were several others who were considerably more advanced, some, like Dragona, almost fluent. Others like the Egyptian and Dragon had been here before, for Dragon it was his fourth consecutive year; both also had been taught by Mima before.

Around eleven each morning there was a break when most headed for the open courtyard, the sun and a cigarette; for Kay and I a chance to discuss progress.

Kay's class was mainly made up of Argentines, Romanians, Montenegrins and a lone Cypriot and by coincidence Kay and I both gravitated towards the Montenegrins in our respective groups.

There were clearly some in Kay's class who were only in Santa Severina for the sun and the fun (and can you blame them?) and were not really interested in coming to grips with learning a new language. Although the language element took up every morning, Monday to Friday, outside those times the students were free. There were excursions to the sea at Crotone almost every afternoon and longer excursions at weekends; also on two afternoons a week there was a well-attended voluntary art class led by our friend Enzo Ziparo.

Although we were always invited to participate in all these extra-curricular activities we had our own lives to lead and a busy schedule to keep up with. We were just grateful that there was never any homework other than the revision people chose to do by themselves. Kay and I, swots that we were, each wrote up notes every afternoon in the hope that some might actually stick.

Each evening in the square, whether or not there were any other events there, most of the students were out enjoying themselves and, as most were female, this in turn brought out the young men of Santa Severina to practise strutting their stuff.

It was a month I recall with fondness in a summer like no other. We were accepted by our fellow students as part of their 'group'; we burnt the candle at both ends – went to school, did all the other 'chores' we had to do at the *orto* or at Silvana's house and still had the energy to head up to the square to have a drink or three with our international friends. And all of this in temperatures that rarely fell below 35 degrees and for a short time even topped 40 degrees.

Santa Severina's erstwhile prison was located at the far end of Via Grecia – not a particularly striking building, just a house with a high fence that had served another purpose in another age. That summer there were half a dozen refugees living there, some from Nigeria, the rest from Somalia, all male. They loved their football (that's soccer to all the Americans out there) and could often be seen kicking a ball around in the new car park opposite their temporary home.

Someone had the bright idea of arranging a game between them and a team from LALEO. The school's self-appointed team manager had the wisdom to overlook me in his selection but I was asked to come along as their mascot. I did.

Picture the scene. It's gone nine on a warm summer evening. Sitting around a small, concrete-tiered amphitheatre are most of the LALEO's students in full female voice. They are watching a floodlit six-a-side football game between six Africans and a dozen (only six played at a time) assorted Europeans, South Americans and fellow Africans. Somewhere inside the netted 'stadium' there is an ageing Irishman with nothing better to do. This could only be Santa Severina.

Back at school it was strange how an ex-headteacher and his nearest neighbour in age should have become the naughty boys of the class. Dragon and I forged an unspoken alliance and knew how to wind up Mima in Italian ... in a nice way of course.

We had been learning Italian's simple past tense, most often used when in English you would say 'used to' as in 'I used to go to school' meaning 'I went to school'; something that happened regularly in the past. Having learnt how to form the tense and when to use it, several people were chosen to initiate a conversation with a friend. I was first and Mima asked me to choose somebody with whom to discuss what pets we used to have when we were young. Naturally I chose Dragon.

I asked him if he had had any pets when he was young. He answered "No, and you?" I answered "No". Our conversation was over. Mima stared blankly at us ... we had done as asked and said only eleven words in total. There was a brief moment of silence and then everyone was laughing and eventually Mima joined in, shaking her finger from left to right as she did so. She saw the funny side but wasn't going to let us get away with it. I changed my story and admitted to having had a black cat when I was young; Dragon could not be broken.

At the end of the course there was an exam, both written and oral and everybody came away with a certificate saying that they had participated.

As we were doing the written paper, Mima left the room for about five minutes ... long enough for Dragona to furnish her co-patriots with all the answers; I was offered Dragon's second-hand version but declined.

The oral was directed by all three teachers and was rather a strange affair with people coming and going to watch and to try and work out what *they* might be asked when it was their turn ... certain people had larger audiences depending on their popularity and how many wanted to heckle. It was fun and had its embarrassing moments and I was under strict instructions not to be in the room when Kay did hers.

Bruno's logic in creating such a school in Santa Severina was simple enough. He knew that most of these (mostly) young people would never forget their time here and some would not only return but they might bring with them a wife or a husband, maybe even their children. They would create a bond with this place that would be as hard to break for them as it was for us. All this Bruno knew and understood; and of course he was right.

Each month when these young people had to return home there were scenes of great distress in and around LALEO; many, many tears were shed. Bonds and relationships had been forged, some temporary, some permanent; and every month there were two or three special stories to bring a lump to your throat, some between students from different continents, some between students and people from Santa Severina, even one between teacher and student.

By the end of the month our Italian was probably better, it was hard to quantify. We were told we could 'do' another month if we wanted but July had taken its toll and we thought we should at least *try* to have a break.

Things at the *orto* had reached a peak and though there was still some harvesting to be done, the rise in temperature was making it difficult and I had decided that I really didn't want to yank that pull-cord in that 'subterranean hell' ever again.

We had enjoyed it and we were glad we did it but, with August only a day or two away, for the moment we'd both had enough.

———————

One evening there was a late-night LALEO-organised disco in open space behind the castle where there was a small amphitheatre-shaped square. Kay decided to stay at home but I felt duty-bound to show my face; I went with Giuliano.

It was gone one in the morning and I'd had enough of the

music and the wine and walked up into the square where I joined a table of four men outside Carlo's bar; I knew them all, three were from Santa Severina and one from nearby San Giovanni in Fiore. I wasn't really part of their conversation, I was listening and re-adjusting to voices rather than loud music and soon became aware that this was a discussion rather than a cosy chat. Generally the voices were calm but once or twice there was an increase in octaves as one or another strove to get a point across.

I began to take more of an interest and gradually came to the conclusions that of these four, three were atheists and only one a believer and that this was the essence of their late-night discussion. I wasn't completely sure that I'd got this right, mainly because it wasn't what you might expect in such a place. I left around two and walked home.

It was only when I got home that I realised that somewhere, somehow that evening I had mislead my keys; I also knew that Kay always slept with earplugs. It was almost another two hours before she eventually heard me; I had decided that the best option was to sleep on the doorstep and try ringing every time I woke up to readjust my contorted body.

The next day I retrieved my keys from Carlo's and within a couple of hours word of this unfortunate episode was common knowledge. Enzo Ziparo thought it particularly funny and regularly used to tease me about it ... until two weeks later when he did the same himself and spent longer on the doorstep than I did; he felt really sorry for himself, even more sorry when he did it again a week later!

For the record, I did check up whether or not I'd correctly interpreted that early morning discussion at Carlo's. I had.

Summer sun and fun

July and August in Santa Severina were (and are) different to other months. Of course the weather and the entertainment in the square are factors in this and for us that first year our time at LALEO made things special. But these were not the only factors.

Many Santa Severinese have apartments by the sea or in the Sila mountains. It's a matter of taste, there are those who want to bask in the heat and sun by the sea, there are others who prefer to cool off in the Sila mountains where, at this time of year, it is generally about 10 degrees cooler.

At the same time many of those with out-of-town houses or apartments were keen to take advantage of August, the month when most Italians take their holidays, by renting out their property at the sea or in the Sila. In July therefore there was a significant migration of people *to* the sea or the Sila who then returned in August which in turn coincided with an influx of Santa Severenese who lived in the north but chose to return home for the holidays. Put simply, the population fell in July then increased significantly in August.

Although the town's population was lower in July, few were very far away. Silvana and Raffaele's apartment at Le Castella, for example, is no more than a forty minute drive; similarly

Franco Severini's house in the Sila. So if there was something happening in the square of an evening you were just as likely to bump into someone who was actually spending the month by the sea but had just come back for the evening.

Of course those that fled to the sea and did not own an apartment there would rent instead, usually the same apartment in the same town or holiday village that they'd been going to for years: Stumpo's wife's family had an apartment at Strongoli and they themselves had a small place in the Sila; Bruno had an apartment at Praialunga another holiday village north-east of Le Castella; Enzo and Franca rented the same apartment every year at Botricello, as did Vittorio and Anna Clara. And when they came back to Santa Severina of an evening to see a particular show or concert, they could stay overnight in Santa Severina and sleep at home.

Some people made the move to the sea in July and continued to work in Santa Severina or (more likely) Crotone, they just got up a bit earlier and drove to work as usual ... then in August they had their holidays.

Santa Severina's holiday rituals and relocations were something this new, more worldly generation had almost made into an artform.

People noticed quite quickly that we were not ones for parking ourselves on a beach. Almost every time we walked up to the square, we ran the gauntlet along Via Grecia of those who would always ask the same question, *niente al mare?*, you don't go to the sea? It became a sort of standing joke and after we stopped trying to explain the truth (we prefer being here / we prefer the mountains / we just don't do the sand-in-every-orifice thing) I tried to think up more elaborate and unlikely responses.

Then again, there was so much happening in Santa Severina at this time that we didn't need to be anywhere else, didn't need to sit on a beach or by a pool or in the mountains. We had a our balcony and when we weren't up in the square of an evening we'd sit outside with a glass of red wine in a heat that you could almost touch.

Santa Severina's summer programme included two major music festivals both of which Stumpo had more than a hand in: a festival of Mediterranean music and, later, a festival of Arab music. Before and in between these two there were all sorts of other one-off theatrical events and gigs, from jazz to classical, from traditional to rock.

For me by far the most memorable event was the week-long residency in Santa Severina by L'Arte del Gesto, a theatre group like no other I had ever seen ... this was their fifth visit to Santa Severina, so we were probably the only ones taken by surprise.

Every day they put on two shows, usually one in the square and one somewhere else around the town. But they were wont to turn up when you least expected them ... early one evening Kay and I set off along Via Grecia en route to the square when we unwittingly got involved in a Baroque-style musical experience. We stopped to listen and watch; all the children were out, open-mouthed drinking it all in.

One of the women in period costume grabbed hold of me and took me off to dance with her while some of her male colleagues did the same with the watching women. I whispered sweet nothings in her ear (actually I shared my Irishness with her) and she told me she'd chosen me because I looked typically Calabrian; she was obviously not from these parts.

In the square itself of an evening, just as it was getting dark, a drama would unfold incorporating the most lavish costumes, music, dance, mime ... and stilts. Stilt-walkers such as I had

Awesome open-air theatre

never seen before, some as tall as a first-floor balcony, not just incredibly skilful walkers and but also amazing dancers.

What was unforgettable was the look on the children's faces, even those for whom this was the second or third time they had seen such things. They stood momentarily fixed to the spot, eyes wide open, mouth caught halfway between speech and awe; we shared their wonder.

All too soon they were gone and all Santa Severina had to offer was lots of music and more conventional entertainment.

At home we decided that we would like to paint the house inside from top to bottom ... except for the hall and the Lion King wall. I sent a text message to Silvana to ask if she minded. Five minutes later the phone rang ... it was Silvana who was surprised that we had to ask. "Of course you can", she said, "it's your house" which, strictly-speaking it wasn't. Still we felt it was important to ask.

So most of August we spent covered in paint – when we did venture out, mostly evenings, we had to explain the fact that people had seen less of us. Some even jumped to the conclusion that we might, after all, have gone *al mare*, to the sea. In fact we did go once on August 15, the annual holiday knees-up known as *Ferragosto*, the mid-point of the summer. That evening we went to Le Castella, for an impromptu party with the Gerardi family and their friends from all over Italy ... the only common factor was that everyone, except us, was holidaying at Il Tucano.

When we told people we were painting the house, they were surprised that we, two pensioners with no obvious background in the painting business, should actually do it ourselves. Many Calabrians would have paid for someone to come and paint the house, the notion of DIY was catching on but many still believed that such things should be left to experts.

The painting finished, there then followed a series of 'showings'. All the Gerardi family had to pop in and go round room-by-room; it was like the private view of a new exhibition without the nibbles and wine. Non-family neighbours popped in to look and to wonder at what we had done which, in all truth was nothing exceptional; fame of our skill spread, the more so because we had done it all in August when most people were too drained by the heat to do very much except wait for the cool of the evening.

September was just around the corner; a year earlier we had spent every waking hour preparing for our move to Santa Severina. It was time to take stock, to reflect on a year like no other.

———————

In September, the day after our anniversary, my brother Trevor, Neff's father, and his wife Angela came to stay for four days. Their visit coincided with the only four days when there was no music, *absolutamente niente*, up in the square.

Aware of the irony of this after such a busy summer, Stumpo got to work and invited us to come to Marina di Strongoli one evening for a pizza. We arrived at La Vespa expecting no more than to share the evening with Stumpo, Francesco and Carmen. But this was Stumpo and, as gradually others arrived, all involved in the Festival of Arab Music, we realised that, like it or not, we were in for a musical evening courtesy of Domenico Francesco Stumpo and his wily ways.

This impromptu gathering in an otherwise empty *pizzeria* was Stumpo's way of ensuring that Trevor and Angela would experience an evening of Calabrian hospitality and music before they returned home.

———————

A shift

I warn you, this chapter is going to be a bit on the reflective side. Brace yourself.

I realise that somewhere in this story a shift has taken place. I'm not sure when exactly but know that I have changed from being a mere observer of what it was like to come to live in Santa Severina ... I have ceased to be a visitor and become a resident.

When we arrived in Santa Severina the previous September our support group was centred on the people we knew in and around Le Puzelle and people like Carlo whom we had known before. Of course these people still remained close friends, but we had increasingly become independent of them.

This second wave of friendships was centred around Stumpo, Enzo Ziparo, Franco Barone, Franco Severini, Tonino Parisi, Lamb-In-One-Leg, Lina's extended family, Agata, Vittorio and Anna Clara, and of course the Gerardi family and almost everyone along Via Grecia.

There was a third wave also based at Le Puzelle where there were regular meetings of Santa Severina's Rotary Club – both Vincenzo and The Good Doctor were past-presidents, indeed this is how we first met The Good Doctor. From time-to-time we were invited to their functions but I think they realised that the Rotary wasn't our thing. Nevertheless it was through these get-togethers that we made new friends from Santa Severina and the surrounding towns including Crotone. Stumpo was a member but the idea was anathema to our mutual friend Enzo Ziparo; on the other hand Enzo's older brother, Felice was a member as was *il sindaco*, Bruno Cortese.

And there was a fourth wave: most of the rest of the population of Santa Severina.

Many people still thought we were living here for a while, an indeterminate period as opposed to *per sempre*. But even these people soon realised that this was not the case; people who hadn't seen us for a week or so often jumped to the erroneous conclusion that we'd sloped off back to England and would say as much when we next met up. Our response was always the same, "No, we're always here, maybe we haven't been out as often or not in the square when you are.".

So gradually people were treating us differently, we had become part of the fabric of Santa Severina, less like *gli inglesi* and more like Santa Severinese, though referring to us as *gli Inglesi* was still a shorthand way of identifying us ... even Silvana still did this.

Like the chronology of this story there were many inter-connecting strands that brought us to this point and for Kay and I, individuals in our own right even though many people here often saw us as one, our recognition of this shift did not necessarily coincide.

I became aware of it that balmy night when I was with Giuliano in the *piazzetta* behind the castle. The disco music was taking a long-overdue break and I wandered over to the railing that looked down on the lights of the lower town. I was picking out landmarks, places I knew by day but had never seen at night. I was in melancholy mood. Giuliano joined me and lit up a cigarette, his smoke wafting down into the blackness below and the lights beyond. I broke our few moments of silence.

I don't recall whether I was speaking to Giuliano or talking to myself when I said, "I have just realised that this is where I will die." Not a particularly profound statement, nearer to stating the obvious, but one which had just occurred to me and as such indicated a distinct shift in my life ... and my death. It threw Giuliano, he didn't know what, if anything, to say. Being Giuliano he just rested his hand on my shoulder and probably put it down to a surfeit of red wine. Of course he could have been right.

I had left my home in 1966 and moved to England; language-wise no great change. Even so, it was a move that made me part of a different culture and a culture which, in terms of its openness and the fact that its politics was based on philosophical considerations and not a person's religion, was profoundly different to the one I left behind in Northern Ireland.

So I had 'previous'; I wasn't exactly making a habit of it (twice in forty-two years?) but to make such a change was something I had experience of. This move begged another question ... in 1966 I was sure I was moving to a place that suited me and my outlook on life better ... but was the same the case in 2008? The answer a year earlier would have been "Let's see"; the answer as I looked down on the lights of the lower town that evening had moved on to, "I think so".

There was no single reason for this shift; I had no checklist that I was mentally ticking. There were things that impressed me about living here, things I relished in; there were also some things I found irksome or worse. Perhaps now *is* the time for that list.

Something that I thought about before we came here was those same religious overtones to day-to-day living that I disliked so much about my place of birth. Here I was moving to a country that many saw as the homeland of wall-to-wall Catholicism, of the absolute power of the Church. But our experiences on holiday already belied this notion ... the Pope may well have had his stance on birth control in a country ninety percent Catholic but it didn't stop the people buying condoms when they had the need.

I had met more non-believers in and around Santa Severina than anywhere else I have ever lived; Franco Severini's words appeared to have some resonance when he said that Calabrians were generally indifferent to the Church. It must also be remembered that the only west-European country to almost vote for what would have been the first democratically-elected communist government in the world ... was Italy.

On the positive side of this reflective checklist was Santa Severina's young people, from kids to teenagers; almost without exception they were a joy to be around. Hitherto I had never seen a group of children, none older than ten, sitting in a restaurant, adult-less, enjoying each other's company, talking reasonably to each other, eating their pizza and not playing with it or throwing it around. Nor had I ever seen a group of adolescent boys doing exactly the same, a few having a beer but most with soft drinks. No rowdiness, just respect for others sharing their eating space.

And out in the street they were the same, unbelievably polite and courteous and not just to us but to all other adults. I'm sure there were a few bad apples in these various baskets but, if so, they didn't seem to infect the others. But it was more than mere politeness, it was a maturity and a respect that can only have come from their parents and as such no surprise as we had been the beneficiaries of this ourselves.

People had a respect for what we had done. This was not something we sought or expected but it soon became clear that many people realised that we had done what they could not have done. In our sixties we had moved to a foreign country, a foreign culture and a foreign language. More than any other question, we were asked was *perchè?* why?

In addition, the young people themselves were able to experience a sense of freedom that in recent years had been suppressed and virtually wiped out in other countries by a pernicious press and lemming-like parents.

From about the age of three the young Santa Severinese is out and about with his or her brothers and sisters. They play in the streets; the walk up to the square together; they nip into Carlo's for a packet of crisps or to use the toilet; they speak to adults in an adult way; they laugh; they have fun; they kick a ball; they play hide and seek; they ride their bicycles.

Alessia and her friends, for example, would greet Kay and I in the street with enthusiasm, fondness and the Italian double-kiss. It was how they were brought up and it was unbelievably refreshing.

I suppose linked to what I said about the older youths was the general lack of crime. Indeed when somebody did do something anti-social it was such a rarity that it bordered on the inconceivable. It was not unusual to see a key left in a front door or to have a lost wallet returned unpilfered ... I speak from personal experience regarding the latter.

Also, it must be remembered that Calabria was lumped together with other parts of Italy, mainly Sicily and Naples, through its mafia connections. The Calabrian *'ndangheta* was notorious, some even said worse that the Sicilian mafia. Its base was in Reggio Calabria but most, if not all, Calabrian towns had had (perhaps still had) some 'connections'.

In its favour Santa Severina had Bruno Cortese, *il sindaco* who would have nothing to do with such people and, by coincidence, it was Bruno's brother, Renato Cortese, who led the Calabrian police unit (the SCO) charged with finding and bringing such people to justice. Renato and his team were very thorough and very successful.

Not unrelated to all the above was the sense of family we discovered in Santa Severina.

When I say 'the sense of family' I do not imply that the family *per se* is by default an important institution or factor in people's lives. I am in no way elevating the family into some sort of sacrosanct unit. There are families here and elsewhere that I would not have relished being a part of; though mainly elsewhere.

Families can be stifling or liberating or somewhere in between; they can be geographically round the corner from each other or at the opposite end of the country (or world) and still be stifling or liberating. It goes without saying that I favour the liberating end of the spectrum.

Here in Santa Severina I observed that many families somehow seemed to have a genuine fondness for each other's company, helped each other and were part of something special to them without the need to participate in some of the unseemly shenanigans that others seems to find acceptable. Of course, I'm not suggesting that this has never happened or doesn't go on, just that it didn't seem as prevalent as I've observed elsewhere.

There is probably a cultural and historical explanation and perhaps in time it might change; that said, I like it the way it is. And this is the essence of why the Gerardi family became special to me. Generally my own family was at the liberating end of the spectrum but I never had the chance to see it through. True we had out fights and squabbles (my two brothers and I) but our parents were pretty open and of their time. Having fought in the Great War, my father was not altogether enamoured with, for example, my interest in the German language and culture but nevertheless he had helped fund my trip to Bad Honnef when I was a teenager. When, I called my mother to say that I had decided to stay in Germany and would not be returning to school as planned, she didn't shout at me or slam the phone down – we just had a reasonable conversation even though I could sense she wasn't best pleased. Quite rightly she trusted me to change my mind.

I never had 'the chance to see it through' because I don't know what might (or might not) have been, what would have happened had they lived long enough to ever visit me at *my* home in England or see and know their grandchildren. These things were not to be. I know what I would have wanted it to have been like and it was a sense of this that I belatedly recognised in the extended Gerardi family.

You will have gathered that I had grown to like this place, that I felt at home here ... but what about the downside, those things I found 'irksome'? Here are a few:

When the man in the Post Office, seeing that we just want to post a letter, lets us jump the queue.

When queues elsewhere take on a flexible element and become more lateral than linear.

The fact that it is a largely male-based society though this is changing.

The fact that there is ADSL about eight kilometres away but not yet in Santa Severina, nor likely to be.

The fact that arrangements, particularly relating to a job needing done, are sometimes open-ended.

The fact that we live in two time zones, what I call 'normal' time and Italian time with its element of elasticity.

The perceptible change in the media in following the lead

of other countries to indulge in shows based on psycho-babble and mumbo-jumbo ... everything from 'true' ghostly encounters to interminable conspiracy theories.

The fact that the 'black' economy is endemic, particularly in Calabria, though there are moves afoot to counter this.

There are three other things that are worthy of a lengthier discourse, things sometimes a little more than 'irksome'.

Dogs. No, like the rest of the world, it's more the owners of dogs that are the problem: dogs might do their business on the pavement but it's up to their owners to do something about it. Unfortunately the concept of doing something about it hasn't really permeated to Calabria. I simply wish it would. It's not a huge problem in Santa Severina compared to, say, Crotone, but a problem nevertheless – if it weren't for the good street lighting, walking home at night could involve an unpleasant surprise.

The second area is a problem in southern Italy generally and on the whole not as prevalent in Santa Severina – unfinished houses and other buildings. This happens when families build a house for one generation and half finish the next storey for the next generation. Coupled to this is the fact that when a building has been completed there is a tax to pay. Santa Severina is generally a clean and tidy place – one of the reasons we like it – but there are other towns in Calabria where there is less civic pride and where the general ambience is of a work-in-progress.

Then there's the state of the roads. It starts at the top with Calabria's only *autostrada*, the A3, that links the region's southern-most point, Reggio Calabria, with the rest of the road network north of Salerno in Campania. It is Italy's only *autostrada* without tolls because nobody would ever pay them.

The A3 was originally 'completed' in 1974 but was substandard even then and has since undergone a complete rebuild ... they say it has never seen through-traffic without roadworks. It is no exaggeration to say that there are thirty-somethings for whom it has been a work-in-progress *all their lives*. I understand the end is in sight and that it will be completed (again) in 2014, forty years on.

In some places other roads are not a lot better, particularly local roads. Repairs, when they are completed, tend to be piecemeal and as such often ultimately exacerbate the problem. But, as before, there are signs that this is changing; Italian engineers have shown themselves to be consummate road-builders in the past as is evidenced by the majestic lines of the *Strada Statali* between Crotone and Cosenza as it cuts through and weaves across the Sila mountains.

My reference above to the 'elasticity' of Italian timekeeping is based on many examples, most of them not really very serious. They relate mainly to the time of a meeting and sometimes also to the location. In respect of the latter, Calabrian directions can sometimes be misleading.

One evening I arranged to have an *aperitivo* with Domenico Faragò in the square at six, I arrived on time but by six-twenty I'd decided I must have got it wrong and went home. Just after six-thirty, I had a call from Domenico wondering where I was so I explained that I'd been there as arranged but was now back home. He was genuinely surprised that I'd not waited as he was only twenty-five minutes late!

It took Stumpo and I at least six months to actually meet at the allocated place at the appointed time. Part of the problem was probably my fault in terms of not understanding the language sufficiently, part Stumpo for forgetting that I wasn't Calabrian.

There were so many examples when we didn't get it right – once we even passed each other going in opposite directions and another time compounded the absurdity of it all by passing each other twice. When we eventually *did* get it right we hugged each other as much in surprise as with relief.

We found it difficult to break the habit of not being punctual for arrangements and it did eventually have its upside in that gradually people started fitting in with our concept of time. But there were sometimes things beyond our control; when, for example, Enzo would mention an event in the square the conversation would go something like this:

Enzo: coming to the see the band tonight?

Me: what time?

Enzo: at nine.

Me: is that normal time or Italian time?

Enzo: about ten then.

Me: see you at ten-thirty.

Enzo: ten-thirty sounds fine.

The posters for this imaginary gig will all have had the time as nine ... Calabrian time.

In defence of 'Calabrian time' it has to be said that most Italians consider that there are two levels of arrangements, formal and informal. The former are the important ones when most will try to arrive on time; the latter are the 'flexible' ones where getting the right day is a bonus.

Stumpo completely threw me one evening when he was due to eat with just me (Francesca was with her sister in Rome and Kay was in the UK); he was due at half-seven. At seven-twenty the phone rang and and I remember thinking to myself ... this'll be Stumpo to say he's going to be late.

I was half right. It was indeed Stumpo *and* he was actually going to be on time ... he just rang to tell me that he'd asked our mutual friend Alessandro (who was clearly at a loose end that evening) to eat with us. I had ten minutes to rustle up an extra serving of the planned three-course meal.

The problem with directions was something that took a little longer to work out, but eventually we got there.

Our first experience of this was when I asked for directions to the dentist's ... the one I mentioned earlier who is also a doctor. I spoke to someone at Le Puzelle and was given clear enough directions. I was to go the *bivio*, the junction, turn right and carry on towards the church; on the left, just before the church, I would find the dentist's. I did as instructed and spent about twenty fruitless minutes trying to locate the dentist's *studio*.

The problem was that I had been given directions from Le Puzelle; the person directing me was in fact directing herself from where she was and not us from our house at the top of the hill.

A similar thing happened when Raffaele gave us directions to a shop in Crotone which involved turning right at a roundabout ... problem was he was mentally approaching the roundabout from one direction, we were approaching from another. This time I worked it all out a bit quicker and only spent about ten fruitless minutes in the wrong part of town.

Some time later a friend from nearby Rocco di Neto asked us to eat with him; we accepted and asked him where he lived. He told us what we already knew – Rocco di Neto. We waited, but that was it. But where in Rocco di Neto we wanted to know. He shrugged his shoulders in a way that said we'd recognise it when we saw it, that everyone knew where he lived. Next we narrowed it down to the main street, a main street that was well over a kilometre long. Eventually we dragged some more basic information out of him and finally we knew which side of the road and had a number.

Carlo and Anna Maria: a day to remember for all sorts of reasons

Births, marriages and deaths

By coincidence our first experience of all the above in Calabria centred around the same family, the Tigano family.

Carlo and Anna Maria were scheduled to marry in September 2009 and we were invited to the wedding. But just before Christmas 2008 disaster struck when Anna Maria's brother-in-law died.

The problem was that many families recognised a period of one year's mourning before any other kind of celebration, such as a wedding, could take place. For there to be an exception, both families would have to agree that this particular celebration could go ahead.

For our friend Carlo this was a very difficult time. *His* family were happy for the wedding to take place as planned but this death, particularly as there were two young girls fatherless, clearly had more implications for Anna Maria's extended family. For a period it was all up in the air and poor Carlo was unsure what would happen but eventually all was resolved and it was agreed that the wedding could go ahead in September as intended.

Early in June disaster struck yet again when Carlo's mother died.

As close friends of Carlo and many of his family, we knew we would have to go to the funeral, in Calabria an event which normally takes place within twenty-four hours of the death and in Santa Severina traditionally at five in the afternoon. We had no idea what to expect.

We walked to Carlo's house with Raffaele and waited outside with other friends until the family emerged and the coffin was carried up to the church. We followed behind.

Inside the church (our first time inside) we signed the book of condolences and stood at the side throughout the ceremony which lasted about an hour. At one point everyone shook hands with everyone else near to them and at the end people formed a queue to shake hands with or embrace the family before leaving the church.

Two things struck us. Firstly the general informality of it all. Few people apart from the close family were dressed formally (I, unusually, was one of those). Secondly, people came and went during the service to sign the book and many more arrived towards the end to join the queue to greet the family. It felt more like a celebration of a life and, though it included a mass, not many people participated in this part and those that did were almost all women.

Historically Santa Severina was a rural community and the time of the service and the general informality were a reflection of when people used to come in off the land to attend such events. They came as they were and sometimes they were late, sometimes they had to leave early, sometimes they only had time to pay their respects to the family ... the important thing was that they came and not when they arrived or how they were dressed.

I found such informality refreshing. In no way did it detract from the importance or the mood of the occasion. People came as they were and they came because they wanted to demonstrate a moment or two of solidarity with and compassion for the family. Nobody needs a collar and tie to show such humanity.

The next day I asked Carlo about the wedding and he told me that, before she died, his mother had gathered together the family and said that, should she not survive her illness, then she wanted the marriage to go ahead as planned.

And now, it being September, the day was fast approaching … the only downside was that Giuliano couldn't come as there was another Santa Severina wedding that day and the reception was at Le Puzelle where he was on waiting duties.

Trevor and Angela had just returned to England. Our wedding anniversary was on the Thursday, my birthday the Friday and Carlo and Anna Maria's wedding on the Saturday. Then came the *temporale*.

A *temporale* is a storm but in Calabria the name is usually given to a storm that is particularly vicious like the one we experienced the previous November when we were entertaining our friends from Le Puzelle.

There had been another at the beginning of July that actually lifted a manhole cover outside our front door and another by the back door as the water rushed through the huge underground drains, negotiated four sharp bends in quick succession and shot over the edge of the hill by Silvana's house with incredible speed and force.

September's *temporale* was worse. It began on my birthday and that evening washed away the ramp to the bridge over the river Neto and in so-doing denied easy access to the *Strada Statali*. There was another, longer way round, via Attilia where, the next morning Carlo and Anna Maria would wed.

The wedding itself was a wash-out. It rained most of the time and though Anna Maria was clearly putting a brave face on things, Carlo never stopped smiling ... I think he was just relieved they had got this far after everything that had happened.

The reception was at an *agriturismo* near the coast south of Crotone and Kay and I set off the long way round, there being no bridge across the Neto. We were one of the first cars to get to the Crotone area and to head out on the winding road south. We were also the last to get through for, moments later, a tree came crashing down to block the road which meant that everyone else, including the bride and groom, had to take a lengthy detour.

In Calabria it is the party after the actual nuptials that is the important thing ... when we arrived at the *agriturismo* there were already many people there who'd come just for the food and fun. It was all about eating, drinking and dancing and was a revelation. Although everyone had allocated seats there was a bit of spontaneous re-arranging and we were invited to join another table with some friends.

I remember texting brother Trevor, who like Neff, had really taken to Carlo and wanted to be kept up to date with the wedding ... he didn't believe me when I told him that, foodwise, we were on course number eight and that I thought there were at least five more to go.

Throughout Carlo beamed like the cat who'd got the cream.

A few weeks later, when Carlo and Anna Maria returned from their honeymoon, a Mediterranean cruise, they chose a warm October day to get dressed up once again in their wedding finery to have all their photos retaken. *Temporale* or not Carlo's wedding was, as the record shows, a bright, sunny day.

Early the following August their daughter Giovanna was born; she was named after Carlo's mother.

Carlo's wedding party did not hold the record for number of courses. The following year I attended the wedding of Angela's daughter, Anna, when Kay was in England. I left around eight in the evening by which time we had been eating for nearly five hours.

Not counting the welcoming alfresco buffet, we had just finished course thirteen when I decided I could take no more. By my reckoning, excluding the wedding cake, there were five more courses to go.

Since the death of Carlo's mother, Kay and I had taken a keener interest in what we called the 'death board'. There were several such boards around the town but there was one just outside the nearby *Scuola Media* where we normally parked the car. In larger towns such as Crotone there is a whole wall given over to such funereal announcements; surprising enough we called this the 'death wall'

Whenever someone died (whether living in Santa Severina or from Santa Severina but living elsewhere) there were two things that happened in quick succession: there was a sonorous peel of bells, the *campana a lutto*, that people recognised as meaning that someone had passed away; this was soon followed by notices, about A3 in size, which were posted on the various 'death boards'. These gave details of the deceased and of the funeral arrangements.

We were sitting outside Carlo's once when the *campana a lutto* sounded and immediately everyone else in the square was trying to find out the name; many assumed that Carlo would know as bars are generally focal points for such information. On this occasion he didn't know and it turned out to be a Santa Severenese living in Torino.

On a few occasions we had completely missed the death of someone we knew. Once I asked Carlo why we hadn't seen Roberto recently and when we had finally sorted out *which* Roberto, he told me he'd been dead for six months. Roberto Borda had been a kindly man, someone who had made us welcome when we first arrived and many other times thereafter. Had we known, we would have gone to his funeral.

Anton was a bit of an enigma. Although he generally frequented Carlo's bar, he kept himself very much to himself. That said, he looked like an interesting character but all we knew about him was his name, that he was retired and that he smoked a lot. So when Kay went to England in May, I made a point of trying to get beyond the occasional nod of recognition and *buongiorno*. I succeeded but still he remained something of a mystery.

During the summer we got to know him better and sometimes we sat together outside the bar at the far end of the square nearest the church and had a *gelato*, an ice-cream, with him; *we* had the ice-cream, Anton stuck to his cigarettes and beer.

It was the day of another funeral, not anyone we knew but an occasional acquaintance of Anton. We were talking funeral rituals and in particular Anton was eyeing up all the people sitting, standing, hovering outside the church waiting for the end of the ceremony when they would slip inside to shake hands with the family.

He didn't actually say he disapproved but it was the impression he gave. He told us to watch ... "You'll see, they'll all know when the service is over and there'll be a rush for the door and in they'll go and join the queue."

We'd seen this for ourselves and, to be honest, I really couldn't see a lot wrong with it; the people closest to the family, the ones that mattered, were all probably inside and the others had turned up to pay their respects. Nevertheless it was comical to watch.

The service drew to a close. Someone by the church door gave the signal and the various groups of men (they were all men) stationed at different points around the square headed nonchalantly, unashamedly for the church. Anton pointed, "See I told you so, look at them."

At which point he excused himself and headed straight for the church himself. *Volevo solo presentare le mie condoglianze,* just wanted to pay my respects, he said, as he winked at us.

Part three

The second year and beyond

The learning curve became less steep and, for others, our 'novelty' factor was increasingly wearing off. We moved on from being mere observers of life in and around Santa Severina to becoming contributors to it.

At home

A week before Carlo's wedding we had an unexpected caller ... we *had* been expecting him but for such a long time that we'd almost forgotten he was even coming.

Every Friday we had even shared a standing joke with Raffaele for it was always on a Friday that we could expect Enzo *idraulico* to arrive to fit the central heating boiler. And then one Friday it actually happened ... there he was standing on our doorstep next to said boiler, not unaware that he had taken us by surprise.

Despite his legendary unpredictability, we liked Enzo a lot; he was a fast, efficient and tidy worker and had all the pipework sorted and everything hooked up to the gas, including our cooker, before the end of the day. Only problem was, apart from the cooker, it didn't work. Worse still, Enzo couldn't find what the problem was. We would have to wait for a visit from a technician from the company that supplied the boiler. So close yet so far.

The technician turned up sooner than anyone expected and so, about two weeks later, just at the beginning of October the system was finally online. We could hardly believe it ... we had central heating and hot water even if, with the weather still quite warm, we didn't need the heating just yet.

That first winter *with* central heating we were much warmer but also cautious about how we used it; we didn't really have any idea how much it was going to cost and so the times when it appeared less than efficient were generally self-inflicted. We didn't make the same mistake twice.

Apart from the boiler, our only other major purchase for the house had been our bedroom suite and assorted useless heating devices. The house was generally well furnished but gradually, as we began to see it as our permanent home, we added to it things that made our life easier. For example, to take advantage of the various gluts of vegetables, week in, week out, we had bought another freezer and put it next to the sink in the utility room where it could serve another purpose as a shelf.

Our arrangement with Silvana and Raffaele was based on an annual contract which we all signed; it was a contract between friends that basically said that we would take care of the house inside (and that anything we bought would remain our property) and that they would look after and maintain the structure.

But this arrangement was flexible as I turned my hand to some things that were Raffael's province while he did things that were probably our responsibility. When, for example, a water pipe burst in the kitchen, Raffaele was there within minutes and while Kay and I saw off the water and dried up, he replaced the pipe. When the same thing happened in the utility room over a year later, I did it all myself. The fist time one of the straps that operate the outside shutters snapped, I watched as Raffaele replaced it; the second time this happened I did it.

Calabria's older generation did not turn their hand to DIY in the way that we were used to. For a start, twenty years ago such all-purpose stores did not exist. Silvana was genuinely impressed when she said one day, *tu puoi fare tutt'*, she really was surprised that 'I could do everything'; not quite everything I replied modestly.

And we helped them out too, not just with the annual summer watering while they were at Il Tucano, but as and when their computer started playing up even I, an Apple-man through and through, was available to sort out their PC problems.

During our second summer we had had enough of the perennial mosquito and fly problem and decided that, before the following summer, we'd do something about it. The bedroom doors onto the balcony and the window to the spare room upstairs both had mosquito screens so we needed to deck out the two remaining doors and two windows. The problem was that there were times in the summer when we did not want to block out the light; times when we wanted the windows open but not offer an open invitation to any winged visitors with an appetite for blood.

I measured up everything and ordered it all on the internet. Naturally I spoke to Raffaele about it first and when I told him they'd probably arrive in about ten days he looked at me as if I was from another planet.

Calabrians are used to waiting for things; ordering two doors and two windows from a local outlet would not necessarily guarantee delivery the same year. We, on the other hand, knew that internet-based companies couldn't afford to work like this and that my delivery estimate was probably about right. Ten days later, not only had they all arrived, but I had finished installing them; Raffaele was speechless.

For the record, we scarcely saw a fly in the house the next summer and any mosquito bites we did have were almost certainly picked up elsewhere.

Of course, were we to leave this house we could theoretically take the mosquito screens with us, though the likelihood of them fitting any other doors and windows is remote!

I mentioned earlier the other winged visitors we sometimes had around the balcony, the birds. So we decided in the winter that we'd do what we'd done in England and feed them. Kay and I went to a lot of trouble for those ungrateful Calabrian birds. Kay ordered the feeder from England and I rigged up a pole to the balcony railings so that we could sit inside and watch as the peanuts we supplied free of charge were devoured.

But did the little buggers accept our invitation to indulge in a free food-fest on our balcony? No they did not ... they clearly had not read any of the interesting ideas for feeding the birds in winter that are part and parcel of every gardening book in the known universe.

We put up signs (in English and Italian) with large arrows indicating the location of said feeder *and* that it was free. Not a bite. Not a dicky bird. There are just some birds you cannot help!

One day the door knocked. It was a young man called Andrea who lived at the top of our road. Andrea told us about his *fidanzata*, Rosella, who was still at school and needed to pass an exam in English in order to go to the college in Crotone. He wanted to know if we could help her.

I suppose it was inevitable that this should have happened. We had met an English woman who lived with her Calabrian husband in Crotone and who told us there was quite a demand for private English tuition. For all sorts of reasons this was the last thing we wanted to do but we didn't like to let people down, particularly neighbours and particularly ones with the surname Gerardi and cousins of 'our' side of the family.

We suggested that Andrea bring his girlfriend to see us and we'd see if we could help; this first chat and assessment would be free... truth be told we weren't sure if we could accept any payment and, if so, how much.

Rosella was our first student; she passed her exam and later came back for more.

While working on the Gerardi *vendemmia*, the grape harvest, we got chatting to one of Santa Severina's two barbers ... the one I didn't normally go to.

Antonio Bruno told us about his daughter Pamela who was doing a degree in Social Services at Cosenza University; to obtain the best degree Pamela would have to pass an exam in English. The only problem was that when Pamela was at school she was taught French.

Pamela was our second student; she passed her exam so well that she decided to try for a higher level. She passed that too and we were invited to her graduation party.

Naturally I felt duty-bound to change my barber; I can't remember when I last paid for a haircut.

Since then we have had three other students: Mario, the son of Aurelio who lives above us, just wanted to catch up at school; Giovanni comes from Rocca di Neto and was studying engineering at Cosenza University and, like Pamela, needed to pass an exam in English as part of his course; Fabrizio is the brother of Andrea and his *fidanzata* is from the Ukraine (naturally they met at LALEO) and Fabrizio just wanted to be able to communicate with her better in their only common language, English. I think Fabrizio's motivation is by far the best.

So sometimes our home feels like a school. However, we have had to draw a line and tell people that we don't take anyone who isn't at least at the *Liceo* (fifteen-plus). We know that were we to do otherwise, our home would literally become a school.

The problem we have with such a scenario is that we have come to value our freedom; we love to wake up in the morning and know that there is nothing he *have* to do. We were invited to visit the British Institute in Crotone and then to join its teaching staff; we declined but it was difficult and the woman in charge was quite insistent. We were more insistent as the idea of such a commitment, several days a week, every week, horrified us.

When, for example, Giovanni, cancelled his lesson on one occasion we were really pleased for this gave us an unexpected taste of freedom that particular afternoon ... it was being let out of school early.

As if this wasn't enough we have other things that keep us off the streets. As you will have gleaned, I dabble in writing and always seem to have plenty to do in that area.

Kay reads a lot, makes soap and shampoo bars, knits and embroiders. Our friends' babies are decked out in the beautiful clothes she makes for them and her internet-based project page is bursting at the seams.

Each morning when we get up, these are the things that will occupy our minds till we walk up to the square for a coffee with Carlo. But a day of doing our own thing at home is a rarity; something or someone else always turns up. But this is what we have come to expect and we take it in our stride.

We stuck to our original decision to watch only Italian television for two years; two years and two months it was when the satellite dish was finally attached to the balcony and we allowed ourselves the linguistic luxury of watching programmes and films in English.

Earlier that year too we had finally said goodbye to our little *chiavetta* that had served us so well for one hundred internet hours per month. There was a new kid on the block in the form of an unlimited service relayed from a telecommunications mast atop nearby Monte Fuscaldo. We were number seventeen to take up the service and it was amazing to once again have reasonably fast and unlimited access to the world-wide web.

About a year after it was installed, Aurelio's son Mario, who had just acquired his first computer, found that he could 'piggy-back' the wireless signal that Kay and I shared and the family thought they should pay us for it. Naturally we declined but decided instead to set up a more direct, reliable and secure service from our system to his. I bought an ethernet hub and some cable and one Sunday Raffaele, Aurelio and I installed a direct link up into Mario's bedroom.

We were an unlikely trio but we worked well together and had a lot of fun solving any problems we encountered. Indeed Raffaele was so impressed with how it worked that he decided he'd like to be linked in too and, breaking a habit of a lifetime, ordered the cable online that day.

The very next day I received a letter from our internet provider telling us that the system had been under-subscribed and would be terminated in ten weeks. What we hadn't realised eighteen months earlier was that the service was dependent on there being a minimum uptake from the town and that number was never achieved.

But, as ever with these things, another door opened and we now have a similar system which picks up its signal from across the valley at Scandale; it costs less each month and is twice as fast. And, of course, Raffaele and I did a little bit more bonding when we worked together to take a cable underground between the two houses. I also learnt all sorts of useful DIY words that morning.

Life on the edge

It was January 2010. We woke to a day like any other ... though I have to confess that we were up and about a little later than usual.

At first nothing appeared unusual about that day ... until, that is, we noticed that there were a few men wandering about wearing bright orange jump-suits; a few also seemed to have climbing gear strung about their person. Whatever it was they were doing didn't appear to galvanise them with a sense of urgency.

We had a leisurely breakfast before embarking on our daily constitutional ... a walk up to the square for a cup of coffee. We nodded to neighbours as we went and then one asked if we'd heard it. *Cosa?* What? we asked. *La frana.* This was a new word but it didn't take long to get the gist ... there had been a landslide quite close, a bit of the rock, of Santa Severina, had broken off and tumbled down into the valley below. Later we got the whole story from Raffaele.

It was midnight and the Gerardi family were all in bed when the noise woke everybody. Silvana and Raffaele were convinced it was an earthquake – not an unreasonable assumption as the recent devastating quake in Abruzzo was still fresh on people's minds.

They took the children downstairs and checked for news on the television ... an earthquake would have been headline news. Nothing. They wrapped up and went outside where others were gathering and it wasn't long before people realised there had been a *frana*, a piece of Santa Severina had broken off, one house had lost part of its garden.

The *frana* happened about sixty metres away from our house; some people were a lot closer and, later, two families had to relocate. The noise, as the huge chunk of rock that broke away and broke up as it tumbled down the hillside, was heard by people all across the town and was the main topic of conversation for days.

Living so close, we were frequently asked what it sounded like, were we frightened, what did we think it was? People were amazed that we'd slept through the whole thing.

Later Raffaele explained that the bit that had broken off was just round the corner on the wetter north side of the hill; he said the drier east side, where we lived, was fine.

———————

On the land

At the beginning of our second year in Santa Severina the *vendemmia*, the grape harvest, was later than usual because of the weather ... though in truth there is no set time as it depends on so many factors: type of grape, pruning and tying-in techniques, the weather, the location, the soil.

Aurelio was behind schedule and we wanted to help so, on the day after Carlo's wedding, all the Gerardi family was *in campagna* cutting, carrying and pulping the grapes. It was very satisfying work, the more so because at the end of the process, just after Christmas, there would be such a glorious outcome.

Even that day the weather was capricious and there was a freak thunderstorm right over the Gerardi land (and literally nowhere else) so all thoughts of the traditional post-*vendemmia* open-air party were dispensed with and a more low-key snack was the order of the day as everyone tried to make up for time spent sheltering from the elements.

Helping with the *vendemmia* was something we did every year thereafter and our contribution developed into a specific task that we alone did ... we carried the *cassette* full of grapes from the vineyard up to the *magazzino* where they were pulped ... and afterwards we partied with the Gerardi family. We also contributed to the party by bringing something to eat with us and a few bottles of beer.

At first when we could sense a resistance to trying whatever it was we brought ... still prevalent was the notion that *stranieri* cooked strange food and there just might be an un-Calabrian ingredient lurking within. When people tried something they did so out of politeness rather than relish.

But gradually this wariness dissipated as they were introduced to flavours and recipes that they found themselves liking against their better judgement; in one case I prepared something I'd made before and within minutes the plates looked like they'd been attacked by a shoal of piranha fish.

In early November we decided to give the *orto* another chance and planted some vegetables that would over-winter well and produce a crop in the spring – broad beans, peas, onions and garlic. We knew we wouldn't have to water very much and that when we did we could use the water by the house and not the *pozzo romano*.

We're not sure what happened to the peas but very few germinated; on the other hand the broad beans, garlic and onions all looked in good condition and didn't need much attention. We were looking forward to the spring and harvesting the fruits of our labours.

Our cultivating prowess already part of Santa Severinese folklore, it was only a matter of time before we would be asked to be involved in Santa Severina's incarnation of the world-wide project known as Slow Food.

Locally this was a project emanating from *il sindaco* Bruno Cortese with the aim of inculcating into the local children of primary school age an interest in how food is cultivated and harvested. There was to be a public meeting, to which we were invited, to watch a presentation about implementing the project in Santa Severina. Our names were mentioned at this meeting as being consultants (the first we heard of it) and we even got asked to choose the plants the children would grow. A small plot of land off Via Grecia had been earmarked to become the *Scuola Elementare*'s own little *orto*. As a teacher at the *Scuola Elementare*, Raffaele was very much involved and clearly he was the one behind our involvement.

It all got under way very fast as the land had to be prepared before it was too late to plant anything and all too soon the day dawned when the schoolchildren arrived to do their bit of planting.

It may seem strange in an area with such an ingrained agricultural tradition that the children should even need to learn about growing food slowly, the natural way. It has to be remembered, however, that Italy is as influenced by the global media as anywhere else and these days television adverts assault the senses and push fast food in Italy just as they do everywhere else. Linked to that there is the general disinclination of the young to work on the land, even in a 'helping dad' capacity. Slow Food is a way of clawing back, of trying to help children see and appreciate what is right in front of them.

Unfortunately there was a problem with the project here in Santa Severina ... the land was not close enough to the school. There was no way the children could easily tend it on a regular basis. In addition, there was no way over the winter months that the children would be allowed to walk the seven hundred metres to and from the *orto*. For vegetables that would normally be planted in the spring and which would need more watering and weeding, the problem is exactly the opposite – having to go to and from the *orto* and work in the heat of the sun.

A worthy project but one that was ultimately unworkable here in Santa Severina.

In the spring it was time for us to check on our broad beans, onions and garlic and the few meagre peas. The garlic was pathetic, not even as large as we'd cultivated in England. We were bitterly disappointed ... until we discovered that many other people were selling garlic that was just as small. So we harvested it and were still using it almost a year later. The onions were, we think, spring onions or scallions and as such another disappointment as I was picturing large red onions by the sackful that would keep us going for a year.

The few peas that germinated gave us a couple of meals but at least the broad beans didn't let us down; an excellent harvest and we had a new freezer to store them in.

Also in the spring we had our second crop of kumquats, what the Italians call *mandarini cinesi*, Chinese mandarin oranges, from our little tree on the balcony. After some research on the internet and bearing in mind the size of the yield, we decided that we could probably make just over half a litre of brandy-based kumquat liqueur. So we did. And the following year we made kumquat chutney ... who knows what we'll find to do with a surfeit of kumquats in years to come? Kumquat may?

That second spring in the wake of our latest *orto* adventures we decided that come the summer planting season, we'd give it a miss. The main problem for us was the watering and the commitment entailed to water properly. Like with the English teaching in Crotone it was a commitment in terms of specific times of the day, almost every day and that, more than anything, was something we'd done for years and something we loved not having to think about.

At the same time we were approached by one of the *vigile urbano*, the local policemen, who wanted us to go and look at some land with him. He drove us out along the road towards Altilia, a *frazione*, a small part or hamlet, of Santa Severina where Carlo's wife Anna Maria was born and where they were married. His land was impressive, had water and good access from the road ... and he wanted to know if we would like to work it. He wasn't looking for any payment, he just thought it would be better for someone to work it than to let it lie fallow.

I was very kind offer and we acknowledged it as such but we knew this was going to be a busy year – one of Kay's daughters was pregnant and she was planning a couple of visits to England – and that we couldn't give it the commitment it deserved.

That summer and autumn we did nothing land-related except indirectly with the on-going search for a good cheap source of red wine. Eventually we found it at Marina di Strongoli, a small *cantina* that Stumpo knew well and that produced some fine wines ... we paid only 60 euro for forty litres and, as often as not, come away with some other goodies and half a dozen eggs.

Behind Le Puzelle there was an old vineyard, at one time overseen by Roberto Sculco, our friend who had died in 2008. Since Roberto's death it had not been looked after and Vincenzo decided to have a local 'expert' look at it to ascertain whether or not it had any wine left in it.

By chance we happened to call in that particular day, the day when Vincenzo was told it was finished; the age of the vines coupled with the land's neglect brought wine-making to an end at Le Puzelle. Vincenzo had suspected as much and, thinking aloud, went on to say that the land would make a good *orto* for Le Puzelle's restaurant ... you could almost hear the penny drop as he fixed his eyes on us and, without saying a word, asked if we were interested.

In one sense this was a surprise, in another not so because

it was something we had once talked about. There was something about the idea that was like the missing link in a perfect circle. This was the place that we'd come to every year for three years on holiday. These people were people we loved dearly and the idea of working with them (as opposed to for them) had a particular appeal. We said, yes ... depends.

The 'depends' bit was to do with the availability of water and we left things in a state of uncertainty, save to say that we were not averse to the idea. Nevertheless Vincenzo insisted on shaking my hand as if it were a done deal.

It did happen. Vincenzo sorted out the water and eventually by the following spring there were over one thousand plants flourishing behind the Le Puzelle. It was incredibly hard work and too many plants were bought and, though we sometimes helped out with the watering, it was not our responsibility.

English and American visitors to Le Puzelle were surprised to find that the two old codgers working their socks off just outside their windows while they holidayed, spoke English just as well as they did.

At the time of writing we don't know what's going to happen next year ... maybe they'll find someone a bit younger.

———

When the *temporale* hit Santa Severina the day before Carlo's wedding it devastated the approach ramp to the road bridge across the river Neto and thus severed access to the Crotone-Cosenza *Strada Statali*; for some people it theoretically denied them access to their land.

The road collapsed late on Friday evening but by Sunday morning it had re-opened. Indeed it it doubtful if it ever closed despite the bollards and warning signs that suggested the contrary. You see, the Calabrians don't really 'do' closed roads and no access signs; if there's room for a car, then the road is deemed to be open and any obstructions put there by officialdom are generally moved aside little by little until, first an *Ape*, then a car, then a van, then a truck, can just squeeze through.

This is what happened that September. People wanted access to their land and so, despite the fact that half the road had disappeared into the Neto, what was left was wide enough for a car to pass through. Within days everybody, even trucks, was using it as if nothing had happened; they were also using their common sense when it came to observing the fact that there was a part of the road effectively one-way. In other words, life went on.

The same happened on the road to San Máuro when a bridge was partially destroyed by flood water ... the key word was 'partially' and all the road signs saying there was no access, no through traffic, were gently pushed aside and access found and policed by sensible driving.

In both the above cases, we were, like everyone else, just ignoring the signs and carrying on regardless.

When is a road not a road?

Festivals and celebrations

The Italians have a lot of festivals, a few have a political significance but most have a religious connotation and every town also has its saints day. The national holiday in the middle of the summer, *Ferragosta*, had religious origins (the Assumption of Mary) but, for most, this seems to have been lost in the mists of time as they enjoy themselves in the sun. Quite simply they love to party.

Locally the *vendemmia*, the grape harvest, and *Capodanno* became two of the annual events we shared with the Gerardi family. But there were others and some of these in turn started to take on new element because of our participation.

The winter festive season in Calabria has four key dates: 7/8 December (*Immacolata*), 24/25 December (*Natale*), 31 December/1 January (*Capodanno*) and 5/6 January (*Befana*). They are all family occasions though the first and last are generally for immediate family. In Santa Severina on all four there is a *falò* in the square, a bonfire, often accompanied by some impromptu music, a few demijohns of red wine and maybe some pasta and/or potatoes roasted in the fire.

The Italians also manage to squeeze in another festival in late February/early March, a movable date based on Easter and called *Carnevale* when the children dress up and go a-door-knocking. In places like Venice this is a proper Carnival, the Italian equivalent of Mardi Gras.

In our first January in Santa Severina, Befana (Epiphany) seemed to pass us by but, thereafter, we have ended up as guests at various houses and once again it's been something of a food-fest. On one such occasion we spent the evening at Nino and Antonietta's house with the rest of the Gerardi family.

After the food, the children were restless and wanted to go up to the square to see the *falò*. Silvana, Rosanna (Aurelio's wife) and Kay and I said we'd go too but first I nipped back to the house to fetch one of the Chinese lanterns I'd been telling the children about.

The square was buzzing with families walking up and down or standing round the bonfire near the church. We went into the middle of the square and Kay opened out the lantern and all the Gerardi children wrote a message on the white tissue paper before we lit the 'basket' so that the lantern filled with hot air and was ready to lift off.

While this was going on we realised that everything in the square had come to a halt and that almost everyone had formed a circle round we four adults and the children to see what we were doing. When the lantern eventually lifted off all eyes were drawn skyward as it rose higher and higher and eventually disappeared out of sight. There was spontaneous applause.

As we walked back home, Mario, Aurelio's son, was in reflective mood. He asked us if we realised what we'd just done and without waiting for an answer went on, *avete iniziato una tradizione, dovrete farlo ogni anno*; Mario was telling us that we'd started a tradition and that now we'd have to do it every year.

He was right of course. What had begun as a simple bit

of fun for the Gerardi children had become, in the blink of an eye, an event that involved many other people. Alessia, Francesco and Mario expected that the following year there would be another Chinese lantern in the square. And there was.

In Italy Easter Monday is called *Pasquetta* and every year, weather permitting, the Gerardi family gets together at the house in the country for an *alfresco* lunch ... it's like a celebration that the weather is on the turn and that summer is just around the corner. And every year, included in the party is Raffaele's sister, her husband and their younger daughter, Eleanora.

A long table was laid outside and everyone brought their culinary contributions and tucked in. As ever on such occasions there was so much food and wine that people were in dire need of sleep or exercise afterwards. The first year we went down the exercise route and decided to go into the nearby fields in search of *asparagi selvataci*. Kay and I, Silvana, Rosanna and Raffaele's sister; there were also four children, Francesco, Alessia, Mario and Eleanora.

The search for *asparagi* soon wore off when the children spotted a hill that was crying out to be climbed and I was the only adult willing to accompany them on this expedition. It was hard work, particularly for Alessia, the youngest, but she made it and everyone felt a surge of pride at having got to the summit from where the rest of our party, the other adults, looked like ants down in the long grass below.

Getting down was probably more difficult and I had to give Alessia a helping hand on a few occasions. The children all ran excitedly to the other adults, exhilarated by what they'd done and where they'd been.

Fast forward a year and it's a day or two before *Pasquetta*;

Silvana appears at the door to confirm that we'll be coming as before and then, almost as an aside, mentions that the children are looking forward to climbing the hill again ... with me. The little sods had remembered and it had become, in their eyes, something that we, the five of us, did at *Pasquetta* and, by implication, would always do. It had become a tradition.

Not that I minded of course, the more so when I saw how little help Alessia now needed, how confident she had become. On top of the hill the second year, unknown to the adults below, I agreed to do this every year provided that, when *I* was not able to physically do it, they would carry me to the top. In the mistaken belief that I was joking, they agreed.

It was mid-summer and we had spent a warm evening at Carlo's sharing a bottle of red wine. The music on the stage had long ended but the square was as busy as ever with people of all ages still walking up and down, sitting at the bars, relaxing in the warmth of the evening ... nobody, it seemed, was keen to get home.

Reluctantly we decided it was time to go and that, instead of our normal route home, we'd walk the long way round, down the steps past *La Locanda del Re* and right by the old bank (which had closed several years earlier but left behind a functioning cashpoint/ATM) then under the old arch which once supported the town's west gate and on along Corso Aristippo and past our first little house. We paused momentarily by the wall to have look and marvel at the fact that we had once lived there before continuing along the cobbled street towards where there seemed to be a gathering of people. This was not unusual on such an evening, people would often sit outside their houses into the late evening just to keep cool.

But this gathering seemed a little different and in the middle of what appeared to be an impromptu street party we could hear music and see our friend Tonino. Tonino waved at us to come and join him and the others and by the time we got there he had two glasses of red wine already poured. Tonino explained what was going on.

He introduced us to the groom and the mother of the bride. The bride herself was at an upstairs window looking down, Juliet-like, on the assembled masses. The groom, her Romeo, had arrived with his musical friends to serenade his wife-to-be ... in fact, as it was gone midnight, they would be husband and wife before the day was done.

This is a particularly southern Italian celebration when a party is thrown outside the bride's home after the groom and his entourage have arrived 'unexpectedly' to serenade the bride; the groom supplies the entertainment and the bride's parents, the buffet. The serenade is the opening gambit in a day of feasting and partying.

We stayed for about half and hour and sloped off home despite entreaties to stay on for a while longer. As we headed round the curve that linked west with east, we were still marvelling at this wonderfully simple pre-wedding custom; it was particularly refreshing as it involved everybody, young and old, male and female and, of course, all the neighbours. *And* it put the absurdities of the hen- and stag-party into perspective.

A year or so later a neighbour's daughter was getting married and we stayed up till about one in the morning awaiting the groom and his friends; nothing happened so we went to bed. The next day people asked us where we'd been ... didn't we hear the music and the dancing? As with the *frana*, we'd slept through it all ... apparently the groom turned up at three!

By contrast, on a dark November evening I chanced upon our Australian friend Col at the barber's. Col, an artist, was nearing the end of his month's residency in Santa Severina. Shorn, we decided to have an *aperitivo* together at Carlo's where we bumped into his sponsor, Bruno Cortese, now Santa Severina's *ex-sindaco*.

Bruno invited us (and Kay) to a pig roasting somewhere in the countryside; it was all rather vague but we arranged to meet an hour later. I returned home to break the news to Kay.

We met up with Bruno at the *bivio* below and followed his car down and out of Santa Severina along a little-used track to an isolated farmhouse; there were about a dozen cars parked along the lane, another half dozen closer to the farmhouse. From inside a sort of makeshift marquee we heard voices and joined an exclusively male gathering, glasses and oiled bread in hand, awaiting the arrival of the roasted pig, *la porchetta*.

Kay was aware that in this place she was one of a kind but the men, there must have been be over thirty, most of whom we knew well, made her feel at home. She soon relaxed, aided and abetted by a glass of wonderful red wine and a plateful of tiny roasted potatoes.

The pig, having been cooking for over five hours, arrived on a large wooden platter and assumed pride of place. We were all told to take *our* places so that the feast could begin.

And a feast it was, with more of those roasted potatoes, oiled bread topped with cherry tomatoes, beans, chick peas and mushrooms to accompany a thick slice of succulent pork, followed by apples, walnuts and roasted chestnuts – all the fruits of the countryside.

There were a few toasts, much laughter, some singing, a bit of dancing. As midnight approached it was time to return to Santa Severina as another unexpected day, one of many in this unpredictable little town, was coming to an end.

But it was only that first time that it was unexpected ... when it happened again the following November, we realised that once more we had become part of an annual event, a celebration of the bounty of the pig and all the fruits of the nearby countryside. True, this particular gathering was by invitation only but there were probably other such celebrations going on in other farmhouses around this time of year.

There is one celebration where 'by invitation only' doesn't work. When a new restaurant, bar or even shop opens it is traditional to have an *inaugurazione*, an open-house party with lots of free wine and soft drinks and appropriate food.

We have been to a number of such *inaugurazione*, from a restaurant in Rocca di Neto run by a Santa Severinese to an *enoteca* (wine bar) in Cotronei. At the restaurant there was a whole range of food available while at the *enoteca*, the sort of bar food you would expect to eat there normally. All of it was, of course, *gratis*.

A few years ago a new restaurant opened in Santa Severina, at the *bivio* on the main road. It too had an *inaugurazione* but with an unfortunate twist ... it was 'by invitation only' to the great and the good of Santa Severina. Not surprisingly all the other potential customers who *weren't* invited were a tad peeved and to this day, apart from some passing tourist trade in the summer, it remains empty every evening.

Every year, on the last Sunday in May, there is a peculiarly Italian festival. It's strange because not many Italians, certainly here in Santa Severina, have ever heard of it. It's called *Cantina Aperta* and is when, in each area of the country, one local *cantina*, winery, opens its doors to the local community. In the province of Crotone this would normally be a *cantina* in the nearby Cirò wine region.

Like me, Stumpo enjoys a glass of wine and it was through him that I first got to hear of this little gathering; at the time Kay was in England on grand-mothering duties.

It was a beautiful spring day and the *cantina* Malena

was already buzzing when Stumpo and I arrived to try the wine, taste the food, listen to the music and walk round the grounds. And it was all *gratis*, absolutely free. I estimate there were about two hundred people in total and the next year it was much the same even with the participation of the local vintage car folks and their wonderful vehicles and scooters.

On both occasions Stumpo and I (and Kay the second year) were the only people from Santa Severina ... I'm hoping that next time round we can persuade a few others to come along and that one might just offer us a lift so that we can enjoy even more of that wonderful Cirò wine.

That first year at the pig-roast Kay was the only woman there and so the following year she thought she'd give it a miss and make it a real boys' night out. She was not uninfluenced by the fact that on that particular night there was an unusually persistent storm, a spectacular *temporale* with lightning that momentarily seemed to illuminate the whole countryside.

So I arrived by myself and every single person asked where she was; they weren't being polite, they genuinely expected her to be there and were surprised that she wasn't.

On the wall I noticed a photo of a similar gathering a couple of years earlier and there were definitely other women there. I suspect that the women *chose* not to come ... they probably just wanted an evening in without their husbands!

At the end of this particular evening I was given a plastic plate covered in tin foil ... an ample portion of succulent *porchetta* to take home to Kay.

To and from

After our first year in Santa Severina there followed a flurry of comings and goings the first of which was when Kay decided to spend a week in England early in October; by coincidence, I received an email from Neff in Chicago.

It was straight to the point: "a little bird has told me that Kay will be in England for a week ... I think I will need to import a drinking partner around the same time.".

Kay and I flew together to London and I flew on to Chicago to spend a week with Neff and Jo. When we were doing the rounds of friends to say our goodbyes I could sense an element of incredulity that I could leave Santa Severina one morning and the next day I would be in Chicago. Many found such a scenario truly *incredibile*.

Kay and I met up a week later in London and then flew on to Rome where we missed our connection to Lamezia and had to transfer to a later flight. Finally, around ten in the evening, we left Lamezia Airport, having first filled in all the necessary forms for our missing luggage which was apparently still in Rome.

We picked up the car and ten minutes later were on the fast dual carriageway heading east towards Catanzaro and home ... when the car suddenly died a horrible death.

I was pitch black, the road was unlit, cars and trucks were shooting past incredibly fast ... and we'd no idea where we were exactly. The latter became relevant five minutes later when I was trying to explain our location to the central command of the breakdown recovery service that was part of the car's insurance. I knew roughly where we were but couldn't recall how many exits we'd passed.

Half an hour later we had a call from the local operative who was already en route to us; he was on the right road but we weren't where I said we might be. I asked him just to keep coming, we were definitely on that road and that eventually he'd find us. He sounded less than convinced.

As it happened we were about a hundred metres beyond an exit, the exit at which the breakdown recovery man said he would leave the road if he couldn't find us ... but luckily he saw the on-off orange glow from our hazard warning lights and continued on past the exit where he found two very relieved *stranieri*.

They pulled the car onto the back of their truck, dropped us back at Lamezia where we knew there was a hotel and gave us a telephone number to call in the morning to see what the prognosis was.

We booked into the hotel and then headed for the nearest bar ... it was thirty-six hours since I had woken up in Chicago; thirty-six hours since I had slept.

The next morning the mechanic confirmed what I already knew ... the problem was serious, it would take at least three days for them to rebuild the engine and it would cost eight hundred euro. We arranged to return on the Friday.

Back to Lamezia Airport we went to hire a car to get us home; we also recovered our 'missing' luggage at the same time and by lunchtime were back home in Santa Severina where people kept saying *auguri* to us and pointing to the car

... they'd spotted the change of car, jumped to the conclusion that it was new, and were congratulating us on our purchase!

When we returned to pick up the car, the mechanic, a man in his sixties, had laid out on a bench every single part of the 'old' engine that had been damaged or replaced – he wanted us to see what he had done, to know that he hadn't tried to pull the wool over our eyes. He talked us through it all and demonstrated how it was the pistons had become so badly bent and distorted. It was refreshing to deal with someone so fastidious and open and, like Enzo *meccanico* back in Santa Severina, his workshop was methodically organised and, given what went on here, almost spotless.

Another ex-client from Bristol stopped off for a few days to introduce her new boyfriend and had to suffer the usual tour of hotspots. We didn't know it at the time but Sharon and Bill were our last new visitors for almost ten months when another former client, Steve, stopped by.

In February we returned to the UK so that I could visit my new granddaughter, Cara, and other family. I only stayed a week, Kay a fortnight.

Apart from seeing Cara, this journey was memorable for another reason ... it was the first time we used the newly inaugurated service to and from Crotone Airport ... less than a forty-minute drive away. Crotone to London via Milan or Rome with Alitalia was just what we'd been hoping for, perhaps I might never have to drive to Lamezia again.

Crotone Airport must be one of the smallest in the world; it's like flying to and from someone's back garden. Everything is on a small scale, from the security area to the baggage reclaim belt. I love it; a joy to leave, a joy to return to. We also found the route to and from Milan generally more convenient and reliable as Milan Linate is much smaller than Rome and therefore less prone to delays.

Kay returned to the UK in May for the birth of her first grandchild, Ivo, while I focussed on a project that had been ten years on the back-burner but now was almost a reality ... retracing DH Lawrence's footsteps in his *Sea and Sardinia*.

I won't bore you with the details, they're all in my book *Keeping up with the Lawrences*, suffice to say that my partner -in-crime on the nine-day trip was Neff and later he stayed for a few more days in Santa Severina to bond again with Carlo.

Just before we set off on our adventure I had also spent a couple of days in Zurich with another son and daughter-in-law ... and another new grandchild, Christopher.

Back in Santa Severina, I spent much of the rest of May writing up notes from the Lawrence trip in preparation to getting down to the nitty-gritty and writing the book itself which in turn took much of the summer.

Kay's focus was still with her grandson back in England so she decided to return for most of August to help out; it also gave me more space to write.

My abiding memory of that time, apart from the fact that Kay wasn't there, was that there were one or two Santa Severinese (women) who found it difficult to get their heads round the fact that Kay and I could survive independently. True, they weren't to know that we were in almost daily contact, but nevertheless, even with the evidence of their own eyes when Kay did return, I could still sense disapproval from this minority.

And curiously, they weren't finding fault with me, Kay was the bad apple for not staying by my side; she it was who had left me all alone in Santa Severina to suffer the slings and arrows of outrageous fortune. This really angered me and I made a point of learning how to say in Italian "mind your own bloody business" in case it was a phrase I might need. Sadly, after all that effort, I never did get to use it; once or twice it seemed only a matter of time. Maybe next year, I thought.

In September we took s short break in Sicily and spent a week in Marsala in the south-west of the island. On our way home we stopped at Lamezia to pick up Steve, an ex-client from Bath who organised music festivals as well as performing.

Stumpo and Enzo soon got wind of another muso in town and there followed several evenings of unrehearsed, bawdy revelry as these two tried to impress and get in on one of Steve's festivals. They might well be lucky.

It was while Kay was in England for Ivo's birth, that I started to have a problem with the car. It wouldn't always start when I turned the key ... in a few days it went from bad to worse and when I went to see Enzo *meccanico* it was at that very moment that it decided not to start at all. Enzo was pretty sure that the key's code was faulty and asked if I had another. I told him I had two at home so he drove me there but I was unable to find either. I had to abandon the car at Enzo's.

I guessed that Kay probably had one with her in England so rang to see if she knew where the other was and discovered that she had that as well. I was in Calabria with a key that didn't work; Kay was in England with two keys, at least one of which I hoped would work. As it happened this was only a few days before Neff, now London-based, was due to fly to Crotone en route to Sicily and the start of the Lawrence trip ... we had arranged to met in Milan Airport as I was on my way back from Zurich from *my* grandfatherly duties. Kay got the keys to him in London he brought them with him to Italy.

Car-less, I had two problems to solve ... how to get to Crotone Airport to fly to Milan en route to Zurich and how to get back from the airport with Neff, two keys but no car.

Step forward the Gerardi family.

Raffaele apologised for not being able to take me to the airport; he was teaching that day but would be free the day Neff and I returned to Crotone and would pick us up. As it happened that week Attilio was in town and when he heard of my predicament he simply said that he'd take me to the airport, he'd pick me up at ten the next morning.

At two minutes to ten the next morning I was packed and standing by the door, more than a little nervous bearing in mind what I knew about Italian punctuality. It was ten o'clock. I stuck my eye against the front door's security lens. Nothing, nobody. I looked at my watch, willing it to be running fast and walked up and down the hall a few times. I looked through the lens again ... all I could see was Attilio's mop of white hair, his hand poised to ring the bell.

En route to the airport Attilio shared with me his knowledge of cars and their keys and was convinced that the problem lay elsewhere, it was definitely not the key's code. He was sure Enzo's diagnosis was wrong; I hoped *he* was wrong.

When Neff and I returned to Crotone, Raffaele was waiting as promised. But he had a surprise for us ... he'd taken the covers off his pride and joy, his beautiful Alfa Romeo, charged its battery and driven it to the airport to collect us. He chauffeured us door to door, from Crotone Airport to Enzo *meccanico* in chic, Alfa Romeo style.

Nervously I tried one of the keys Neff had brought from England. The engine turned first time. Enzo *meccanico* looked very pleased with himself and his diagnosis and dramatically waived aside all attempts at paying for such expertise.

Neff and I would, after all, go to the ball; we would drive to Sicily the following morning to follow in Lawrence's footsteps.

The place and the politics

Santa Severina sits atop a lump of rock, *un scoglio*, that from time to time can show its unstable side. These days most people approach the town from the main road that runs north-south (the front cover image is the view from the south). The views are spectacular whatever the approach but it is from the east, and the old disused road to Crotone, that *lo scoglio* derives its other name, *la nave di pietra*, the stone boat.

This is the view that in the past those travelling from Crotone would have seen and in my opinion its the best view of all and a side of Santa Severina which we only discovered after we'd been living here a few weeks; it does indeed look just like a stone boat.

For seven or eight months of the year the surrounding countryside wears a verdant overcoat but in the summer months the sun parches the land and though the dusky, sage-green of the olives still hold their colour, yellows and browns now dominate the landscape. You could be forgiven for not expecting the land to recover from such ferocious punishment, but it always does; come the end of September it breathes a sigh of relief and prepares itself for the seasons of recuperation.

As I've mentioned elsewhere Santa Severina is a tidy place.

The *piazza* from the castle; Carlo's bar and the Town Hall are on the left

It is endowed with enough historical edifices to make it an occasional tourist hotspot. It has sufficient places to stay and a couple of restaurants. Its distinct oval-shaped square, with its central *rose dei venti* design that illustrates the names and direction of the eight local winds, is bounded by the church at one end and the castle at the other. Historically and aesthetically it has much more to offer than many other similar-sized towns in the area.

Many ordinary things made it unique: the language school for young people (and a couple of oldies); the renovation of every street in the *centro storico*; the new car park and access road at one end of Via Grecia; the adjacent gardens and walkway down to the ruins of the town's ancient eastern gate; the small complex for camper-vans at the edge of the town; the new car and coach park by the *bivio*; the new walkway up to and along the walls of the castle; the road lighting on the road bridge across the Neto.

What all these things had in common is that they were projects of Bruno Cortese, *il sindaco* of Santa Severina up to the end of March 2010.

Bruno had been *sindaco* for ten years (two five-year terms), at the end of which he was obliged to 'retire', though he could stand for election again after a five-year break.

As *sindaco* he was a one-off. He was accessible to everyone: dignified, open, warm, intelligent, *simpatico*, interested and interesting. Like everywhere else, Santa Severina has its classes: it's working class, its agrarian class, its middle class, its upper class and all groups in between. But somehow Bruno forged it into a place where, other than income, people from every shade and aspect of life seemed to be on talking terms and genuinely open to each other. True, the Rotary Club is the Rotary Club and seems to derive its membership from the same social group but the day-to-day ambience of the town was generally a refreshing blend of people who respected each other for whom and what they were.

We had made friends from every strata of Santa Severinese society, from Antonio whose claim to fame was that he always wore sleeveless T-shirts throughout the year and could play the *fisarmonica* (accordion) to retired headteacher Franco Severini; from Marina our Russian neighbour to her nearest neighbour, diminutive dynamo Antonietta, erstwhile baker, prison cook and aunt to Enzo *idraulico*.

So a change at the top was inevitable but there were two types of change on offer as election fever gripped Santa Severina that March: there was complete change from Bruno's centre-left alliance led by his chosen successor, Salvatore Giordano, or the centre-right grouping of Diodato Scalfaro. Each party put forward twelve potential councillors and though we knew people on both lists, Raffaele and Enzo's wife Franca were standing for election with Salvatore. Everyone had one vote ... Kay's would go to Franca, mine to Raffaele.

The hustings took place in the square from a small raised platform erected for the occasion; there were speeches from both candidates and their representatives and these were always listened to with quiet respect. We listened with varying degrees of understanding but, had I been voting on passion and clarity, as opposed to policies, my cross would have gone next to the name of Antonella Parisi, one of the centre-right's chosen representatives.

Everyone knew that, with Bruno out of the equation, the voting would be close. But it was even closer than expected and their were two recounts before the final result was announced; truth be told we had already heard it unofficially before it was announced.

The exact result depends on your point of view. The winning centre-right party of Diodato Scalfaro won by eleven votes or, as the centre-left like to think, they lost by six votes ... the logic being that if six people had voted the other way, *they* would have won. Which of course is also true.

This election result heralded major changes in Santa Severina and most of Bruno's uncompleted projects remained in that state. The LALEO was cut right back that first year to virtually nothing with only a small increase the next summer when Dragon returned for the fifth time. His view on things was particularly interesting for he had observed Santa Severina in its formative years under Bruno and could make a more reasoned comparison than residents like us. He could hardly believe the changes. The LALEO itself was a shadow of its former self; the numbers were lower, the atmosphere had changed and there were scarcely any excursions; he gave the impression that he would not be back.

L'Arte del Gesto have not been invited back; that look of awe that we saw on the faces of Santa Severina's young has been lost; there is still music and other events in the square during the summer but these have been cut right back as have the music festivals. Of course, as ever, the reasoning has always been 'the crisis' but I seem to remember that this started in 2008 and not just after Santa Severina's mayoral election two years later.

Stumpo and Francesca moved back to Cotronei.

Can one man make such a difference? I and other Santa Severinese have had to address that question over the last couple of years and I am aware that a significant number of those who voted in the new *sindaco* have since regretted it. On the other hand there are probably those who voted against him and are happy with the way things turned out ... though, at the time of writing, such people seem harder to find.

Don't get me wrong, most people accept that the new man at the helm, Diodato Scalfaro, is a really nice guy, *molto simpatico*, and he has always been courteous to us. Perhaps the problem is that he is just not a *sindaco*, he doesn't yet seem to have that blend of charisma, gravitas and the common touch that personified Bruno. Even now, if the two were in the square at the same time and you were to ask a stranger which one was *il sindaco*, they might well point to Bruno as he still looks the part. He is still respected for what he achieved and there are some who hope that he can be persuaded to stand again in 2015. Basically, for anyone, Bruno would be a hard act to follow.

Of course there have been some constructive changes: the visitors' entrance to the castle is at the front and not round the back where it used to be; the bi-weekly market has moved from the castle car-park to the square where it seems more at home; the unsightly rubbish tip on the town's main access route, which definitely did not say 'Welcome to Santa Severina', has gone; and there is free wi-fi internet access in the square.

So, despite some of the reservations mentioned earlier, Santa Severina remains a good place to be, even if it is not as lively as it once was and, of course, some people prefer it that way – after all they voted for it.

Santa Severina clearly has its political divide but with a few exceptions people see beyond the divide and respect what they like in a person even if they don't agree with their politics. Tommaso Rizzuti is a case in point. A native of Santa Severina, Tommaso is a school secretary who works and lives in Florence but always turns up in Santa Severina at holidays or when there is an election. He always votes Communist or as near as he can get. (It should be remembered that voting Communist in Italy does not have the same resonance as it would have in, say, the UK or the United States. For Italians this a normal part of the political process and one which has none of those irrational reds-under-the-bed connotations.)

The day of the election, just as we left the polling station (*la Scuola Elementare*), we bumped into Tommaso and confirmed that we'd voted for Raffaele and Franca. Next to him was standing Diodato Scalfaro and at the time we had no idea that these two were in fact great friends.

Tommaso later told us how, as youngsters the two of them were inseparable and went on to wax lyrical about his friend's many qualities but finished off his potted biography with something along the lines of ... of course politically we are poles apart.

Other political adversaries have said much the same thing ... that he was a really good person but, in their opinion, just not *sindaco* material. We shall see. Maybe he has a surprise in store; maybe being *sindaco* is something you grow into ... a bit like coming to grips with the Italian driving experience.

For me, Tommaso's way of looking at things was a new experience; I had always tended to dislike everything about my political adversaries. You will have gleaned I was somewhere along the Bruno continuum when it came to local politics, so you will understand the shock I experienced one day at Carlo's when *il sindaco* paid for our coffee.

At first I felt a little awkward, particularly as I could see that, in the background, Carlo was aware of the irony. *Il sindaco* was probably repaying a kindness we had shown his daughter and her best friend Alessia. At the time it was a strange moment but I got over it and socially I have shared other moments with *il sindaco* and warmed to his company ... Santa Severina is such a small place it's hard not to rub shoulders with all sorts of people, people that, if we had more of the language, we might conceivably view differently.

It is almost certain that we have 'friends' that we would like less were we to understand them better; perhaps too

La nave di pietra and other aspects of *lo scoglio*

there are others whom we have hitherto misjudged and, with more understanding, might be deserving of a second chance, a reassessment. If such a scenario ever arises I might even have to re-write this book.

Is is also worth mentioning that, political shenanigans notwithstanding, Santa Severina is not southern Italy's equivalent to Stepford, a place where everyone wears the same satisfied smile. It is not like that and there are certainly several 'oddities' about the town – outlandish, reclusive, isolated, eccentric individuals have a place here as everywhere else; in some cases their stories are as bizarre and incredible as they are unique. The fact that we fitted in is evidence enough.

Apart from their individual characteristics, they have one thing in common ... they are all harmless. To go into details would be impertinent but one such person, whom we first 'met' when we were on holiday, deserves discreet mention.

At first Gaetano (not his real name) was puzzled by us. He saw us almost daily but never made any sign of recognition; having lived in Santa Severina all his life, he thought he knew everybody. It took him two years to feel comfortable in our presence and even then he rarely acknowledged us.

It was almost another year before he felt able to respond to our simple *buongiorno* overtures; but eventually he did. On one occasion I heard him mutter to nobody in particular *sono ancora qui* ... they're still here.

We will probably never know where and how we fit into his order of things for it must surely not have been easy for him to process us and allow us to enter his sense of place. The fact that Gaetano managed to do so was some sort of milestone for all three of us.

Bruno found it difficult not being *il sindaco*; at first he looked lost, unaccustomed to not being at the centre of things, to not having the fingers on the pulse of Santa Severina.

But before leaving office he had invited Col Madden, an Australian artist, to spend a month in Santa Severina. Everything that could have gone wrong with this venture did and the exhibition, originally scheduled for the castle, was eventually held in a back room at *La Locanda del Re*. I assumed this change of venue had its origins in the murky world of *sindaco* and *ex-sindaco* rivalries.

Bruno had asked us to take Col under our wing and help out with the language and over the month we three got to know each other well; we sometimes ate together at home or at *La Locanda del Re* and often met up at Carlo's for a drink. And of course we went to the pig-roast together. Unlike other artists of my acquaintance Col was surprisingly philosophical about the change of venue.

It was the evening of the exhibition and the room was buzzing when Bruno asked for silence and made a short speech, outlining the origins of the project and praising the artist's work. He went on to say that Col would make a short speech which I would then translate into Italian.

The look of horror on my face was genuine … I had no idea that Bruno was going to spring this on me and, of course, there was no way out of it, I was on the wrong side of Bruno to make a bolt for the door. Had I known in advance, I could at least have faked an attack of laryngitis or even asked Col what he was going to say and prepared a quick translation.

To this day, I have no idea what Col *did* say or how I translated it … I was just glad that I'd had a couple of glasses of wine earlier and that somehow I was able to 'wing' it.

This was Bruno's great skill: he could galvanise people into doing the impossible in any language.

———————

People *particolare*

In Italian the word *particolare* has more subtle meanings than the English word 'particular' – ideas such as special, unique, peculiar (in the good sense), eccentric, even funny, come to mind. In using this word to describe the people in this chapter, I include all the above to varying degrees. In some cases I am just bringing lives – and deaths – up to date and there are one or two new faces.

In the autumn of 2009 Giuliano told us that a Romanian girl, Roxana, was coming to stay with him; he and Roxana had met about four years earlier when they had both worked briefly at the restaurant *La Locanda del Re*. Roxana's second visit to Santa Severina turned out to be more permanent though the couple did travel back to Romania in February 2010 to get married.

Three days before the wedding Giuliano's father died so the church service was postponed and a civic service held instead. The following year they returned to Romania and they married again in late February; earlier the same day their daughter Giulia was christened in the same church.

Giuliano had always been a friend, a unique, hard-working young man with a sensible head on his shoulders, a person that we knew we could always rely on; the feeling has been mutual.

Since he and Roxana returned from Romania with Giulia that friendship has flourished and sometimes it feels like we are Giulia's grandparents. One of her real grandparents, Giuliano's mother, also lives in Santa Severina so there is no danger of usurping her role.

Soon the family will return to Romania for a month's holiday and they will have visitors for a few days when Kay and I turn up to stay. Giuliano asked us to come to Romania for two reasons: firstly out of simple friendship and wanting to share his origins, his homeland, with us; but he also wants us to return to Santa Severina and tell people what Romania is like. This second point is important to him for, he argues, if *we* say it's not backward and that they do have cars and good roads and electricity then people will believe *us*; even if they don't always believe him.

Lina, Barend and family returned to Santa Severina the following summer and we often spent time together at Carlo's or eating at each other's apartments. Barend, Naseer and I did some more bonding and went off in search of wine. Naturally we never came back empty-handed but we remained uncertain as to whether we had bought the best wine out there at the best price. Clearly more research had to be done.

The family returned to Holland at the end of the summer where, we found out later, Lina and Barend went their separate ways. Lina has not been back to Santa Severina since.

Gina and Franco closed their restaurant late in 2009 and moved north to Verona to be closer to their son. A personal loss as I don't believe I have ever tasted such wonderful wild rabbit before or since. Their families remain in Santa Severina so we got the odd bit of news every few months,

Gino working here, Franco working there. But, we are told, they are back working together in a new venture ... they have opened a fish 'n' chip shop in Verona!

Not long before our second Christmas at Santa Severina we bumped into The Engineer, Antonio, at Carlo's one evening. He was working on a project in nearby Scandale and living at our 'old' house in Corso Aristippo and our paths only crossed when he had less than a month remaining in Santa Severina.

We liked The Engineer but locally we seemed to have been the only ones that did so for, before we met, he had not made many friends in the town. He hailed from Caserta near Naples and perhaps it was simple regional rivalries that seemed to put some people's backs up; perhaps too *our* friendship was based on the fact that he spoke good English. *He* found it truly bizarre that we had ended up here in Santa Severina and, in some strange recognition of this, named us Bonnie & Clyde.

We sometimes ate together at our house or at the *centro storico*'s only restaurant *La Locanda del Re* and when he left we kept in touch – indeed I met up with him later in Naples while researching *Keeping up with the Lawrences*.

La Locanda del Re is a Santa Severina institution, and the kingdom of chef Ciccio Guzzo. Eating out is not *abitudine* in Santa Severina; people tend to do so on special occasions rather than for pleasure. But Ciccio, ever the entrepreneur, plastered the whole area, particularly all the surrounding restaurant-less villages, with posters advertising what *La Locanda del Re* had to offer. Which is why, on most evenings, many, if not most, of his clientele are not locals.

La Locanda del Re is a comfortable, homely place where we try to eat about three times a month; out on the verandah in summer, by the fire in the corner in winter. The staff are mostly the family of Ciccio's Polish wife, Eva.

One winter Ciccio suggested that we could use the restaurant for some sort of English conversation group ... of course he had an ulterior motive in that he wanted to learn some English himself. Every Saturday at six we met in a back room, up to half a dozen people, just to talk in English; each week we had a theme that people knew about in advance. There was no cost and sometimes some people would stay on and we would have a pizza together.

By the time the early evening light returned in late March, everyone was ready for a break ... and of course Ciccio had learnt how to greet and treat any English-speaking tourists that might drop in during the summer.

One of Bruno's projects included forging links between the elderly of Santa Severina and five other areas in the European Union. One of these was Anglesey in north Wales and when it was Santa Severina's turn to host an event we got invited to the dinner afterwards to keep the Welsh happy.

We went to the dinner (at an *agriturismo* on the road to Altilia) with Stumpo and Salvatore, the latter in his seventies was a renowned local *mandolino* player. It was a fun evening with lots of Calabrian music, traditional food (including tripe and goat) and local wine but the most memorable part was meeting and getting to know Salvatore.

Thereafter we became good friends, the more so when we realised that we actually knew his son and his daughter.

Fast-forward a year and a bit ... it's mid-summer and Kay and I are enjoying a late afternoon *gelato* up in the square in the company of Anton when Salvatore joins us. He tells us he's a bit nervous as he's playing that evening and hasn't played for a while. He looks in need of moral support and when he asks if we'd like to come we think it's the least we can do. He says he playing with Franco Barone, gives us directions and a time and is gone. Anton tries to clarify the directions so we think we've got it pretty much sorted. Nothing could have been further from the truth.

At the appointed hour Kay and I arrive down at the *bivio* and are looking for a *piazzetta*, a small square where there might conceivably be some music that evening. We walk and re-walk round the whole area; it's as dead as a dodo. It's now a good half hour beyond the appointed time (nothing unusual there) so we return to the car and are heading back up into the town when we pass a car going the other way with Franco Barone and Salvatore. I do a u-turn and follow them.

They park up in a small open space by some apartments; we park behind them. Franco is surprised to see us and with a flick of the head asks what we're doing here in a way that suggests it might be more than mere coincidence. We explain that Salvatore said there was some music that evening and invited us. Salvatore is nodding approvingly; Franco still a tad unsure.

When, guitar in hand, Franco goes to an apartment and knocks the door, we realise the awful truth. Salvatore had invited us to a private party, a family gathering and, what's more, a family we'd never met before. We try to beat a hasty retreat but the apparent head of the family, a woman, insists that we stay and join them.

It was an extraordinary evening, the more so because it was entirely unexpected and because we met two amazing sisters; of course we enjoyed the music too.

The sisters, both in their seventies, left Santa Severina in the sixties and followed their father to France where they had lived ever since. Both had married Frenchmen, had families in France and French grandchildren. Their husbands were with them in Santa Severina as was the granddaughter of one couple and the grandson of the other. Salvatore fitted into the equation because he was brought up in the same part of Santa

Severina as the two girls, they had been childhood friends. Guitarist Franco Barone didn't know the family any more than we did – he was there as Salvatore's accompanist.

Both sisters spoke fluent French as did their grandchildren, both of whom also spoke reasonable English. They had bought this property in Santa Severina as a holiday home and came back every summer to revel in the past, renew old friendships and, in our case, make new ones.

And that's what happened. We got to know them and their extended families who came and went over the summer from France. One of the grandchildren, Antoine, stayed the whole summer and every other day or so rode his scooter up the hill and popped in to use our internet signal ... he was also planning a six-month trip to Australia the following spring.

We spent another evening with the whole family, without the music this time, and know that every summer we'll do the same again.

And then there's Tonino Parisi. I have no recollection of how or when we first met Tonino ... it's as if he just grew on us and became part of our circle of friends. We definitely didn't know him when he ran his Sexy Shop in Crotone ... a short-lived idea that perhaps might have worked in some parts of Italy but Crotone was not one of them. But then everyone else here also claims not to have known him then.

When he opted for a more orthodox career in one of Crotone's supermarkets we certainly saw more of him. Eventually too we got to know his two young daughters who normally lived with their mother in Crotone but spent some weekends and holidays with Tonino. Despite the separation the girls clearly loved spending time with their father in Santa Severina.

In his spare time Tonino evolved a Facebook page called Noi di Santa Severina where he had gathered together all sorts of memorabilia, mainly photos, relating to Santa Severina and its people. I got all this second-hand from Kay as I don't (and won't) 'do' Facebook. It's called having a life.

So I suggested to Tonino that what appeared to be a random mix of photos on the Facebook pages could function differently as a website, a site organised into themes which could even have some sort of chronological element. Unknown to him at the time I had already bought and registered the name.

One evening he came round to eat and, having plied him with sufficient wine, I showed him what I had in mind. To say he was enthusiastic is an understatement ... he was bursting with excitement and energy and once I'd shown him how to edit and operate the site he was like a man possessed. Ever the showman, he launched it on Christmas Day.

However, less than a year later, he decided that he couldn't keep up with both and the website was cast adrift and floated off into the ether. But the Facebook site remains and seems to grow from strength to strength ... it is, I believe, Tonino's third child.

I took a copy of *Keeping up with the Lawrences* to show The Good Doctor. He was impressed but wanted to know when he could read it in Italian. I shrugged my shoulders in Italian. The next time I saw him he had a plan, the first part of which was to sell me two tickets, at twenty-five euro a time, to a quasi-Rotary function in Roccabernarda just after Christmas. Part two of his devilish scheme was when, at said dinner, he introduced me to Victoria Kelly.

Unfortunately before he made any introductions he said he wanted us to meet an American friend and, as it happened there was another American there too, the Richard Gere-lookalike husband of the sister of someone we had met at other Rotary functions. So, when we were introduced to said sister and *her* American husband, I immediately jumped to the wrong conclusion. Just when I'd told him what he already knew, that he was Richard Gere's double but taller (aren't we all, taller I mean?), and got them really confused about translating a book, up pops The Good Doctor with Vicky in tow.

Vicky's partner is a local teacher, Pasqalino, and they have three bilingual children, Sam, Viola and Chloe. She is a native of Minnesota, speaks Italian like a native and The Good Doctor had seen fit to sanction our union in the hope that Vicky might ultimately provide *him* with an Italian version of *Keeping up with the Lawrences*. That remains a work in progress but what was important about that evening was that we met our first native English speaker since we'd been in Calabria.

For a decade or more Vicky had run the Mississippi English School in Roccabernarda ('Mississippi' because north America's longest river rises in Lake Atasca, Minnesota) which took pupils from all the local towns and villages. She and her school were so well known in the area and many of Santa Severina's children have been pupils, that it is remarkable that our paths hadn't already crossed until, that is, The Good Doctor took it upon himself to play linguistic cupid.

Early in the new year Vicky invited us to come to Crotone one evening "to meet the rest of the guys". In fact when we got the seafront pizzeria *Il Gambero Rosso*, I was, in the old-fashioned sense, the only guy there. What everyone had in common was that they were all native English speakers who had married Italians from the Crotone area; Kay and I were the only 'all-English-speaking' couple. Having had some experience of the ex-pat community elsewhere I was not sure how this was going to pan out.

I needn't have worried. Our hostess, Tessie, was Canadian and wife of the chef, Sergio; together they ran *Il Gambero Rosso*. There were two others from Canada, Ida and Mira, two from the UK, Sarah and Joanna, and a South African who was returning home for good the next day. Well, *almost all* were native English speakers, there was also Colette, the token linguistic *straniere*, half French, half Greek, born in Egypt and fluent in five or six languages including English. She was always invited, they said, because everybody really liked her.

*

Apart from Roberto Sculco, Roberto Borda and Carlo's mother we have lost some other friends.

During the 2010 World Cup (that's the *soccer* World Cup) we met and got to know an unlikely friend in the form of one of Santa Severina's two priests, Don Misiti. He was, I'm guessing, in his late sixties, he always looked undernourished and perhaps not in the best of health. But he loved his football.

Many times throughout that summer we sat at Carlo's or sometimes outside the *gelateria* in the corner of the square near the church and talked soccer. Talked and argued is closer to the truth but in a friendly, tongue-in-cheek way. Never did we talk religion.

One afternoon he shared with us that he was off to Genoa the next day for some tests; he was flying from Crotone. It was obvious that didn't like the idea of these tests, we could sense his unease. When we said our goodbyes we shook hands and wished him well. We never saw him again.

We understand he did return to Calabria and went into a nursing home but in September that year he died. His funeral was on the same day as Lamb-In-One-Leg's and we missed both. We had been for a short holiday in Sicily and didn't know any of this at the time. It wasn't until a few days later that we discovered that these two men, both of whom had touched our lives in such simple ways, had died.

The following July, when Silvana and Raffaele were *al mare*, we were going up to the square when we bumped into Rosanna, our upstairs neighbour. She told us that Raffaele's father Ciccio had died and that the funeral was that evening.

Ciccio Vizza lived with his wife in the lower town. His local bar was Bar Stella where we often used to stop for a beer on the way back from the *orto* and where we first met him. He was a large man and had survived throat cancer and spoke with the aid of a voice box. We often used to buy him a beer or he would buy us one. When we first met we didn't know who he was or why he was buying us drinks; all was revealed when I went to thank him and he said he was Raffaele's father.

He was an incredibly popular man and the church was bursting at the seams for his funeral. For us it was an emotional time, not just because we knew him and had seen him the day before he died, but because we could see how it effected Raffaele, Silvana and the children. A very sad day.

The day that The Good Doctor sold me the tickets for the Rotary dinner, I was just leaving the room when he had another thought. *Aspetta*, he said and I waited while he got up from his desk and walked to a cupboard. He took out a package and handed it to me. *Buon Natale*, he said. Inside was a Calabrian cake, one of many such offerings at this time of year that keep local dentists happy.

By the time I'd said my thank yous and told him how *molto gentile* he was, I had worked out what happened: this was almost certainly one of the many gifts his patients had given him and he was passing the surplus on to other patients such as me. As I passed through the waiting room, I said goodbye to those still there ... and just hoped that nobody recognised the bag I was carrying.

The Good Doctor and his ways never ceased to take me by surprise ... I was fifty euro lighter but had a cake I hadn't been expecting.

On food and eating

When we stayed at Le Puzelle on holiday we ate there almost every evening. We ate the normal Italian five-course dinner – *antipasto, primo piatto, secondo piatto, dolce* and *liquore,* accompanied by rich, red wine – and, not surprisingly we both put on weight. Regularly I put on about eight to ten pounds every summer in Calabria.

Now this wasn't a problem because, in England, we generally ate well, often oriental food, and soon lost all those extra pounds; in less than a month back home we both returned to normal ... until the following year, that is.

Living in Calabria was a whole new ball game.

First of all Italians, and Calabrians in particular, are, as I have mentioned elsewhere, almost obsessive about their local cuisine. In most supermarkets there are rows and rows of pastas, every brand, variety, shape and size imaginable ... and yet a pasta like *pizzocherie* which is traditional around the Lake Como area in the north of Italy is treated like a foreign food and you need to be dedicated to find it anywhere.

Real foreign foods can be even more difficult to find and when you do they are generally expensive. A good example is basmati rice. When we first came to Calabria we found one source and even then it could only be bought in small, expensive quantities. We eventually discovered somewhere where we could buy one-kilo packets at a very reasonable price ... it was a German-owned supermarket.

The same was, and still is, true of other non-Italian ingredients such as soy sauce, coconut milk and other oriental foods, they are sometimes available in small, expensive quantities. I am, of course, talking about Calabria; I know that further north in Naples and Rome these are generally available.

I had to go to Rome for a day to visit the American Embassy and left Crotone on the early morning flight and returned in the evening. Inside my briefcase I carried another bag large enough for my secondary mission ... a visit to Rome's Chinese quarter which I knew was close to the central station around the Piazza Vittorio Emanuele II.

I was like a kid in a sweet shop and soon my extra bag was bursting. I bought everything I needed in the same small supermarket and chatted to the Chinese owner about the problem we had in Calabria. She was surprised and said, "But the Chinese are everywhere". I agreed and told her that there were several Chinese communities in and around Crotone and Catanzaro but that they only sold clothes and knick-knacks. I still live in hope that she took the hint, saw this as a marketing opportunity, and headed south.

But finding the ingredients for cooking something other than Italian cuisine is only half the battle ... you also have to have the opportunity to use them.

Calabria being Calabria and Santa Severina being Santa Severina, planning a week's menu is fraught with difficulties. For us it is simply almost impossible to plan ahead with any certainty. Take this week: yesterday we ate at home; tonight we eat at a charity function organised by The Good Doctor; two days later we have lunch at Le Puzelle and some time in the next few days we promised the owner of a new *pizzeria* that we'd pop in. Two days ago, the only one of these arrangements we had planned for was The Good Doctor's function. We will be lucky if we eat at home for four evenings; four consecutive evenings is almost unheard of.

And when we eat out, apart from in a restaurant or pizzeria where *we* have control, it is generally a food-fest; the notion of eating one, maybe two, courses is almost unheard of in Calabria. This has historical roots in a land where, until recently, the notion of a feast, of celebrating 'plenty', was something that came round one or twice a year if you were lucky, and in the winter was associated specifically with the slaughter of the pig and the eating and preserving of every single part.

These days, in times of relative plenty, Calabrians enjoy what historically they never had. They always had the basics, the local fruit and vegetables, all year round, now they have the trimmings: beef, pork, lamb, chicken, rabbit, wonderful cheeses and cold meats and, of course, lashings of olive oil.

So Calabria is not the best place to be if keeping slim is a daily struggle and/or you suffer from lack of will-power and/or have a penchant for the wares offered by the local *pasticceria* such as Le Antiche Delizie in Santa Severina.

We have both put on weight, not masses, but enough to make us aware that it is something we should keep an eye on. We have, for example, cut back on olive oil; we never used a lot but now that I have found a source of rapeseed oil (in, surprise, surprise, the same German-owned supermarket), we use that instead. We try to eat less pasta and more rice, basmati rice rather that the creamy *arborio* rice used for risottos.

Recently Italians in general and Calabrians in particular have become more aware of the health implications of a fatty diet and increasingly are choosing the leaner cuts of meat, cutting back on their cheese intake and having their cholesterol checked. The packaging in most supermarkets has started to proclaim goods with less fat and low in cholesterol; television adverts are doing the same. That said, finding a lean equivalent of bacon is still like looking for a needle in a haystack.

———————

Most people living abroad seem to miss something that can only be bought 'at home'. For many English it is Marmite, for Americans probably peanut butter. Neither of these have I seen in Calabria.

When people come to visit from England they always ask what, if anything, can they bring. For me this is easy – oats, oat bran and sunflower seeds, the basic ingredients of our morning muesli and the ones difficult to find here. Calabrians aren't big on cereals unless they're of the Kelloggs variety. Raw cane sugar is also a problem ... when an Italian packet says it's cane sugar, it invariably means demerara sugar.

So, imagine my surprise when I was wandering round my favourite Chinese supermarket in Rome to find, as well as Marmite and peanut butter, Quaker oats and real raw cane sugar. Naturally I stocked up with these too.

My host asked me about Marmite. She sold it because people kept asking for it but she didn't know what it was or how it was used. I enlightened her ... and now she's the official Marmite expert in Rome's wonderful Chinese quarter, il quartiere Esquilino.

———————

A last word on language

Our month at LALEO had given us some of the basics of the language that we had never learnt. Had we been learning Italian at school we would probably have assimilated things like numbers and the conjugation of verbs by rote. But we never had that experience and often had to work backwards to try and work out why people said what they said.

Had we been younger we would have absorbed the language like the young, like sponges; but we weren't and we just had to take it in as best we could.

In 2009 there were new residents in the old prison, an Iraqi family, mother and father and five children four boys and a girl. They were refugees from the war and clearly used to a better life in Baghdad where, I gleaned, the father, an accomplished artist, had worked as a teacher for the boss-man, one Sadaam Hussein.

Sarah, the only girl, was also the youngest, and soon became friends with Stumpo's daughter Carmen. She also befriended us and there were times when we all had a pizza together: Kay and I, Stumpo and Francesca, Carmen and Sarah.

What was so incredible was the way in which, literally

within months, Sarah became almost fluent in a language that used a completely different alphabet to her native Arabic and even read in the opposite direction. It was both amazing and frustrating to witness and at the same time profoundly humbling. There was a time when Sarah could communicate better than all her siblings and both parents and was, essentially, the family's interpreter. She was seven.

The family moved several times within Santa Severina before settling in the apartment that we had once considered moving into near the *bivio* ... when we visited them there we were surprised to see that the awful concrete staircase that had put us off had finally been replaced with marble.

The family later split up temporarily, some remained in Santa Severina with their father, the others, including Sarah, moved north with their mother in search of work.

We must have been making some sort of headway because the woman who effectively told us off for not coming to grips with the language, and whom we didn't meet again socially for almost eighteen months, actually praised our progress as we shared an evening meal together.

Even so we still had feelings of inadequacy and were pretty sure that each day we learnt three words and forgot two.

Kay continues to speak with a near-perfect accent while I still defy all logic and stick to my guttural inheritance which I'm hoping will become endemic in Calabria before too long. I continued to have difficulties with certain people and not with others and am no nearer to working out why other that what I've already said on the subject.

Sometimes we continue to get the wrong end of the stick and don't always appreciate the full story; we can both come away from listening to the same conversation with completely different ideas of what was going on; this is particularly frustrating when there is an arrangement involved. I have noticed too that, as we improve, so those who made allowances for our lack of understanding do so less ... in a curious way it sometimes feels as if we have returned to a variation of square one, just on a slightly higher plane.

The night the car broke down on the way home from Lamezia illustrates the importance of coming to grips with the language. We are not living in an area where everyone, including those who work in the breakdown recovery service, speaks English. Santa Severina is not southern Spain, nor is it Tuscany; here we cannot rely on people understanding us in *our* native tongue. It is no more than a bonus if they do.

That evening on the busy *Strada Statali* we *had* to get the message across; we *had* to get help. And it wasn't easy, given that we didn't know where we were and weren't sure even how the system worked.

We had also become adept at avoiding the sorts of situations that, in normal circumstances, might result in a confrontation, the sort of thing I might have relished in English. Taking an Italian stance is a skill we haven't got, particularly on the phone when it is difficult to judge the other person. But that's exactly what happened when we hit a problem with our internet service and an Italian friend, who made the call and did the initial talking, unexpectedly handed me the phone to have it out with the company's local rep.

What made matters worse was that I knew this guy spoke good English (he'd lived and worked in the United States for a dozen years or more) but he also knew I was going to have a moan so he made it more difficult for me than it should have been by steadfastly refusing to speak any English. Nevertheless it was a strangely exhilarating experience as I thought I did reasonably well and got over the points I wanted to make.

Apart from Bruno's bombshell at Col's exhibition, such extreme language events are few and far between. Normally it's the pleasantries of life that we have to deal with and generally I leave these to Kay while she leaves me to do the floor show like when I foolishly decided to tell Ciccio (*La Locanda del Re*) an Irish joke ...

I explained to him that the Irish were going to outflank the Americans, the Russians, the French and the Chinese with a new space project to send a manned space mission to the Sun, his reaction was as predicted: *Ma, non è possibile ... il sole è torrido!*

Then, in hushed tones, I went on to explain that we had a cunning plan to overcome the problem of the sun being a tad on the hot side ... he came closer, as I checked to make sure we couldn't be overheard ... I whispered in clandestine tones that *we Irish* were going to travel at night, *andiamo a notte!*

I can still hear his laughter and since then every English-speaking visitor to the restaurant has had to suffer the same story told in Italian. And, should I be there at the same time (as has happened twice), I am forced to translate his version; not to repeat mine in English but to provide the English subtitles for *his* Irish joke told in Italian. Once, when I wasn't around, he got into such difficulties trying to tell the story to four Irishmen that he phoned me to ask if I'd come and help. I did.

As well as being a talented musician, Francesco Domenico Stumpo writes about music and presents papers on obscure musical themes at various specialist conventions that are held all over Italy and elsewhere. Such discourses are initially presented several months in advance and have to go though a selection process; they also have to be in English. So, regularly and with little warning, I get an email attached to which is Stumpo's latest musical masterpiece; my job is to translate it into English.

This apparently was originally Vicky's job but Stumpo I think decided that my need to practice and learn was greater than hers ... and yes, Stumpo also knew Vicky but omitted to mention that there was an American living a few kilometres away.

So, thanks to Stumpo, what I don't know about the Calabrian oral tradition and the story of Ucciali, the videos of pop-idol Tiziano Ferro and the Calabrian lyre is simply not worth knowing.

*

Trying to master the language has had its highs and lows but I think we are both now reconciled to the fact that we'll never be fluent Italian speakers but that we'll probably continue to improve at our own rates and in our own ways in the vain hope that our mistakes and gaffes will gradually become fewer.

This was something we had *not* expected when we first came here, but it's the best we two ageing English speakers can do. We've given it our best shot.

———————

It was when four young American Rotarians were staying at the Le Puzelle for a few days that I made my contribution to world peace and understanding between nations. Kay was in England and Vincenzo asked if I would take them on a tour of the town and, if necessary, act as their interpreter.

It was market day and the busy square was basking in a warm summer sun. We were working our way round the stalls when I happened to notice a couple of friends at another stall and couldn't resist doing the introductions ... it was simply too good an opportunity to miss.

That was the day, in the square in Santa Severina, four Americans were introduced to two Iraqis. My American friends were momentarily taken aback but, quick to notice the absence of horns and blood-dripping fangs, soon warmed to the irony of the occasion. They all shook hands and I realised then I had missed my vocation as a peace envoy.

Just the sort of thing you might expect to happen in Santa Severina.

———————

Yesterday

It is two weeks after our fourth Christmas in Santa Severina. All the eating indulgences are finished: *Natale, Capodanno, Befana* and, for us, Giulia's birthday too.

We have started work again with Giovanni to prepare him for his exam at the end of January when, out of the blue, he asks us to eat with him and his parents that evening.

Giovanni's father is a *gommista*, a man who repairs and supplies tyres, their home is above his workshop in nearby Rocca di Neto where Giovanni is also a town councillor. When we arrive outside, a disembodied voice from two or three floor up tells us just to turn the key in the door and come on up. Naturally, being *straniere* and thus not used to leaving keys in locks, we bring the key up too.

Giovanni and his mother, Lupina, meet us on the first-floor landing and we wait while Giovanni takes the key back down to replace in the door. Beyond the second floor the marble staircase ends and we climb further up on rough concrete stairs to the floor above. Lupina apologises for the change in decor.

Giovanni holds open the door to a huge open space, enclosed by terracotta-red unrendered brick and with no internal walls; I guessed close on 300 square metres. At one end there is a long table, the whole width of the room, and there are probably about twenty people, nearly all of Giovanni's extended family standing round the wood-burning stove on the back wall. We do the round of introductions, hoping that we are not expected to remember all the names.

In a clear American accent Giovanni's father, Pasquale, offers us a glass of red wine and, picking up on the obvious question in our gaze, explains how, in the late eighties, he used to live and work in the Queens and Long Island districts of New York ... something Giovanni had mentioned but I had forgotten.

More people arrive: more family, friends and some of Giovanni's fellow councillors, including *il sindaco* of Rocca di Neto. More introductions; more names to forget.

Kay and I look at each other with that same look that has characterised much of these last few years. It is the look we give each other when we realise that, once again, we have got it all wrong, when something has turned out to be nothing like what we had expected. As ever, we should have known better.

It goes without saying that this is the foreplay to another Calabrian feast.

The table is decked with all sorts of wonderful Calabrian dishes and they keep coming with predictable regularity. It is hard to resist such wonderful fare; hard to say no to pasta infused with the rich flavours of the countryside or pork that just falls off the bone; hard to refuse that next glass of local red wine or that special liqueur that seldom graces the supermarket shelves.

And the Calabrian women who prepare such feasts have come to realise that their menfolk will probably not help with the washing-up ... so they use plastic plates and glasses that can be discarded afterwards. One small step for Calabrian womankind.

We drive home still in a state of shock; still marvelling at the kindnesses and hospitality that this family and their friends have extended to us; still uncertain whether this evening was for us, about us or would have happened anyway without us. Probably nobody knows the answer to this. It just happened.

Back in Santa Severina, I text Giovanni to tell him we have arrived home safely; he calls me back immediately and I can hear that the party is still a work in progress. Once again I thank him and his family for their hospitality.

I omit to tell him that this evening was now at the top of our list of evenings that took us by surprise. It was an unforgettable mixture of new friendships, wonderful food, fine wine and lots of ribaldry. An evening all the more enjoyable because, despite everything that has happened to us these past three years, it was completely unexpected.

Epilogue

It was April 2011 and Kay's friend and ex-colleague, Teresa, was visiting us for a few days. On her last evening we went to Le Puzelle to eat.

Towards the end of the meal Elvira came and sat with us for a chat; a few minutes later Vincenzo joined us. Because Teresa was there, Elvira was speaking in English. Then out of the blue Vincenzo, who speaks little English, grabbed everyone's attention when, in hushed tones, he said "Top secret" and looked at Elvira.

Elvira was beaming as she told us she was pregnant. She went on to explain that only her parents knew and that she wanted it to remain a secret until she had passed the three months milestone; she knew that, given her age, things could be difficult. As far as the other staff were concerned she was off work with a virus.

This was carrying the notion of expecting the unexpected to a new level. We were delighted for them both, particularly so because we knew this is what Elvira had always wanted but never expected to happen.

Vincenzo and Elvira took everything in their stride and all went according to plan.

Eleanora was born in late October.

This feels a fitting place to end. The two people that we first met back in 2006 when we happened upon Le Puzelle as a place to holiday are still dear friends; special friends who have just embarked on *their* adventure.

On the other hand, *our* adventure is almost over.

We have now spent more than three years scratching around atop the hill that is Santa Severina and have come a long way from those first tentative days when we were trying to make ourselves understood in the *Angrafe* with neither the language nor the confidence to tell the man there that we were right and he was wrong.

We have settled into the normality of life in and around the town and somehow have become an integral part of the community. Most people will still call us *gli inglesi* but this is just a shorthand for identifying us quickly as our names do not trip off the Italian tongue easily.

Now we look forward to sharing Santa Severina with the next generation and in particular Giovanna, Giulia and Eleanora, as they learn to laugh, to play, to walk, to talk and perhaps to understand what is *particolare* about this place.

In the meantime we will continue to struggle with the language in the certain knowledge that each of those little girls will soon out-strip us as they head onwards and upwards.

Of one thing I am certain ... that somewhere, sometime, in *their* stories there will be a place for us.

Niall Allsop ...

... was born and educated in Belfast, Northern Ireland, but began his working life as a primary school teacher in London and in 1971 took up his first headship.

He left teaching in 1981 to pursue a career as a freelance photo-journalist specializing in the UK's inland waterways and wrote extensively in this field both as a contributor to several national magazines and later as author of a number of related titles, one of which, in a fourth edition, remains in print.

By the early 1990s he was a graphic designer and the in-house designer for an international photographic publishing house in Manchester before becoming a freelance graphic designer based in the south-west of England.

In September 2008 he and his wife, Kay, moved to Calabria, the toe of Italy, where they enjoy a sort of retirement and where they continue to struggle daily with the language in a small hilltop town where they are the only English-speaking people.

Since moving to Calabria he has written several books with Italian themes, also a memoir relating to his teaching career and another about experiencing prostate cancer – see following pages.

Stumbling through Italy
Tales of Tuscany, Sicily, Sardinia, Apulia, Calabria and places in-between

In September 1999 Niall Allsop and his wife Kay flew to Pisa and stepped onto Italian soil for the first time.

Within six months they returned and thereafter they visited Italy at least twice a year, usually to the most southerly provinces of Apulia and Calabria and the islands of Sicily and Sardinia.

They knew they holidayed differently to other people and in Italy, despite the lack of language, they found themselves somehow drawn into people's lives and homes; they had experiences and encounters that seemed to pass others by.

Stumbling through Italy is the prequel to *Scratching the Toe of Italy* and is the irreverent chronicle of their Italian travels and the many remarkable and colorful people they met there up to the summer of 2008 ... when, finally reconciled to the inevitable, they returned to Italy one last time. Which, as they say, is another story.

Also includes chapters on the idiosyncrasies of the Italian language and the Italian driving experience.

> ... above all else, an entertaining book, a book packed with characters, stories and anecdotes, frequently amusing, often enlightening, sometimes thought-provoking, never dull.

> ... it's fun and informative ...

> It's the people of the different regions that we get a real sense of with Stumbling—their daily lives, their families, their feuds, their celebrations.

> ... brings to life with affection and humour a whole cast of characters ... against a background of the glorious colors of southern Italy and Sicily.

Amazon Reviews of *Stumbling through Italy*

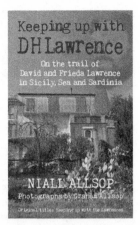

Keeping up with DH Lawrence

On the trail of David and Frieda Lawrence in Sicily, Sea and Sardinia revisited

In January 1921 DH Lawrence and his wife, Frieda, left their Taormina home in north-east Sicily and set off on a nine-day excursion to and through Sardinia and back to Sicily via mainland Italy. Lawrence's account of their journey, *Sea and Sardinia*, was published later that year in New York.

Keeping up with DH Lawrence is a contemporary account of making the same journey, as far as possible keeping to the same route, the same time scale, the same mode of transport and the same overnight stops as Lawrence and the queen-bee, his pet name for Frieda.

Like *Sea and Sardinia*, *Keeping up with DH Lawrence* is written in the present tense but there the comparisons end for the irascible Lawrence was not a tolerant traveller, was not what the Italians would call *simpatico*.

Lawrence travelled at a time of heightened tensions in Europe after the Great War and these are reflected in his outlook and the people he encountered, most of whom he gave appropriate nicknames such as Hamlet, the Bounder, Mr Rochester and the Sludge Queen.

Niall Allsop and his nephew traversed the same route in a different world, a brave new world of iPods and tele-communications masts, and here they met Julius Caesar and Cicero, Wonderwoman, Red and Mr Irritable ... and many more colourful and interesting characters brought to life on the pages of this unique travelogue.

> ... more than once [I] wished they'd taken me along with them.

> [Niall's] penchant for the odd glass of wine or three ... had me reaching for my own glass as his journey rattled along. I learnt a lot and laughed a lot.

> ... fairly rattles along as [they] encounter all sorts of interesting characters ... and have as many off-the-wall encounters in their nine days as I do in a year

Amazon Reviews of *Keeping up with DH Lawrence*

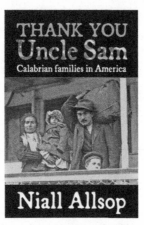

Thank you Uncle Sam
Calabrian Families in America

It has been estimated that twenty million Italians emigrated in the hundred years between the 1860s and the 1960s. The majority of these went to start a new life in the United States of America and of these by far the majority left behind family and friends in southern Italy.

From within southern Italy it was individuals and families from Calabria and Sicily—the areas of the most endemic poverty and perennial economic hardship—who formed the bulk of those who emigrated around the turn of the new century.

Post-war, in the fifties and sixties, America once again drew many from these same areas of deprivation, people for whom the post-war boom was something that was happening elsewhere.

As a resident of Calabria, Niall Allsop had met people who talked of family members in America, some of whom had emigrated as far back as the early twentieth century. Then, in the square of Santa Severina one summer, he met Gino Sculco from New Jersey who was enjoying a vacation back in the town of his birth. Gino explained how his father had emigrated in 1920, returned to Calabria and emigrated again in 1960, the second time accompanied by one of his sons. In 1967 Gino and his wife Sina followed in their footsteps.

Niall Allsop was so intrigued by the Sculco family's story that he decided to travel to America to find out more about what motivated them and other Calabrian families to emigrate. He was also curious to find out what happened once they got there. *Thank you, Uncle Sam* is the result of that curiosity.

Niall Allsop presents a heart-warming study of Calabrese families in America. His book helped me understand and better appreciate my roots, as a Calabrese-American

Amazon Review of *Thank you Uncle Sam*

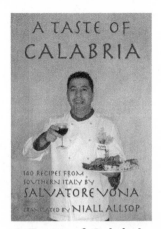

A Taste of Calabria
140 Recipes from Southern Italy by Salvatore Vona
Translated by Niall Allsop

Salvatore Vona is the chef at Le Puzelle, an *agriturismo* (converted farmhouse accommodation) near the small hill-top town of Santa Severina in the Calabrian province of Crotone.

As well as providing holiday accommodation, Le Puzelle is well-known locally for its cuisine and many Calabrians and others travel considerable distances to wine and dine at Salvatore Vona's table.

Salvatore's book of recipes, *A Taste of Calabria*, began life as the third edition of his popular *I Sapori delle Puzelle* (literally the tastes and flavours of the Puzelle) and reflects the demand, expressed by many of Le Puzelle's English-speaking guests, for an English language edition.

Lovely easy and tasty recipies. Not difficult to follow and giving the true flavour of Calabrian cooking.

Amazon Review of *A taste of Calabria*

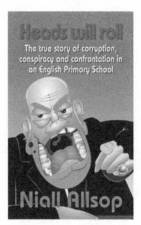

Heads will roll

The true story of corruption, conspiracy and confrontation in an English Primary School

In January 1971 a young, inexperienced teacher took up his position as Deputy Head of a Primary School in a small commuter-belt village not far from London. The School was not what Nigel Allsop (as he was known at the time) was expecting.

The Head of St Patrick's, George Snaith, was involved in a number of unorthodox and illegal practices, only one of which is the focus of this book.

In March that year Allsop witnessed Snaith helping two children during a crucial exam and realised also that the same children had clearly had unauthorized access to the detail of the papers.

Heads will roll is the story of how Nigel Allsop and his teaching colleagues went head to head with Snaith and those in authority who had turned a blind eye to such practices at the school for years.

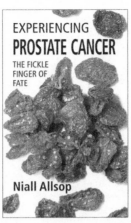

Experiencing Prostate Cancer
The Fickle Finger of Fate

In June 2013, Niall Allsop was diagnosed with prostate cancer and, like many others, survived the experience. He didn't battle against it, fight it, beat it or any of the other clichés that some people love to use ... he just had prostate cancer, was treated for it and got better.

Though, as you might guess, it wasn't quite as simple as that.

For a start, his experience was a little different in that it took place in the south of Italy and was also conducted in a foreign language. Nevertheless the story is universal—the treatments and therapies available no different to anywhere else.

The sundried tomatoes on the cover—which do bear an uncanny resemblance to some images of the prostate gland—are not part of any Italian theme but rather are an example of one of the foodstuffs that, according to which internet site you browse, will either prevent, alleviate of cause prostate cancer.

In *Experiencing Prostate Cancer*, Niall explains how he found the internet to be a minefield of conflicting information, speculation and misrepresentation—most of it meant well, much of it based at best on anecdotal evidence and some of it no more than a sales pitch. This book is the antidote to much of that but then Niall was fortunate in being able to rely on his trusty 'Bullshit Button' to separate the wheat from the chaff.

Experiencing Prostate Cancer does not claim to be a blueprint. It is no more than an irreverent account of Niall's experience ... from his below-the-belt medical history to the mistakes he made when first faced with a high PSA score ... from the treatment he eventually received at the hands of a remarkable doctor to trying to keep a catheter bag from slipping down his leg.

As usual a great book from the author. I have enjoyed all four of his books ...

Amazon Review of *Experiencing Prostate Cancer*

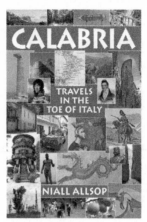

Calabria
Travels in the toe of Italy

Since 1777, when Henry Swinburne travelled in Calabria and wrote about his experiences, there have been a further dozen travellers—including one woman—who have written travelogues in English about Italy's remote toe.

Calabria is a fusion of their experiences and impressions, good, bad and indifferent, and those of Calabrian-based writer, Niall Allsop.

Calabria is not a guide *to* Calabria but rather a book *about* Calabria. Its thematic format, generously illustrated with many maps and over one hundred and fifty photographs, includes chapters on Calabria's history, its earthquakes, its brigands and the mafia, the mountains, superstitions, important people and places and lots, lots more.

Witty, informative and authoritative, *Calabria* is the definitive book in English about Calabria, past and present.

AVAILABLE SUMMER 2016

Made in United States
North Haven, CT
06 March 2023

33629047R00189